Complexity and Co-Evolution

Complexity and Co-Evolution

Continuity and Change in Socio-Economic Systems

Edited by

Elizabeth Garnsey

Reader in Innovation Studies and Fellow, Clare Hall, University of Cambridge, UK

and

James McGlade

Senior Research Scientist, Universitat Autònoma de Barcelona, Spain and Research Associate, Clare Hall, University of Cambridge, UK

Edward Elgar
Cheltenham, UK • Northampton, MA, USA

Published by
Edward Elgar Publishing Limited
The Lypiatts
15 Lansdown Road
Cheltenham
Glos GL50 2JA
UK

Edward Elgar Publishing, Inc.
William Pratt House
9 Dewey Court
Northampton
Massachusetts 01060
USA

A catalogue record for this book
is available from the British Library

Library of Congress Cataloguing in Publication Data

Complexity and co-evolution : continuity and change in socio-economic
systems / edited by Elizabeth Garnsey and James McGlade.
        p. cm.
    Includes bibliographical references and index.
    1. Social structure. 2. Economic history. 3. Chaotic behavior in systems.
I. Garnsey, Elizabeth, 1945– II. McGlade, James, 1950–
    HM706.C655 2006
    306.301—dc22

2006046370

ISBN 978 1 84542 140 3

Printed on FSC approved paper
Printed and bound in Great Britain by Marston Book Services Ltd, Oxfordshire

Contents

Contributors

Professor Peter Allen Head of Complex Systems Management Centre, Cranfield University, Bedford, UK

Sinésio Alves Júnior Centre for Advanced Spatial Analysis (CASA), University College London, UK

Dr James Baldwin Management School, University of Sheffield, UK

Dr Joana Barros Centre for Advanced Spatial Analysis (CASA), University College London, UK

Professor Michael Batty Director of Centre for Advanced Spatial Analysis (CASA), University College London, UK

Simon Ford Centre for Technology Management, Institute for Manufacturing, University of Cambridge, UK

Dr Elizabeth Garnsey Centre for Technology Management, Institute for Manufacturing and Fellow of Clare Hall, University of Cambridge, UK

Dr Paul Heffernan Centre for Technology Management, Institute for Manufacturing, University of Cambridge, UK

Dr Michael Lyons Manager, Strategic Analysis and Business Research Group, BT Group Chief Technology Office, UK

Dr James McGlade Universitat Autònoma de Barcelona, Spain and Research Associate, Clare Hall, University of Cambridge, UK

Professor J. Stanley Metcalfe Co-Director of the ESRC Centre for Research on Innovation and Competition (CRIC), University of Manchester, UK

Dr Robert Murray Department of Mechanical Engineering, University of Sheffield, UK

Dr Ronnie Ramlogan ESRC Centre for Research on Innovation and Competition (CRIC), University of Manchester, UK

Professor Keith Ridgway Director, Advanced Manufacturing Research Centre with Boeing, University of Sheffield, UK

Mark Strathern Complex Systems Management Centre, Cranfield University, Bedford, UK

Dr Belinda Winder School of Social Sciences, Nottingham Trent University, UK

Preface

The aim for this book is to offer stimulus to those wishing to engage with the concepts and tools provided by the emerging paradigm of thought on complexity and at the same time to foster new debate on co-evolutionary issues within the social sciences. The book reflects the growing attraction for social scientists of investigations into the nature and evolution of complex dynamic processes, particularly as they affect human societies in a variety of environments, social, political and economic. More specifically, it identifies the need to move beyond the abstruseness of the current complexity discourse to explore real world applications through a set of empirical examples that demonstrate the connections between abstract issues that have received mainly formal mathematical treatment and the problems faced by decision makers in the contemporary world. The wide variety of representations and explorations presented here – from archaeology through urban evolution, from industrial decline to the dynamics of innovation – suggests potentially fruitful directions for future research into the evolutionary and often counterintuitive behaviour of socio-economic systems.

This book has its origins in the NEXSUS project, a Priority Network funded by the ESRC over a period of four years (2000–2004). The research concerned the broad application of complex systems thinking and approaches to increase understanding on the general theme of sustainability in socio-economic systems. At the core of NEXSUS were six research projects involving the participation of five UK universities (Cranfield, Manchester, Sheffield, UCL and Cambridge). While each project was designed to tackle a different issue, the aim was to try to create interdisciplinary bridges across these problems, leading to common understandings and integration in methodologies. Some of these commonalities are examined in the first introductory chapter and Afterword. In addition to these research aims, NEXSUS has developed a national and international network and fostered the Complexity Society to link a broad-based community of researchers and practitioners concerned with issues of sustainability of socio-economic systems, decision-making in uncertainty, adaptability, the development of networks and the application of evolutionary complex systems.

The contributors to the book show that complexity issues do not reside in some remote corner of science, accessible only to a limited group of cognoscenti. Terms such as 'self-organization', 'phase transitions' and 'path dependence' have entered mainstream usage and the underlying principles involved are essentially simple, involving above all, a change in orientation from the reductionist and static to the systemic and dynamic. They can help generate tractable solutions to a variety of socio-economic questions. For these reasons the complexity perspective has important consequences for managers and policy makers in a variety of fields. But what the contributions also show is that there are no invariable sets of rules or short-cuts by which the human conundrums created by complex dynamic processes can be tackled. Each problem set must be addressed on its own merits and an appropriate methodology devised to which insight can be offered by the tools and conceptual orientation of the complexity perspective. Herein lies the contrast with the normative scientific approach that pursues universalist methods of analysis and interpretation. The complexity perspective acknowledges above all the importance of non-reductionist, pluralistic approaches to interpretation.

We would like to thank the volume authors not only for their cooperation in its making, but for fulfilling the cross-disciplinary aims of NEXSUS and producing thought-provoking contributions. We would also like to thank Simon Ford, the volume's Editorial Associate, and Jane McCarthy and Rosemary Cockfield, who have provided invaluable coordination for the project. Professor Peter Allen was the inspiration for the research programme as a whole.

Elizabeth Garnsey and James McGlade
Clare Hall, Cambridge, CB3 9AL

1. The nature of complexity

James McGlade and Elizabeth Garnsey

BACKGROUND

Over the past decades, theories of chaos, complexity and the idea of a new non-linear science have become increasingly prominent in leading edge research in the physical and biological sciences, and have diffused into the social sciences. Complexity driven research is currently engaging physicists, biologists, ecologists, geographers and sociologists alike, supported by a rapid growth of specialist academic journals and popular science books (see Edmonds 1996; McGlade and van der Leeuw 1997; and Byrne 1998 for useful reviews). However, despite its fashionable status and evident popularity, there is little consensus on just what is meant by the term. In fact, complexity has the unenviable distinction of meaning 'all things to all people' and is characterized by imprecise and generally ambiguous usage.

The new interdisciplinary field, which has somewhat confusingly been referred to as *Complexity Theory*, *Complex Adaptive Systems* or *Non-linear Science*, is essentially concerned with studying the general attributes of evolutionary natural and social systems. Whatever the terminology and specific concerns identified by these approaches, at the most general level they are characterized by particular attention to structural change driven by non-linear dynamics, as well as explorations of the propensity of complex systems to follow unstable and chaotic trajectories. Beginning in the physical sciences during the early 1970s, and gathering pace over the past two decades, 'complexity thinking' has moved beyond the natural sciences and has begun to penetrate the research agendas of the social sciences. As a consequence, complexity is increasingly viewed as an important step towards the construction of alternative evolutionary schemas (for example Byrne 1998; Cilliers 1998). The tendency to treat non-linear relationships as if they could be plotted as linear associations has long been endemic in the social sciences in the attempt to make the measurement of such phenomena tractable and amenable to orthodox mathematical representation. Advances in computing have made it easier to deal with complex non-linear relationships, but thinking in the social sciences continues to be dominated by the search for linear, predictive relationships, requiring heroic assumptions that may distort rather than clarify. The emergence of alternative ways of representing the complexity of things and relationships has opened new possibilities. For some, such as Hayles (1991), this is seen as having potentially profound consequences for conventional epistemological assumptions: 'When a dichotomy as central to western thought as order/disorder is destabilized it is no exaggeration to say that a major fault line has developed in the episteme' (Hayles 1991, p. 16). There is a rejection of the tradition of a two value logic in which order and disorder are dichotomous and opposites and its replacement by a conception of them not as antagonistic and fixed states but rather as stages in a process of dynamic and transformational becoming (Wolfram 2002, p. 1068).

Such ideas have potential for a new understanding of causality, as where effects operate as causes through feedback loops and causes are disproportionate to their effects (Hayles 1991; Reed and Harvey 1992; Gilbert and Doran 1994; Harvey and Reed 1994; Byrne 1998).

There are important implications for the nature of long-term change in the historical and archaeological sciences (McGlade 1995, 1997, 1999; Kohler 1993; van der Leeuw and McGlade 1997; Bintliff 1997; Bentley and Maschner 2001). Echoing this stance, McGlade (2003) argues that a focus on complexity issues is not simply concerned with the adoption of new analytical tools, but rather, represents an ontological shift that alters our notions of causality. What this amounts to is the recognition of the limits of science understood as the use of linear mathematical formalism in describing the world. The implications of this challenge to the Newtonian foundation of western science have been eloquently pointed out by Prigogine and Stengers (1984) and in a series of papers by Peter Allen (for example 1982b, 1990, 1992). In summarizing the key elements of this challenge for scientific research, Wolfram (2002) underlines a recognition of the centrality of Poincaré's conception of deterministic chaos in both mathematics and science, dismissing both randomness, the foundation of stochastic modelling in science, and certainty, the foundation of linear determinism. There is a revalidation of the idea that systems have emergent properties which are not to be understood by reductionist analysis of the systems into lower order components – that is an assertion of holism.

COMPLEXITY: TOWARDS A DEFINITION

This growing interest and increased participation in the complexity discourse has not been accompanied by any clear, rigorous definitions of the term. The main reason for this is that by its very nature as a holistic concept, complexity resists easy reduction to a set of law-like statements or general principles. On the other hand, a historical survey of the literature on complexity thinking as discussed by researchers such as Nicolis and Prigogine (1989), Allen (1982a) and Jen (1990) allows us to assemble a set of characteristics that appear to be generally applicable to a variety of systems spanning cellular biology, the human brain, societal organization and economic systems. These have been summarized by Pavard and Dugdale (2000), allowing them to be expressed as four related properties. These are not exhaustive, but provide a useful starting point.

- Property 1: non-determinism and non-tractability. A complex system is fundamentally non-deterministic. It is impossible to anticipate precisely the behaviour of such systems even if we completely know the function of their constituents. It should be noted that this does not imply that the behaviour of such systems is random in the sense of haphazard; there are causes at work but they operate through complex feedback effects and are unlikely to be detectable by standard measures of association between assumed determinants and presumed effects.
- Property 2: limited functional decomposability. A complex system has a dynamic structure. It is therefore difficult, if not impossible, to study its properties by decomposing it into functionally stable parts. Its permanent interaction with its environment and its properties of self-organization allow it to functionally restructure itself.
- Property 3: distributed nature of information and representation. A complex system possesses properties comparable to distributed systems (in the connectionist sense); that is, some of its functions cannot be precisely localized. In addition, the relationships that exist within the elements of a complex system may be short-range and contain feedback loops (both positive and negative).
- Property 4: emergence and self-organization. A complex system comprises emergent properties which are not directly accessible (identifiable or anticipatory) from an understanding of its components.

Thus, while complexity as a distinctive study area eludes rigorous definition, what we can say at a general level is that complex systems are those systems 'whose aggregate behaviour is both due to, and gives rise to, multi-scale structural and dynamical patterns which are not inferable from a system description that spans only a narrow window of resolution' (Parrott and Kok 2000, p. 2). An important property of complex systems is the way they exhibit self-organizing behaviour, driven by co-evolutionary interactions. This adaptive capacity enables them to rearrange their internal structure spontaneously. They not only cope with but impact on their environment, sometimes collectively shaping it. Such evolutionary properties are manifest in systems such as the human brain, cellular evolution or socio-economic systems.

What the present volume sets out to demonstrate is that a complexity perspective can provide an appropriate context within which to understand the behaviour of socio-economic systems and to provide an analytical framework that forces us to reconsider the nature of causality and the process of evolution. Not surprisingly, as we shall argue below, this poses a number of fundamental questions for the representation and modelling of socio-economic systems.

COMPLEXITY VERSUS COMPLICATION

In coming to terms with complexity issues, we encounter terminological confusion between complexity and complication. Frequently these terms are used interchangeably and the description 'complex' is often inappropriately attributed to systems by virtue of their having a large number of component parts, when these systems are merely complicated. A system of this kind can be understood by taking it apart and rebuilding it, like a watch or clock – the system is explicable through a description of its component parts. On the other hand a system is complex when it comprises non-linear interactions between its parts as well as feedback loops. This means that an understanding of the system is not possible through a simple reduction to its component parts.

Complication has been defined as quantitative escalation of what is theoretically reducible; these observational phenomena are explicable in terms of their component parts (such as relatively stable and recurring physical phenomena). By contrast, complexity belongs to entities for which reductionist explanation is insufficient; thus the isolation of individual aspects of a living system may tell us nothing of the operation of the whole (Chapman 1985).

In effect, complicated essentially refers to either a simple hierarchical structure (weakly complicated) or a hierarchical structure with circuits of influences (strongly complicated). On the other hand, complex is reserved for structures comprising many closed loops between interacting parts (Gardin 1979). The fundamental point here is that for complex systems, particularly human societal organization, no general simplifying assumptions can usefully be applied. Conversely, this does not preclude the possibility of generating meaningful description at the macroscopic level. Hogg and Huberman (1987) have addressed such an issue, tackling the problem of complexity from a computational perspective, and have evolved a quantitative measure of complexity based on diversity. This measure is founded on the number of different kinds of interaction which can exist in hierarchical structures. These findings support the intuitive notion that complexity exists as an intermediate state between perfectly ordered and completely disordered systems.

COMPLEXITY AND CHAOS: THE STRUCTURE OF DISORDER

The dominance of complex interactions renders these social systems endemically unstable, leading to the emergence of erratic, aperiodic fluctuations in system behaviour. These highly irregular fluctuations (previously dismissed as environmental 'noise') in fact contain an elusive and subtle structure known in the mathematical literature as *chaos*. First described in a seminal paper by Lorenz (1963), the important contribution of this work was in demonstrating that chaotic behaviour was a property of *deterministic* systems; the system's instability was not the outcome of extraneous noise.

As a result of subsequent observations in the physical, chemical and biological sciences, there is something of a consensus emerging on the role of chaotic dynamics in systems as diverse as global climatic regimes, biophysical structures, and physiological processes such as blood flow. We now know with some certainty that the seeds of aperiodic, chaotic trajectories are embedded in all self-replicating systems, and these intrinsic non-linear interactions have become the object of intensive study. Such dynamical systems have no inherent equilibrium but are characterized by the existence of multiple equilibria and sets of coexisting attractors to which the system is drawn and between which it may oscillate.

A critically important characteristic of chaotic systems, whether natural or physical, is that the possibility of chaos undermines the idea of prediction in the sense in which it is employed as a fundamental tenet of conventional scientific method. The property that has come to be known as 'sensitivity to initial conditions' (Ruelle and Takens 1971) implies that nearby trajectories will diverge on average exponentially. Consequently, given any observational point, it is impossible to make accurate long-term predictions of system behaviour.

From our current complexity perspective, the discovery of self-induced complex dynamics is of profound evolutionary importance, since we can now identify a powerful source of *emergent behaviour*. The origin of the heterogeneous and asymmetric behaviours observed in the natural – and by implication social – worlds may not prove as intractable as they appear.

Homogeneous structures may indeed have chaotic origins. What is clear is that, far from promoting any pathological trait, the aperiodic oscillations resident in chaotic dynamics may perform a significant operational role in the evolution of a system, principally by increasing the diversity or 'degrees of freedom' within which it operates (cf. Conrad 1986). This in turn may allow us to re-situate problems of adaptation and see a potential theoretical solution in the coexistence of multiple attractors as potentially defining a flexible domain of adaptation, as opposed to any single state. We arrive at a paradox where chaos becomes responsible for *enhancing the robustness of the system.*

In brief:

- Chaos (that is, structured disorder) is an intrinsic property of all complex systems.
- The adaptive significance of chaotic dynamics lies in the provision of increased degrees of freedom in the system, hence the possibility of new evolutionary pathways.
- The presence of chaotic behaviour in complex socio-economic systems means that prediction is severely constrained; thus, the long-term behaviour of economic markets is essentially unknown, regardless of a profusion of historical data.
- Chaos is paradoxical in the sense that it is the product of a deterministic set of events or processes.
- The desire to 'control' chaos may be decidedly maladaptive and counter-productive. For example, in ecological systems attempts to control environmental events can lead to catastrophic outcomes.

COMPLEXITY: EARLY THINKING AND RECENT DEVELOPMENTS

Systems and Cybernetics

While complexity research is a topical concern, the underlying principles are far from new. For example, the central ideas underlying phenomena such as chaotic dynamics, bifurcation, phase transitions and emergent behaviour, have a long history and form the core of studies in non-linear dynamics and Complex Systems Theory (for example Thom 1975; Nicolis and Prigogine 1977; Haken 1977; Allen 1982a, 1982b; Ruelle 1991). Strictly speaking, from a mathematical perspective, it was Henri Poincaré and his work on the three-body problem that produced the first insights on the nature of complex dynamical systems.

The origins of systems based research can be traced to the 1940s with the emergence of information theory as part of the cybernetic revolution and a new approach to understanding the structure and evolution of social and natural systems. This 'systemic' vision was based on the notion of providing a general description of systems as functioning mechanisms that could be broken down into sub-systemic parts as a prelude to analysis. A key process in the functioning of such systems, as originally presented by von Bertalanffy (1968), involves the role of feedback, where the output of a process in turn acts back to affect the input. 'Negative' feedback, whereby an event or process acts to maintain system equilibrium, is opposed to 'positive' feedback, in which case self-amplification occurs, leading to system transformation or collapse. Implicit in von Bertalanffy's General Systems Theory is the notion that societal systems (or indeed any other natural system) can usefully be disaggregated into a number of sub-systems (for example, economic, social, ideological and so on) so that their interdependent causal chains might be more effectively studied. This model of society as a sequence of coupled sub-systems was championed by Kent Flannery (1968, 1972) who declared that 'Culture change comes about through minor variations in one or more systems, which grow, displace or reinforce others and reach equilibrium on a different plane' (1968, p. 120).

From a cybernetic perspective, complexity was generally synonymous with the presence of large numbers of components, a variety of different types or behaviour, and particularly with the presence of extensive interconnections or interdependencies (Wolfram 2002). However, some systems that are merely complicated operate in this manner.

The objectivist nature of systems theory and its mechanistic portrayal of social phenomena rendered it subject to increasing academic criticism even as it diffused widely in the 1970s. A related controversial and contentious approach to understanding complex societal systems involved the social science's espousal of Catastrophe Theory. René Thom's (1975) work on the mathematics of structural stability focused on the capacity of systems of continuous variables to generate discontinuous states through bifurcation, and provoked both fascination and derision across the academic spectrum. Following Thom, some authors (for example Renfrew 1978, 1979) sought to use the methods of Catastrophe Theory to create a theoretical foundation from which a general theory of the collapse of complex societies might be constructed. Essentially a theory of qualitative dynamics, these catastrophe models emerging in geography, archaeology, psychology and sociology have been criticized as overly simplistic and requiring too much *a priori* information, as well as being ultimately difficult to verify. On the other hand, as with all models, they may be useful in clarifying relationships between variables so as to render them more explicit.

In complexity research, perhaps the most influential work has been that of Ilya Prigogine and colleagues with their investigations of 'far from equilibrium' phenomena and the study of system transformation in terms of 'order through fluctuations' (Nicolis and Prigogine 1977; Prigogine 1978, 1980; Prigogine and Stengers 1984). Indeed, it was the introduction of this work into the social sciences, largely through the efforts of Peter Allen (1981, 1982b, 1985, 1990, 1992) which provided the context for the first discussions of non-linear dynamics in the historical and archaeological sciences (van der Leeuw 1982; McGlade and Allen 1986) and led to the first explicit models exploring the nature of chaotic behaviour within prehistoric trade/exchange contexts (McGlade 1990, 1997; van der Leeuw and McGlade 1997).

Complex Adaptive Systems (CAS)

By way of contrast to much of the 'top-down' modelling associated with early systems theory, more recent complexity research has emphasized 'bottom-up' or micro-level theorizing, and this has favoured a move towards multi-agent models as the dominant modelling paradigm for complex systems of the past two decades. Broadly speaking an agent can be seen as an autonomous goal-directed software entity able to interact with an environment or resource (Axelrod and Cohen 1999). Agents can be individuals or a variety of collective entities such as households. Groups of agents, as interacting collectives, are usually defined as multi-agent systems; that is a collection of self-contained problem solving systems. These approaches have notably been used as vehicles or 'test beds' for the exploration of spatio-temporal complexity and have had a substantial impact on disciplines such as physics, urban geography, ecology and biology, from whence they have mutated to archaeology. Their universal applicability has been advocated, most forcibly by those researchers aligned with the Santa Fe group. In fact, it is the emergence of the Santa Fe Institute in 1988, under the guidance of Murray Gell-Mann and Philip Anderson, which has done most to promote the field of complexity studies – albeit within very specific terms of reference. Explorations of complexity and emergent phenomena dubbed 'artificial life' (Langton 1989, 1992), build on research into 'autopoietic' or self-replicating systems (Varela *et al.* 1974). This work on the evolutionary behaviour of self-replicating systems (Kauffman 1993) coupled with genetic algorithm research (Holland 1975), has led to the pronouncement of a general hypothesis that all complex systems emerge and preferentially maintain themselves at the 'edge of chaos' (Langton 1990).

It is worth noting here that one of the key insights claimed for CAS structures is their ability to self-organize through co-evolutionary adaptive mechanisms (Holland 1992; Kauffman 1993). The paradigm of self-organization has a somewhat longer history than CAS research at Santa Fe (Gell-Mann 1994; Kauffman 1995), in the light of the critical work of Ilya Prigogine on non-linear dynamics and dissipative structures (Nicolis and Prigogine 1977; Prigogine 1978, 1980). This paradigm was first introduced to a social science audience more than two decades ago by Prigogine's colleague Peter Allen (1981, 1982a, 1982b).

More recent work into self-organization as a key component in complexity research follows Bak and colleagues (Bak *et al.* 1988; Bak and Chen 1991) whose work in physical systems has identified 'self-organized criticality' as a key aspect in understanding scalar growth. In this evolutionary model, periods of stasis alternate with cascades of change that generate chain reactions between agents. Self-organized critical systems are said to evolve to a critical state; that is one poised between order and chaos (Kauffman 1995; Bak 1996). It remains to be seen whether the claims of those such as Gell-Mann (1994), Kauffman (1995) and Bentley and Maschner (2001) as to the ubiquity of self-organized critical processes at the heart of society and culture will be borne out.

Power Law Distributions

One of the properties claimed for complex systems of all types – biological, social, economic – is that they display power law structures; change occurs at all scales, incrementally and as 'avalanches' (Bentley and Maschner 2001). Complex phenomena are distributed in a highly skewed manner, rather than following the normal, Gaussian pattern. Vilfredo Pareto (1896) showed that the distribution of income in households obeys a power law distribution, but the hold of assumptions that normal distributions are the norm has remained strong in the social sciences, with implications for predictions based on underlying reasoning (statistical significance, confidence levels, standard error). Increasingly, evidence is building up on distributions that are far from normal, such as fossil records that exhibit power law distributions with respect to the magnitude of extinction events and species lifetimes (Newman 1996, 1997).

Generally speaking, it has been observed that real, large systems with many autonomous but interacting components are characterized by power law distributions. Dissipative structures subject to amplification effects are typically subject to skewed distributions (for example, firm and city size). The power law distribution is, in effect, an observed statistical signature of large systems of autonomous, interacting entities including software agents. Power law structures have become a central aspect of agent-based research. Adamic and Huberman (1999) have found that the distribution of visits to Internet websites is also a power law distribution, subject to interaction effects among users. Currently, the growing number of examples of fractal structures and self-organized critical phenomenon signal a fruitful research area; indeed, as Bentley and Maschner (2001) have demonstrated, the future for historically based studies of stylistic variation may yet lie in this direction.

Co-Evolution and Complexity

A key aspect of evolution as it occurs in all complex systems involves the role of reciprocal interactions between agents and processes to form co-evolutionary dynamics. These patterns of interaction, driven by positive feedback, or self-amplifying processes, create mutually reinforcing causal chains. Because the system is constantly evolving, these couplings are continuously updated and/or renewed as part of the process of self-organization.

In the biological sciences, while the idea of co-evolution was already present in Darwin's 'Origin of Species' it was the subject of limited discussion, regarded as an exception to the general trend of selectionist principles. Somewhat surprisingly, it was not until the 1960s that the idea was revisited in a systematic way through the work of Ehrlich and Raven (1964) and their influential study of the association between species of butterflies and their host plants. What they describe is a process of reciprocal evolutionary change in which there are close ecological relationships without genetic information being exchanged between the two or more groups of organisms (Odum 1993).

A classic example from the biological sciences is the co-evolutionary 'arms race'; for example, a plant has chemical defences and an insect evolves the necessary biochemistry to detoxify the compounds. The plant, in turn, evolves new defences that the insect must further detoxify. These reciprocal interactions can be said to constitute a co-evolutionary dynamic.

Beyond the biological sciences, a number of studies have sought to extend the co-evolutionary analogy. Examples can be found in development studies (Norgaard 1994), archaeology (McGlade 1995), linguistics (Briscoe 2000), economics (Fiorillo 2001) and anthropology (Kuznar 2001), with a view to seeking alternative evolutionary explanations in systems where competitive interaction and complex feedback processes occur.

With respect to the concerns of the current volume, a co-evolutionary perspective focuses on the way that self-organizing processes at work in socio-economic systems act to generate the system's evolutionary character. Norgaard (1984, 1994) has presented a co-evolutionary model based on the mutual feedbacks and non-linearities between values, knowledge, social organization, technology and environment. Building on these ideas, McGlade *et al.* point out in Chapter 6 of this volume that Norgaard's model rejects the conventional separation between system and environment, viewing all processes within a holistic, co-evolutionary paradigm. Norgaard invokes the metaphor of biological fitness to account for co-evolutionary development, such that selective pressures determine the relative 'fitness' and hence survival of specific sets of values and beliefs. In a real sense, the operation of co-evolutionary dynamics becomes a prerequisite for any system to be described as 'complex'. The presence of causal loops driven by such reciprocal dynamics is in a sense the motor of evolution (cf. Allen and McGlade 1987).

REPRESENTING COMPLEX CO-EVOLUTIONARY PROCESSES

In essence, models are intellectual constructs that allow us to cope with the world of observation and experience through a process of simplification. This is a ubiquitous feature of human perceptual and decision-making processes, and it is largely through the construction of models that we understand and impose a coherent rationale on knowledge structures, behaviour and events. In another sense, models resemble 'maps' in providing us with a sense of orientation, with simplified schemata with which we can negotiate unfamiliar or alien territory – a means of coming to terms with the 'other'. In order to obtain substantive knowledge of phenomena, the world of science conventionally employs a wide variety of modelling strategies. Although these cover a diverse set of approaches, for convenience, they can be classified into two primary types:

1. Implicit, informal heuristic devices, which are largely unrecognized as having any conscious theoretical basis.
2. Formal, scientific models based on some sort of deductive logic.

It is the second category of model building that is of most concern to us here, for it is a primary feature of much research in the natural and social sciences, and forms the basis of deductive inference and predictability. Within this paradigm, models tend to be seen as abstract analogues of some real world phenomena – surrogate, predictive tools directed towards problem solutions. However, rather than submit to systemic models based on mechanistic prediction and quantitative analysis, our aim is rather to focus on the qualitative dynamics that underpin system behaviour;

that is, we mean to investigate possible dynamical trajectories to which socio-natural systems are prone.

Approaches to modelling complexity phenomena have so far been governed by a relatively narrow focus, directed at the functional development of appropriate computational architectures (for example, multi-agent and dynamical systems approaches). In this volume we look beyond the language and assumptions resident in these increasingly dominant modelling paradigms and examine their applicability to recursive, counterintuitive dynamics. A focus on relationships articulating agency and structure is viewed as central to understanding the nature of complex societal systems. What is really radical about the world as defined by the new paradigm of complexity is that it alters our notions of time and reversibility, of space (action can occur at a distance) and of causality which may be non-proportional. These real complexities need to be factored into our representations. Complexity is no new 'master narrative' or totalizing explanation that can provide formulaic solutions. Rather we need to focus on the way in which this perspective enlarges our capacity to understand human-environment co-evolution as recursive, where small events can have cascading consequences. It is an approach that exposes new dimensions defined by partial connections, fragmented temporalities and multiple mappings. The approach we advocate, congruent with post-modernist concerns but rejecting intellectual nihilism, promotes a model of conceptual pluralism as opposed to strategies based on scientific reductionism.

The crux of this argument centres on the possibility of arriving at various reduced descriptions, that is, proximate solutions which avoid the pitfalls of reductionist explanation. The epistemological problem which this poses rests on the belief that explanations are arbitrary descriptions of a continuous learning process, in contradistinction to explanation as a nomothetic goal. Checkland (1981, p. 279) captures the sense of this when he argues for the replacement of a paradigm of 'optimizing' with a paradigm of 'learning'; thus, the idea of any single 'solution' is spurious. By extension we can define any model representation as the carrier of insight through a variety of related arguments and meanings. What we are stressing here is that all model characterizations of socio-cultural phenomena are necessarily both incomplete and contingent; we need a variety of model scenarios at different temporal and spatial scales. Only in this way can we deal adequately with the dynamics of complex socio-economic systems.

The position we are advocating can be summarized, thus:

- No single map (model) is of itself a sufficient descriptor of a complex system (reality); theoretically, there are as many possible mappings as there are meaningful perceptions.

- Models can thus be considered as discrete knowledge systems reflecting distinct points of view or problem sets. In social–natural systems, understanding is the outcome of the conversation or interaction between a plurality of model explorations or experiments.
- Each model potentially serves a different purpose, just as a geological map, a street map, or an aerial survey, all generate different but complementary information on the landscape. (Adapted from McGlade 2003, p. 114.)

Such statements seem innocuous enough, yet the implementation of such a programme runs counter to the current discourse within which Complexity Theory or Complex Adaptive Systems (CAS) is situated, and indeed, to modelling in the social and natural sciences generally.

It is clear that the representation of complexity is non-trivial and requires the development of new approaches that deal with the scale-dependent and self-organizing capacities of socio-economic systems and not least, their propensity to display counterintuitive structural change. An additional related issue concerns the fact that non-linear causality contains within it the seeds of chaotic phenomena. In fact, the important thing about the presence of chaos within a system is that it offers an alternative model of structural evolution and ultimately of order: it undermines the binary distinction between order and disorder beloved by Western science and instead, draws attention to the role of contingent processes within otherwise deterministic 'ordered' systems. Complexity, thus, may be said to inhabit a domain somewhere between deterministic order and randomness. Within the context of societal systems, it is the model representation of this territory of 'structured disorder' that must concern us.

Representation of the attractors underlying system structure can provide insight into fundamental constituents of dynamical systems and define their long run behaviour. They can be thought of as quasi-stable or metastable configurations in an n-dimensional state space of all possible states the system may inhabit. For social systems, we might usefully see this as a 'possibility space' comprising sub-domains or event spaces which are constrained by human agency. *When systems are recurrently drawn to certain states we can say they are subject to attractors.* Major perturbations in the event space as a consequence of new knowledge, innovations and so on – whether intended or unintended – will precipitate bifurcations, causing the attractor to restructure or alternatively to flip to a new basin of attraction. It is these discontinuous mappings that we must attempt to track in our efforts to make plausible qualitative representations of socio-economic systems.

NEXSUS AND THE COMPLEXITY DISCOURSE

This book explores a set of social and economic problems, involving issues that include path dependence, self-organization, co-evolution, resilience, network connectivity, punctuated change and abrupt discontinuity. They offer a set of broad-based perspectives on the nature of evolutionary processes in complex socio-economic systems. They depart from current fashion by suggesting that understanding complex systems is not to be found by recourse to the neo-Darwinist synthesis, or genetic algorithms, but by the application of holistic multi-level modelling methodologies and an understanding of socio-economic systems at different levels of aggregation. Systems whose evolution is a consequence of emergent properties cannot usefully be understood by recourse to conventional deductive, analytical methods. These tend to be focused at a single level of analysis and to neglect the component elements of the observed system and the emergent properties engendered by the collective activities of many such systems at the next level of aggregation.

While the primary emphasis of the contributions is to focus on the nature of co-evolutionary processes and their role in generating emergent evolution, pathdependence and distributed innovation dynamics, this is demonstrated, not by recourse to any single methodological or theoretical structure, but rather through a spectrum of approaches. This methodological pluralism is intended to demonstrate that the understanding of complexity is not to be found in the adoption of any single set of rules or epistemology (such as is advocated by those wishing to create a new orthodoxy in complexity studies). Rather, the diversity that characterizes the volume's case studies allows the reader to encounter co-evolution and complexity issues in the absence of any over-arching ideological perspective. In this way, the volume offers insights into the nature of evolutionary change through a series of empirical studies spanning the emergent structuring in long-term settlement networks, fractal scaling and self-organized criticality in urban systems, the evolution of capitalism, of production systems, markets and technologies, the evolution of industrial ecologies and the adaptability and resilience of large-scale socio-economic organizations.

ORIGINS OF THE BOOK

The volume represents the results of a multidisciplinary inter-university networked programme (NEXSUS) funded by the UK Economic and Social Research Council (ESRC) and involving researchers from a variety of academic disciplines (economics, urban modelling, landscape archaeology, management science and industrial psychology). While the research undertaken by each group was focused on specific sets of social, cultural and economic issues, all were linked by a common commitment to complexity thinking with a view to exploring the utility of such a paradigm to generate alternative interpretations of complex socio-economic processes.

Cross-cutting Themes

In the next chapter, Allen *et al.* provide a new perspective on evolutionary behaviour in the social sciences. Models are constructed to explore the dynamics of cooperation and competition and to demonstrate the role of synergetic practices in generating unanticipated evolutionary outcomes. Another important theme addressed by the volume involves the application of complexity theory to the evolution of cities and the settlement landscape. In Chapter 3, Batty *et al.* explore the application of some of the classic analytical themes of complexity theory such as phase transitions, fractal geometry and self-organized criticality. These are explored within the context of the emergent evolution of cities, the focus being on 'bottom-up' rather than 'top-down' structuring. The study argues that the spatial form of cities is intrinsically fractal, based on the repetition of simple patterns at all levels of the spatial hierarchy. McGlade addresses the long-term evolution of socio-spatial systems in Chapter 4, focusing at a more macro scale in analysing the evolution of landscape over the *longue durée*. Drawing on palaeo-environmental, archaeological and textual evidence, the study explores the structural development of a specific landscape, tracing its evolutionary history from the first prehistoric imprint until the early Medieval period. This period, spanning more than five millennia, is characterized by distinctive human-environment signatures or ecohistorical regimes. These constitute particular social, environmental, politico-economic interactions that define structural attractors as self-organizing emergent phenomena. The study suggests that the trajectory of history has no inherent teleological drive towards increasing complexity, but rather should be viewed as a sequence of contingently determined, though path-dependent transitions.

The complex nature of market economies forms the central focus of the contribution by Ramlogan and Metcalfe in Chapter 5. This study looks at the problem of structural change in modern knowledge-based economies, in particular the role played by innovation and competition dynamics. Beginning with a critique of modern macro-economic theory, the chapter presents an alternative model that views the economy as a complex adaptive system driven by positive feedback processes. A key feature of this study is the construction of a dynamical theory of innovation and competition as a co-evolutionary process, thus presenting a useful comparison with Chapters 2 and 7.

Co-evolution and self-reinforcing dynamics are also at the centre of the study by McGlade *et al.* in Chapter 6, which traces growth, decline and regeneration in the evolution of the South Yorkshire coal industry. Here, the interactions between coupled sets of processes linking values, knowledge, resources, social organization and agency are set within a co-evolutionary model that forms the basis of an understanding of the resilience of the socio-economic system. Results suggest that industrial collapse occurred as a consequence of a conflict between embedded value systems and an unwillingness to confront a rapidly changing knowledge base ushered in by changes in the global economy. A lack of institutional flexibility (resilience) sealed the industry's fate. This latter theme provides a good example of 'lock-in' effects that are frequently the outcome of the operation of path-dependent processes that are a common feature of complex non-linear systems.

A key aspect of a complexity perspective with respect to production systems involves the role played by emergent processes. This is the focus of Chapter 7 by Garnsey *et al.* The creation of novelty and its subsequent retention or elimination by evolutionary mechanisms is a central theme in complexity studies. By examining the evolution of three information and communication technologies, this chapter explores linkages between variety generation, selection and propagation. Tensions are identified between the benefits of variety to meet diverse user needs and the value of standardization to facilitate exchange. Interactive innovations are subject to amplification forces since the usefulness of products and service increases with numbers of users. Interoperability requirements, the facilitation of complementary technologies around a standard and user switching costs contribute to the emergence of dominant designs and standard protocols. These operate as a form of attractor, reducing the variety of possible states of technology but enabling complementary product and process innovations. Incremental innovations can result in radical transformation (analogous to a change in phase state) through technology fusion where complementarities are in place. Co-evolutionary processes that operate as technologies mature and industries consolidate lead to selection and propagation processes inimical to innovation, a finding that links this chapter to the one on declining industries. The need for renewal of diversity is shown to be all the greater in the light of multiple forces operating to erode difference.

The Afterword draws together the themes of the contributors and considers how the ideas highlighted by co-evolution and complexity dynamics can help to improve our understanding of socio-economic systems. Using examples from the volume, the chapter reflects on how a complexity perspective can potentially impact on policy in uncertain environments. A key aspect is seen to reside in the role of models and their capacity to generate a clearer understanding of the complex, counterintuitive dynamics resident in socio-economic systems.

The similarities and differences between the contributions derive both from their empirical context and from the various ways in which they are informed by complexity perspectives. The NEXSUS project has made it possible to find commonalities between projects that would not usually be grouped together. These studies show that complexity-based research is ready to move from theoretical reflections and abstract modelling to in-depth application to systems and situations in the social sciences.

Thus while the contributions of the present volume cover a wide spectrum of subject matter, the issues that unite them include co-evolutionary processes and the representation of complex non-linear sets of relationships: that is with the construction of appropriate models as a means of exploring evolutionary dynamics. A theme that runs throughout the contributions to this book is the recurrence of positive feedback or self-reinforcing processes. Broadly speaking, it is the existence of processes such as reproduction, cooperation, and competition at the interface of individual and community levels which can, under specific conditions of amplification, generate unstable and potentially transformative behaviour. This is clearly the case both at the level of population dynamics and equally within complex exchange and redistribution processes. Instability then is essentially a product of the presence of these self-reinforcing or auto-catalytic structures operating within sets of human relationships and at higher aggregate levels of societal organization. Of crucial importance to an understanding of these issues is the fact that networks of relationships are prone to endogenous transformation, independent of the application of any external force or perturbation.

REFERENCES

Adamic, L.A. and B.A. Huberman (1999), 'The nature of markets in the World Wide Web', IEA5, http://ssrn.com/abstract=166108.

Allen, Peter M. (1981), 'The evolutionary paradigm of dissipative structures', in Erich Jantsch (ed.), *The Evolutionary Vision: Toward a Unifying Paradigm of Physical, Biological and Sociocultural Evolution*, Boulder, CO: Westview Press, pp. 25–72.

Allen, Peter M. (1982a), 'Self-organization in the urban system', in William C. Shieve and Peter M. Allen (eds), *Self-organization and Dissipative Structures: Applications in the Physical and Social Sciences*, Austin: University of Texas Press, pp. 132–58.

Allen, Peter M. (1982b), 'The genesis of structure in social systems: the paradigm of self-organization', in A. Colin Renfrew, Michael J. Rowlands and Barbara A. Segraves (eds), *Theory and Explanation in Archaeology*, London: Academic Press, pp. 347–74.

Allen, Peter M. (1985), 'Towards a new science of complex systems', in Shuhei Aida *et al.* (eds), *The Science and Praxis of Complexity*, Tokyo: United Nations University, pp. 268–97.

Allen, P.M. (1990), 'Why the future is not as it was', *Futures*, July/August, 555–69.

Allen, P.M. (1992), 'Modelling evolutionary and complex systems', *World Futures*, **34**, 105–23.

Allen, P.M. and J.M. McGlade (1987), 'Evolutionary drive: The effect of microscopic diversity, error making and noise', *Foundations of Physics*, **17**, 723–38.

Arthur, W. Brian (1988), 'Self-reinforcing mechanisms in economics', in Phillip W. Anderson, Ken J. Arrow and David Pines (eds), *The Economy as an Evolving Complex System*, Redwood City: Addison-Wesley, pp. 9–31.

Axelrod, Robert and Michael D. Cohen (1999), *Harnessing Complexity: Organizational Implications of a Scientific Frontier*, New York: The Free Press.

Bak, P., C. Tang and K. Wiesenfeld (1988), 'Self-organized criticality', *Physical Review A*, **38**, 364–72.

Bak, P. and K. Chen (1991), 'Self-organized criticality', *Scientific American*, **264**(1), 46–53.

Bak, Per (1996), *How Nature Works: The Science of Self-Organized Criticality*, New York: Springer-Verlag.

Bentley, R.A. and H.D.G. Maschner (2001), 'Stylistic change as a self-organized critical phenomenon: an archaeological study in complexity', *Journal of Archaeological Method and Theory*, **8**(1), 35–66.

Bintliff, J.L. (1997), 'Catastrophe, chaos and complexity: the death, decay and rebirth of towns from antiquity to today', *Journal of European Archaeology*, **5**(2), 67–90.

Briscoe, E.J. (2000), 'Grammatical acquisition: inductive bias and coevolution of language and the language acquisition device', *Language*, **76**(2), 245–96.

Byrne, David S. (1998), *Complexity Theory and the Social Sciences*, London: Routledge.

Chapman, Graham P. (1985), 'The epistemology of complexity and some reflections on the symposium', in Shuhei Aida *et al.* (eds), *The Science and Praxis of Complexity*, Tokyo: United Nations University, pp. 357–74.

Checkland, Peter (1981), *Systems Thinking, Systems Practice*, Chichester: Wiley.

Cilliers, Paul (1998), *Complexity and Postmodernism: Understanding Complex Systems*, London: Routledge.

Conrad, M. (1986) 'What is the use of chaos?' in A. Holden (ed.), *Chaos*, Manchester: Manchester University Press, pp. 3–14.

Edmonds, Bruce (1996), 'What is complexity?', in Francis Heylighen and Diederik Aerts (eds), *The Evolution of Complexity*, Dordrecht: Kluwer.

Ehrlich, P.R. and P.H. Raven (1964), 'Butterflies and plants: A study in coevolution', *Evolution*, **18**(4), 568–608.

Fiorillo, F. (2001), 'Rate of growth and sector specialisation coevolution in a Kaldorian export-led growth model', *Structural Change and Economic Dynamics*, **12**(1), 91–114.

Flannery, Kent V. (1968), 'The Olmec and the Valley of Oaxaca: a model for interregional interaction in formative times', in Elizabeth P. Benson (ed.), *Proceedings of the Dumbarton Oaks Conference on the Olmec*, pp. 119–30.

Flannery, K.V. (1972), 'Cultural evolution of civilizations', *Annual Review of Ecology and Systematics*, **3**, 399–426.

Gardin, Jean Claude (1979), *Theoretical Archaeology*, Cambridge: Cambridge University Press.

Gell-Mann, Murray (1994), *The Quark and the Jaguar: Adventures in the Simple and the Complex*, London: Little Brown.

Gilbert, Nigel and Jim Doran (eds) (1994), *Simulating Societies: the Computer Simulation of Social Phenomena*, London: UCL Press.

Gilbert, Nigel and Rosaria Conte (eds) (1995), *Artificial Societies: the Computer Simulation of Social Life*, London: UCL Press.

Haken, Hermann (1977), *Synergetics*, Berlin: Springer-Verlag.

Harvey, D.L. and M.H. Reed (1994), 'The evolution of dissipative social systems', *Journal of Social and Evolutionary Systems*, **17**, 371–411.

Hayles, N. Katherine (1990), *Chaos Bound*, Ithica: Cornell University Press.

Hayles, N. Katherine (1991), *Chaos and Order*, Chicago: University of Chicago Press.

Hogg, T. and B.A. Huberman (1987), 'Phase transitions in artificial intelligence systems', *Artificial Intelligence*, **33**, 155–71.

Holland, John H. (1975), *Adaptation in Natural and Artificial Systems: An Introductory Analysis with Applications to Biology, Control and Artificial Intelligence*, Ann Arbor: University of Michigan Press.

Holland, John H. (1992), *Adaptation in Natural and Artificial Systems: An Introductory Analysis with Applications to Biology, Control and Artificial Intelligence*, Cambridge, MA: MIT Press.

Jen, E. (1990), 'Aperiodicity in one-dimensional cellular automata', *Physica D*, **45**, 3–18.

Kauffman, Stuart A. (1993), *The Origins of Order: Self-organization and Selection in Evolution*, Oxford: Oxford University Press.

Kauffman, Stuart A. (1995), *At Home in the Universe: The Search for Laws of Self-Organization and Complexity*, Oxford: Oxford University Press.

Kiel, L. Douglas and Euel Elliott (eds) (1996), *Chaos Theory in the Social Sciences: Foundations and Applications*, Ann Arbor: University of Michigan Press.

Kohler, T.A. (1993), 'News from the North American southwest: prehistory on the edge of chaos', *Journal of Archaeological Research*, **1**, 267–321.

Kuznar, Lawrence A. (2001), *Ethnoarchaeology of Andean South America: Contributions to Archaeological Method and Theory*, Ann Arbor: International Monographs in Prehistory.

Langton, Christopher G. (1989), 'Artificial life', in Christopher G. Langton (ed.) *Artificial Life*, Redwood City, CA: Addison-Wesley, pp. 1–47.

Langton, Christopher G. (1990), 'Computation at the edge of chaos: phase transitions and emergent computation', *Physica D*, **42**(1–3), 12–37.

Langton, Christopher G. (1992), 'Life at the edge of chaos', in Christopher G. Langton (ed.) *Artificial Life II*, New York: Addison-Wesley, pp. 41–91.

Lorenz, E.N. (1963), 'Deterministic nonperiodic flow', *Journal of the Atmospheric Sciences*, **20**(2), 130–41.

McGlade, James (1990), *The Emergence of Structure: Social Transformation in Later Prehistoric Wessex*, Unpublished PhD dissertation, University of Cambridge.

McGlade, J. (1995), 'Archaeology and the ecodynamics of human-modified landscapes', *Antiquity*, **69**, 113–32.

McGlade, J. (1997), 'The limits of social control: coherence and chaos in a prestige-goods economy', in Sander E. van der Leeuw and James McGlade (eds), *Archaeology: Time and Structured Transformation*, London: Routledge, pp. 299–330.

McGlade, James (1999), 'The times of history: archaeology, narrative and nonlinear causality', in Timothy Murray (ed.), *Archaeological Approaches to Time*, London: Routledge, pp. 139–63.

McGlade, James (2003), 'The map is not the territory: complexity, complication and representation', in R. Alexander Bentley and Herbert D.G. Maschner (eds), *Complex Systems and Archaeology: Empirical and Theoretical Applications*, Salt Lake City: University of Utah Press, pp. 111–19.

McGlade, J. and P.M. Allen (1986), 'Fluctuation, instability and stress: understanding the evolution of a Swidden Horticultural System', *Science and Archaeology*, **28**, 44–50.

McGlade, James and Sander E. van der Leeuw (1997), 'Introduction: archaeology and nonlinear dynamics – new approaches to long-term change', in Sander E. van der Leeuw and James McGlade (eds), *Time, Process and Structured Transformation in Archaeology*, London: Routledge, pp. 1–32.

Newman, M.E.J. (1996), 'Self-organized criticality, evolution and the fossil record', *Royal Society of London Proceedings B*, **263**, 1605–10.

Newman, M.E.J. (1997), 'Evidence for self-organized criticality in evolution', *Physica D*, **107**, 293–6.

Nicolis, Grégoire and Ilya Prigogine (1977), *Self-Organization in Nonequilibrium Systems: From Dissipative Structures to Order Through Fluctuations*, New York: Wiley.

Nicolis, Grégoire and Ilya Prigogine (1989), *Exploring Complexity: an Introduction*, New York: W.H. Freeman.

Norgaard, R.B. (1984), 'Coevolutionary development potential', *Land Economics*, **60**, 160–73.

Norgaard, Richard B. (1994), *Development Betrayed: The End of Progress and a Coevolutionary Revisioning of the Future*, London: Routledge.

Odum, Eugene P. (1993), *Ecology and our Endangered Life Support Systems*, Sunderland, MA: Sinauer Associates.

Pareto, Vilfredo (1896), *Cours d'économie Politique*, Lausanne.

Parrott, L. and R. Kok (2000), 'Incorporating complexity in ecosystem modelling', *Complexity International*, **7**, 1–19, http://www.csu.edu.au/ci/.

Pavard, B. and J. Dugdale (2000), 'An introduction to complexity in social science', GRIC-IRIT, Toulouse, France, http://www.irit.fr/COSI/training/complexity-tutorial/complexity-tutorial.htm.

Prigogine, I. (1978), 'Time, structure and fluctuations', *Science*, **201**, 777–85.

Prigogine, Ilya (1980), *From Being to Becoming: Time and Complexity in the Physical Sciences*, New York: W.H. Freeman.

Prigogine, Ilya and Isabelle Stengers (1984), *Order out of Chaos: Man's New Dialogue with Nature*, New York: Bantam.

Reed, M.H. and D.L. Harvey (1992), 'The new science and the old: complexity and realism in the social sciences', *Journal for the Theory of Social Behaviour*, **22**, 356–79.

Reed, Michael H. and David L. Harvey (1996), 'Social science as the study of complex systems', in L. Douglas Kiel and Euel Elliott (eds), *Chaos Theory in the Social Sciences: Foundations and Applications*, Ann Arbor: University of Michigan Press, pp. 295–324.

Renfrew, A.C. (1978), 'Trajectory discontinuity and morphogenesis, the implications of catastrophe theory for archaeology', *American Antiquity*, **43**, 203–44.

Renfrew, A. Colin (1979), 'System collapse as social transformation', in A. Colin Renfrew and Kenneth L. Cooke (eds), *Transformations: Mathematical Approaches to Culture Change*, London: Academic Press, pp. 481–506.

Ruelle, David (1991), *Chance and Chaos*, Princeton, NJ: Princeton University Press.

Ruelle, D. and F. Takens (1971), 'On the nature of turbulence', *Communications of Mathematical Physics*, **20**, 167–92.

Thom, René (1975), *Structural Stability and Morphogenesis*, Reading, MA: Benjamin.

van der Leeuw, Sander E. (1982), 'How objective can we become? Some reflections on the nature of the relationship between the archaeologist, his data and his interpretations', in A. Colin Renfrew, Michael J. Rowlands and Barbara A. Segraves (eds), *Theory and Explanation in Archaeology*, London: Academic Press, pp. 431–58.

van der Leeuw, Sander E. and James McGlade (1997), *Time, Process and Structured Transformation in Archaeology*, London: Routledge.

Varela, F., H. Maturano and R. Uribe (1974), 'Autopoiesis: the organization of living systems, its characterisation and a model', *Biosystems*, **5**, 187–96.

von Bertalanffy, Ludwig (1968), *General System Theory: Foundations, Development, Applications*, New York: Braziller.

Waldrop, M. Mitchell (1992), *Complexity: The Emerging Science at the Edge of Order and Chaos*, New York: Simon and Schuster.

Wolfram, Stephen (2002), *A New Kind of Science*, Wolfram Media.

2. Evolution, diversity and organization

Peter Allen, Mark Strathern and James Baldwin

INTRODUCTION

Throughout this book we are discussing the nature and mechanisms that drive change in the economic, social and spatial structures of human systems. This is often supposed to be quite distinct from the evolution of natural systems, since human intention and intelligence is assumed to constitute a qualitative difference. However, we shall show that this is not really the case when the complex and emergent nature of systems robs us of predictive power and knowledge, and makes our actions as exploratory as that generated by genetic variation. When we examine models of natural evolution such as those of *Evolutionary Stable Strategies* (Maynard-Smith 1979), we see that they contain mechanisms of reproduction and mortality whose repeated action over time leads some population types to flourish and others to decline. In other words they are closed models that are only able to discuss single steps in the whole chain of events. These models of evolution do not ask where new 'behaviours' come from, but simply show that, if several are present, then under competition some will grow at the expense of others. The idea is that, in the natural world that surrounds us, such eliminations have already occurred, and what we see is the 'outcome' of such a process, all the marvellously adapted, mutually interdependent behaviours of living creatures. Behind this is the idea of evolution as an optimizing 'force', which has led to the retention of the organisms we see because of their functional superiority. In other words, in this view, behavioural optimality characterizes the organisms that inhabit a 'mature' system. Indeed, this naïve speculation is then used 'backwards' by 'optimal foraging theory', which says that the behaviour of individuals is 'explained' as being optimal within the circumstances within which it resides. Such ideas echo those of neoclassical economics in which the behaviour of firms or individuals is supposedly 'explained' as that which provides optimal profits or utility respectively.

But we disagree with this view. In general, each species is in interaction with others, and therefore evolutionary improvements may lead to greater synergy or conflict between behaviours, and in turn to lead to a chain of responses without any obvious end. And if there is no end, then the most that can be said of the behaviour of any particular individual or population is that its continued existence proves *only* that it is *sufficiently effective – but not that it is* optimal.

Our aim here is to show that the underlying mechanisms that drive evolution are the mechanisms that generate micro-diversity within a system, and how this in turn drives an evolving system structure, characterized by changing structural diversity. This view automatically creates co-evolutionary ecosystems made up of populations whose behaviours are both the mutual responses and challenges to each other.

Diversity is a measure of the number of qualitatively different types of entity present corresponding to individuals with different attributes. It may be that they share some dimensions, but differ on others. This is an important point because it refers to a fundamental issue for evolution – it concerns the qualitative changes that occur in systems and structures over time. This also introduces another important issue – that of multiple levels of description. In evolutionary systems, the internal nature of the interacting individual entities changes over time, as does the configuration of the interactions between these types, leading to a changing overall system performance within its environment. This presents us with a view in which individuals are bundles of their internal components; the local community or organizations they form are bundles of these individual types; and ecosystems and larger structures they form are bundles of these local communities. The essential feature is that of the co-evolution of successive layers of interacting elements both horizontally and between levels. The diversity of the different levels of structure arises through these co-evolutionary processes that are in turn driven by the generation of micro-diversity – diversity at the level below. To illustrate this, let us consider the simplest possible example. Let us consider how a population evolves. It evolves if new behaviour both invades a population and also grows to a significant level in the system.

EVOLVED DIVERSITY OF ECOSYSTEMS

The essential new idea in the foregoing discussion is that in order to 'understand' a particular ecosystem we must comprehend how it became what it is. That is, we must look at its structure as representing the 'accumulation' of successive adaptations to circumstances at different moments in the past. If an ecosystem persists in time, then we should not simply describe it, but rather attempt to establish the 'reasons' for its stability.

The dialogue between population dynamics – the simple reduced model of an ecosystem – and mutations or innovations, is particularly interesting in that it gives rise to what is usually referred to as evolutionary ecology. Consider as an example, the simplest possible ecosystem of a single species, x, growing up to some limit according to the logistic equation.

$$\frac{dx}{dt} = bx\left(1 - \frac{x}{N}\right) - mx \tag{2.1}$$

Providing that in conditions of plenty the birth rate b is larger than the death rate m, the population will grow to a stable, steady state $x^0 = N(1 - m/b)$, where N is the limiting resource. The detailed mathematics of this section is all given in Appendix 2.1.

In order to see what could invade the system, we can consider what would happen to a small amount of 'mutant', x', that is different from x. Now x' is supposed to be different from x, and in that case it may compete with x to an extent β for the limiting resource N ($0 < \beta < 1$). Because of its differences from x we must assume that it has a different birth rate b' and death rate m'. If we think about the population dynamics of this small, initial population, then we will now have two logistic equations, one for x and one for x'. The 'crowding term' expressing the effect of the limiting resource on each of them will also be different, being N for population x, and N' for population x'. We will now have two equations of population dynamics, one with factors b, m and N and the other with b', m' and N'. The crowding effect will be different in each, in that each x is in full competition with each other x, since they are identical, but only an amount β with the x'. Similarly, each x' is in full competition with its own population, but only partially, β, with x.

The question we want to ask is: what kind of x' can invade the system of x? We do not ask whether x' is 'better' or 'worse' than x, but simply whether or not x' *can* invade the system. This question is decided by testing the stability of the pre-existing state: $x = N(1 - m/b)$; $x' = 0$. If it is stable, then x' *cannot* invade the system. If it is unstable, invasion can proceed.

A simple stability analysis shows that the condition for x' to invade is,

$$N'(1 - m'/b') > \beta(N(1 - m/b)) \tag{2.2}$$

If this condition is fulfilled, x' will grow. Thus, if we supposed that a different mutant x' appeared with randomly scattered values of b', m' and

N', then the deterministic equations would allow only those mutants to grow whose parameters satisfied condition (2.2). It would reject all the others.

We can distinguish two different ways that new behaviour can invade the system. One is by 'out-competing' the incumbent within the same niche (same N). The other is to 'differentiate' oneself from the incumbent and avoid the competition by spreading out to feed on new kinds of resource.

In the first case, if the mutation x' is to out-compete x within the same niche, then: $\beta = 1$, and the condition becomes:

$$N'(1 - m'/b') > N(1 - m/b) \qquad (2.3)$$

Hence, as a result of random mutations, evolution within a given 'niche' can *only* lead to increased 'exploitation', or increasingly efficient use of the resources. The important point in this case is that the condition that allows x' to grow also ensures that x must decrease and disappear, as portrayed in Figure 2.1.

In the second case, when a mutant is not in total competition with x, and can feed off a somewhat different spectrum of resources, then $\beta < 1$, invasion is easier, since the value of $N'(1 - m'/b')$ need not be as high. What we shall observe, therefore, in a system with limited resources is that over a long

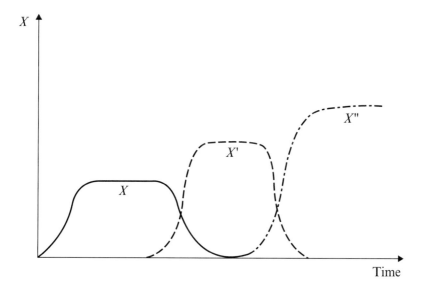

Figure 2.1 Within the same 'niche', we find successive replacement by more 'effective' populations

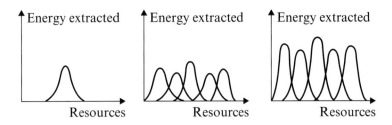

Figure 2.2   The rate and efficiency of exploitation of a resource base increases with evolution

time period an initially empty resource spectrum will gradually be *filled* by different populations, each adapted to a certain range of resources. Also, within any particular range or type of resource the efficiency of exploitation will increase irreversibly. This result can be extended to situations where genetics are explicitly considered, but these slightly more complicated equations do not lead to a different qualitative result (Figure 2.2).

Our model shows quite generally that the only thing that the random occurrence of mutants can do is to *increase the range* of resources exploited in the ecosystem, and *increase the efficiency* of the exploitation of any resource in particular. Of course, these very impressive statements are almost tautological when applied to such a simple system – they correspond roughly to *proving* that, if a species is born more and dies less, then it will grow in the system. It also assumes that the overall structure of the ecosystem (competing populations feeding on resources) doesn't change, for example by a new species emerging that was a predator of x. However, the idea is much more interesting when applied to more complicated ecosystems, where the parameters represented the multiple effects of many interactions and mechanisms, in which case our method could be used to show under which circumstances certain types of evolution would be favoured.

This generalization is indeed possible (Allen 1976). We can suppose that n species are interacting according to some more general dynamic equations, and that in between attempted 'invasions' by new behaviours, the existing system has found some stable condition. The corresponding populations are $x_1^0, x_2^0, \ldots x_n^0$. If some new behaviour, new population or allele, appears in a small amount somewhere in the system, then we want to know whether it can invade or not. The condition for it to invade is that the expanded population dynamics be unstable at the previous situation:

$$x_1^0, x_2^0, \ldots x_n^0 \text{ and } x_{n+1} = x_{n+2} \ldots x_{n+\Delta} = 0$$

Because we had supposed the old system had attained a stable stationary state, then instability can only occur because of the growth of at least some of the invader populations. This means that an evolutionary step can only occur if the invader populations grow in the system, at the existing stationary state, $x_1^0, x_2^0, \ldots x_n^0$ and $x_{n+1}, x_{n+2} \ldots = 0$. This general result has been applied to several different ecological systems (Allen 1975, 1981; Allen and McGlade 1987).

A particularly interesting application of these methods has been to the evolution of 'specialists' or 'generalists' in ecosystems. This example is of great interest because it reflects issues of both the 'strategy' of a particular population or actor, and the connectivity and structure of the ecosystem in which it is embedded. Here we will treat a very simple case of a one-level system, but it nevertheless indicates the potential of the approach. What we do is to consider the birth rate term, b, of our logistic equation, but go into more detail concerning the processes that underlie it.

Underlying the birth rate is the capacity of individuals to feed themselves and to capture and digest food to produce energy with which to 'power' their lives, which will include all the other aspects of their existence, of finding mates, homes, reproducing and rearing young and so on. We will consider a population x that feeds on a food base of a series of food types, each of density c, extracting E units of energy from each meal during a time τ. Each individual of the species x actually eats only a certain width w, of resource types.

We can use the evolutionary criterion discussed above to examine what new behaviours can invade the system. However, we need to make some assumption about the effect that being a specialist or generalist has on the amount of energy per meal that can be extracted. For example, we might assume that there exists an inverse relationship between the amount of energy that can be extracted per particle, and the width of the resource band utilized by an individual, but in fact it is the non-linearity of these two factors that will be important.

Whatever the precise relationship, we find that there are two limiting situations corresponding firstly to a rich system with very high density of resources, and secondly to a poor system with low densities of resources. Using our criterion for instability and invasion to occur, what we find is that for a rich system we shall observe an evolution towards *specialization* in these circumstances.

If, on the contrary, we are in a 'poor' system, evolution will tend to increase Ew, and lead to generalists exploiting a resource width that will depend on the precise form of the curve relating E and w.

This result can be extended to consider the morphological diversity that characterizes evolved ecosystems. If we suppose a resource base of length

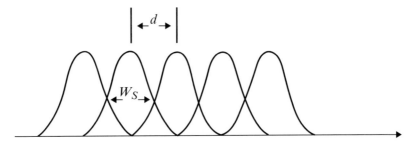

Figure 2.3   *A resource spectrum is supposed occupied by different*
populations, each of width w *and separated by 'distance'* d

L and density *c*, then we may ask how many species we should expect to find sharing these resources as a set of 'not-inconsistent' forms. Robert May (1973) showed that the separation between two species (the mythical Competitive Exclusion Principle) should be proportional to the amount of environmental fluctuation. However, this separation is expressed here in terms of the 'width' occupied by the species, so it is possible to combine our results with those of May to obtain an expression for the expected morphological diversity (in a single level, simple, highly artificial example, of course). If the number of species is *n*, and their 'niche' separation *d*, then we should find that, $d/w = \varepsilon|\sigma^2|$, where σ reflects environmental variability, since $n = L/d$ as shown in Figure 2.3 then:

$$n = \frac{L}{\varepsilon\sigma^2 w_s}$$

That is $nw_s = \dfrac{L}{\varepsilon\sigma^2}$ (2.4)

But the width occupied by a species is given by the variability, *v*, of the species multiplied by the width (degree of specialization) of each individual, as in Figure 2.4,

$$W_s = vW_i \tag{2.5}$$

and W_i is inversely related to resource density *c*. Therefore, we may write,

$$nv = L/(\varepsilon\sigma^2\ W_i) = Lc/(\varepsilon\sigma^2) \tag{2.6}$$

This tells us that morphological diversity (for example, variance of bird's beak) should be proportional to resource volume, *Lc*, and inversely proportional to the degree of environmental fluctuation.

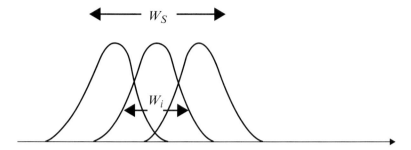

Figure 2.4   The width occupied by a species is assumed to depend on that occupied by individuals, multiplied by some factor of variability

Some partial confirmation of this relationship has been obtained. It concerns 'Darwin's finches' which inhabit the Galapagos Islands and which have been the subject of several careful investigations over the years. As is well known, the islands are home to some 14 species of finch, which are generally not found elsewhere (Figure 2.5). The 'explanation' of their diversity is commonly assumed to be 'ecological release', whereby the empty niches of the islands allowed the evolution of the few original species into the various possible varieties (Lack 1947).

If we consider the particular type of vegetation that each species occupies, then we can draw a more exact comparison. Bowman (1961) completed a careful study of the transitional vegetation and of the finches that occupy it. He identified the diet of each type of finch, measured the beak sizes and variations, and proved that beak size was directly related to the diet. The results of this study are shown in Table 2.1, where the species occupying the transitional zones are shown, together with the manner in which they divide the resources, and the total diversity of beak measurements. One of the most interesting results is that the seed spectrum on large islands is divided between three specialists, except on Chatham, where it is shared by only two. However, the measurements made by Bowman reveal that one of the two species shows a large difference between the male and female, in effect occupying two 'niches'.

Our equation (2.6) successfully predicts the relation shown in Table 2.1 between island size (resource volume) and total diversity that is supported. Such evolutionary arguments however, cannot predict precisely *which* species will occupy a given set of resources or exactly how these resources will be partitioned since this depends on the particular history of the

Notes: (1) *Geospiza magnirostris Gould* – large ground-finch, (2) *Geospizafortis Gould* – medium ground-finch, (3) *Geospizafuliginosa Gould* – small ground-finch, (4) *Geospiza difficilis Sharpe* – sharp-beaked ground-finch, (5) *Geospiza scandens (Gould)* – cactus ground-finch, (6) *Geospiza conirostris Ridgway* – large cactus ground-finch, (7) *Camarhynchus crassirostris Gould* – vegetarian tree-finch, (8) *Camarhynchus psittacula Gould* – large insectivorous tree-finch, (9) *Camarhynchuspauper Ridgway* – large insectivorous tree-finch on Charles, (10) *Camaihynchus pallidus (Gould)* – small insectivorous tree-finch, (11) *Camarhynchus pallidus (Sciater and Salvin)* – woodpecker-finch, (12) *Camarhynchus heliobates (Snodgrass and Heller)* – mangrove-finch, (13) *Certhidea olivacea Gould* – warbler-finch, (14) *Pinaroloxias inornata (Gould)* – cocos-finch.

Source: Lack 1947

Figure 2.5   The finches of the Galapagos: male and female of each species

system. However, this result does show us that there exists a relationship between resource volume, environmental fluctuation, and morphological diversity and that we can actually 'predict' the niches available to different populations, assuming the structural stability of the overall ecology. In other words, evolution leads to a given amount of 'coherent' diversity. But, the motor that drives this evolutionary filling of niches is actually that of micro-diversity generation – diversity produced at the level *below* that of the ecosystem.

Table 2.1   *The morphological diversity of beaks (variance in millimetres)*
            and resource volume for the transitional vegetation found on
            islands of decreasing size

Island	Species	Resources	Total beak variety
Indefatigable	Magnirostris	Large seeds	21.6 mm
Albemarle	Fortis	Medium seeds	20.6 mm
Charles	Fuliginosa	Small seeds	18.9 mm
James	Scandens	Cactus	18 mm
Chatham	Fortis	Large seeds	17.6 mm
	Fuliginosa	Medium and small seeds	
	Scandens	Cactus	
Tower	Magnirostris	Large seeds	13 mm
	Difficilis	Small seeds	
	Conirostris	Cactus	
Narborough	Magnirostris	Large seeds	11.4 mm
	Fortis	Medium seeds	
	Fuliginosa	Small seeds	
Hood	Conirostris	Large seeds and cactus	10.2 mm
	Fuliginosa	Small seeds	
Culpepper	Conirostris	Large seeds	9.6 mm
	Difficilis	Small seeds and cactus	
Wenman	Magnirostris	Large seeds	7.16 mm
	Difficilis	Small seeds and cactus	

THE IMPORTANCE OF MICRO-DIVERSITY

Let us now consider the workings of this 'micro-diversity' and see how it both *drives* evolution – and is also *selected for by* evolution.

Let us return to our very simple logistic equation (2.1) discussed in the section above. Instead of looking at whether a new population can invade the old one, what happens if reproduction is not perfect, so that offspring tend to have behaviours that are spread out around those of their parents, in some 'population character space'? If we consider that initially we have a single 'pure' population type then it will sit on one particular behaviour, *i*. However, the offspring will actually 'explore' behaviours around this in a kind of diffusion outwards in that space. We therefore make a model in which reproduction has fidelity, *f*, of offspring that are so close to their parents as to have the same vital behaviour. Of the $(1-f)$ imperfect offspring, however, we assume that some fraction is simply non-functional, and the remainder are spread around the neighbouring character cells evenly.

Complexity and co-evolution

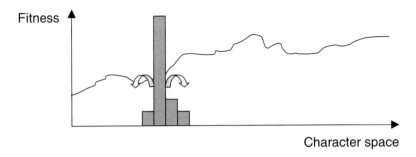

Figure 2.6   A one-dimensional example of the exploration of a character space

This experiment tells us that evolutionary progress – hill climbing – occurs as a result of processes that generate 'diffusion' in character space. Ignorance and error making are very robust sources of such exploration, but clearly random changes in the design of any complicated entity will mean that most experiments are simply non-viable, and only half of those that remain are 'better'. This effectively tells us that there is an 'opportunity cost' to behavioural exploration, and that there will be some 'best' amount of 'exploration' in a given situation, at which the pay-offs found, minus the opportunity cost, is a maximum.

Our model reveals to us a strategic reality – when we are in a new domain, and there is much to learn – then *learning/exploration pays off*. However, when we are in a mature system that has already been thoroughly explored there is no point wasting effort on further exploration. Of course, we can only *know* that there are opportunities or not by actually engaging in exploration, but clearly, unless there is some structural change, the value of exploration falls with sector maturity, and this will lead exploration behaviour to switch to exploitation.

In other words, the presence of populations with different levels of exploration and exploitation (error-making and accuracy) will automatically lead to evolution selecting whichever is most appropriate. So, *evolution will be driven by the amount of diversity generation to which it leads.* Evolution selects for an appropriate capacity to evolve.

COMPLEX SYSTEMS MODEL

This leads us to the general view that is shown in Figure 2.9. This sets out the kind of models that result from a particular set of assumptions. Very common are:

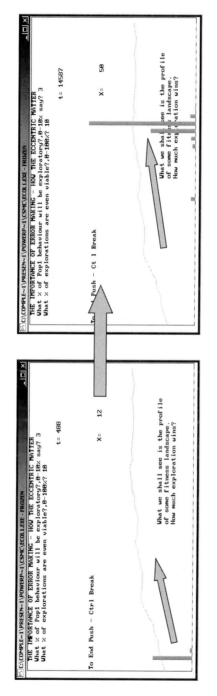

Figure 2.7   Diffusion in character space for a single population leads it to improve its fitness. Left time = 488; Right time = 14 587

33

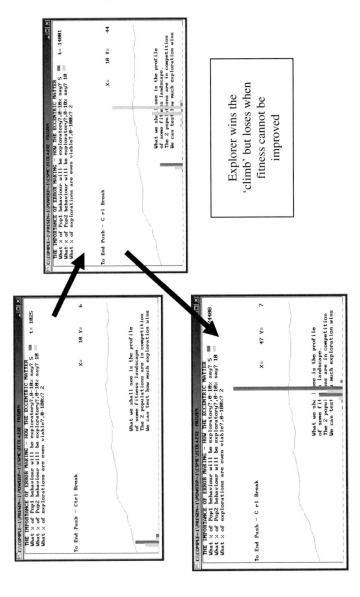

Figure 2.8 If we have two populations that have different rates of 'exploration' then we find that the relative success changes from early exploration to late exploitation

- the assumption of a boundary within which explanation can be found
- the ability to classify the contents and discern the things that matter
- that elements can be represented by average types
- that processes can be represented by their average rates

This succession of models arises from making successive, simplifying assumptions, and therefore models on the right are increasingly easy to understand and picture, but increasingly far from reality. *They lack the underlying micro-diversity that is present in reality, and hence cannot evolve. The model is structurally frozen – but reality is not.*

The operation of a system that is depicted as mechanical may be easy to understand but that simplicity has assumed away the more complex sources of ability to adapt and change. A systems model is a 'description' of the system at a particular moment, but does not contain the vital ingredient of micro-diversity that will really allow the system to undergo structural change and create a new, qualitatively different system, with some new variables and emergent performance. The ability to adapt and change is still present in the 'evolutionary' model that only makes assumptions 1 and 2, but not those of average type and average behaviours. This therefore tells us that the evolutionary capacity is generated by the very behaviours that are averaged by assumptions 3 and 4 – average types and average events. Thus organizations or individuals that show the ability to adapt and transform themselves do so as a result of the generation of micro-diversity and the interactions with micro-contextualities. This tells us the difference between a reality that is 'becoming' and our simplified understanding of this that is merely 'being' (Prigogine 1981).

Another important point to emerge is that it is the micro-diversity that is constantly generated at a *low level* in a system that leads to the evolution of structure, and therefore to the diversity that characterizes the system. If we ask what kind of 'structures' are created by the complex co-evolutionary processes resulting from the constant production of micro-diversity, then we see that it is one in which the structure emerges and evolves towards a baroque rather than a functionally efficient form. Furthermore, however we label its components, and demonstrate the clarity of its systemic structure, reality will always be messier, as there will always be micro-diversity testing the stability of whatever the system appears to be and hence the language we use to describe it. Descriptive language, like conventional system dynamics, will only describe current structure and not capture the dynamic dialectic that is taking place within it.

Another important point is that our understanding of real world situations is really at the level of the 'system model' of causally linked interacting components. Because this is how we understand the world, it follows

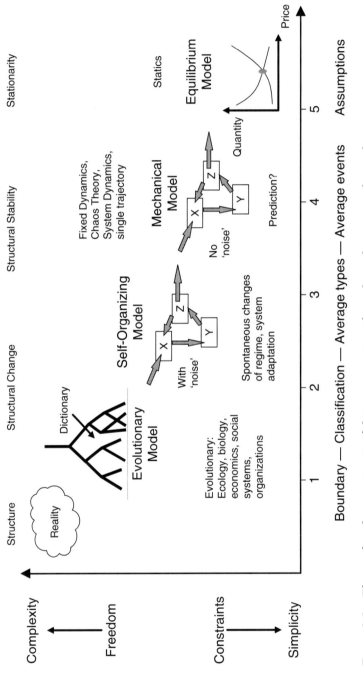

Figure 2.9   *The results of successive simplifying assumptions that take us from a complex evolving system to its mechanical representation*

that it is also how we conceive of ideas for intervention and action. And if we rely on the pure, simple operation of the pristine system, we shall experience failure rapidly, as a result of the actual existence of fluctuations of parameters (assumed to be zero by assumption 4) changing the idealized, smooth mechanical run into a stochastic non-linear dynamical system. In other words, taking into account these fluctuations is equivalent to having contingency plans and responses within the system model. So a simple business plan may rapidly learn to take into account the possibility of fires (for which there is insurance) and breakdowns of various kinds, requiring the engagement of additional repair staff so that they are on hand when these occur. So in the real world a business plan will need to try to include contingency plans for the fluctuations that can be anticipated. However, in an evolving world, with an evolving internal system, new contingencies will definitely occur at some point, and this will call upon the system to respond creatively, or lead to failure. Experienced engineers and entrepreneurs will therefore include feedback and correction responses for the problems they can anticipate, but will always face the problem of potentially new phenomena, resulting from evolution. What we see is that assumption 4, which takes us from a stochastic to a smooth parameter representation, is often successfully 'corrected' through experience of the contingencies that can arise. However, assumption 3, which takes us from an evolutionary system with micro-diversity to a set of interacting stereotypes, will eventually fail as some qualitative change, innovation or new variables emerge in the real system, but which do not emerge in the system representation. This is where strategic issues are separated from operational ones. Instead of mending the system through efficient contingency planning, system re-design will eventually be necessary to deal with the qualitative changes that, over time, will characterize reality.

MODELLING HUMAN SYSTEMS

These ideas can now be transferred to human systems. Behaviours, practices, routines and technologies are invented, learned and transmitted over time between successive actors and firms, so that evolutionary processes arise in exactly the same way.

Emergent Market Structure

The ideas developed in the sections above have been applied to a variety of systems, but here will be applied to the structuring of economic markets, as competition creates ecologies of firms producing goods in different market niches. The fundamental process can be explored initially using a simple model in which we consider the possible growth/decline of several firms that are attempting to produce and sell goods on the same market. The potential customers of course will view the different products according to their particular desires and needs, and in the simple case examined here, we shall simply consider that customers are differentiated by their revenue, and therefore have different sensitivities to price.

The structure of each firm that is modelled is as shown in Figure 2.10. Inputs and labour are necessary for production, and the cost of these, added to the fixed and start-up costs, produce goods that are sold by sales staff who must 'interact' with potential customers in order to turn them into actual customers. The potential market for a product is related to its qualities and price, and although in this simple case we have assumed that customers all like the same qualities, they have a different response to the price charged. The price charged is made up of the cost of production (variable cost) to which is added a mark-up. The mark-up needs to be such that it will turn out to cover the fixed and start-up costs as well as the sales staff wages. Depending on the quality and price, therefore, there are different sized potential markets coming from the different customer segments.

When customers buy a product, they cease to be potential customers for a time that is related to the lifetime of the product. For high quality goods this may be longer than for low quality, but of course, many goods are

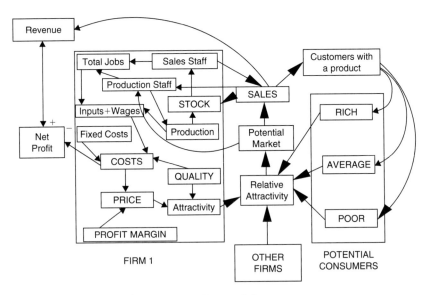

Figure 2.10   The evolutionary market model structure

bought in order to follow fashion and style rather than through absolute necessity. Indeed, different strategies would be required depending on whether or not this is the case, and so this is one of the many explorations that can be made with the model. The model calculates the relative attractivity of a product (of given quality and price) for a customer of a given type (poor, medium or rich). This results in a calculation of the 'potential market' for each firm at each moment, and the sales staff must interact with these potential customers in order to turn them into customers. When a sale is made, then the potential customer becomes a customer and disappears from the market for a time that depends on the product lifetime.

The 'problem' to be solved by the firms in the marketplace is how to find strategies of price and quality that can *profitably co-exist with the strategies of other firms*. This is very like the 'Darwin's finch' problem in which different types of finch emerge and co-evolve as a result of the constant production of micro-diversity from within those that exist. In the economic case, the 'resource pool' is the potential demand from customers for goods or services.

The revenues from the sales of a firm are used to pay the fixed and variable costs of production, and any profit can be used either to increase production or to decrease the bank debt if there is any. In this way, the firm tries to finance its growth and to avoid going near its credit limit. If its losses exceed its credit limit then it goes bankrupt and is closed down.

A very important issue that arises in the modelling concerns the rationality of the manager of the firm in electing to adopt whatever strategy is chosen. In traditional economic theories firms are supposed to act in such a way as to maximize profit. But, here, because the start-up requires an investment (a negative profit) no firms would start. So, if firms do start production, and increase it, then this cannot be modelled by linking the increase in production to the profit *at that time*. Instead, we might suppose that it is driven by the *expected profit* over some future time. But this is clearly difficult to do, because firms go bankrupt – presumably not the expected outcome. And here we see the paradox. In order to build this model to help managers formulate their expectations, the model requires that we represent what managers' expectations are. But this is only a paradox if we believe that the model is about *prediction*. In practice, it is about exploration, the exploration of how we think a market works, and so it is a part of a learning process, which may indeed lead participants to behave differently from their initial intentions, and possibly from what the modellers first expected.

Despite the difficulty in knowing what is going to happen beforehand, firms do start up, production is increased, and economic sectors are populated with firms. Since bankruptcies obviously also occur, then we can be sure that the expectations that drive the investment process are not necessarily related to the real outcomes. In our model therefore we simply have assumed that managers want to expand to capture their potential markets, but are forced to cut production if sales fall. They can make a loss for some time, providing that it is within their credit limit, but they much prefer to make a profit, and so attempt to increase sales, and to match production to this.

We can use our model to explore the effect of different learning strategies of firms. The first example will be a kind of Darwinian method called 'death and replacement'.

a. **Death and replacement**. In this we assume that firms do not adapt their price and quality strategies but pursue them to success or bankruptcy. Following bankruptcy, however, we re-launch the firms into the system with a new, randomly chosen strategy. This either survives or fails in its turn. The model represents a kind of 'Darwinian' model of market evolution in which firms do not learn or change their strategies over time; those random strategies that work remain; and those that don't are replaced by new, randomly chosen strategies.

   A typical long-term simulation shows the 2-D space of mark-up (%) and quality (Q), and the positions of the various firms, along with the strategy, price, profit, present balance and sales of each firm, and the state of the market. Such a simulation shows us that using purely random initial beliefs about possible strategies and random 're-launches' of failed firms leads to a fairly reasonable distribution of the firms in the space of 'possibilities' as well as to good levels of consumer satisfaction at the middle and rich end of the market.

b. **Hill climbing**. In the next version, firm 1 attempts to adapt its strategy by trying out the effects of small changes in quality and mark-up, and moving in the direction of higher profit (hill climbing) that this indicates. What emerges is that firm 1 does indeed succeed much better than when it simply pursued its initial price and quality strategy to bankruptcy. What this leads to is the perception that firms that 'learn' do better than those that fail to learn, and so the learning mechanism has a tendency to spread through firms. Firms that don't learn will have a higher probability of elimination than those that do, and so market evolution will reinforce learning. This is a similar mechanism to that described by the section on Darwin's finches.

c. **All hill climb**. However, if we allow all the firms to 'hill-climb', then their mutual interaction reduces the advantage of learning. There are also fewer bankruptcies in attaining this market structure. We see the 'limits to learning' in which the speed of learning and the frequency really matter and affect the ability to survive and prosper. The whole market evolution is different as all firms hill climb in profit space, moving overall to higher qualities and higher mark-ups. However, for several firms this very sophisticated strategy, involving careful testing of experimental variations in mark-up and quality does not bring success. In that case, it becomes important to see what other strategies are possible, and whether they can result in better outcomes.

d. **Imitation by one firm**. Another strategy is for firm 1 to monitor the market carefully and for it to adapt its production as rapidly as possible to copy whichever firm is currently making most profit. The model allows the imitator to move towards its target. Of course, it may not have the same economies of scale, but nevertheless its presence clearly increases competition at that point in strategy space, and changes the outcome for the market as a whole. For an identical simulation to that of the 'Death and Replacement' strategy we find that firm 1 discovers which firm is most profitable and imitates their strategy. This strategy can also emerge as a ploy to avoid bankruptcy. In the earlier case, firm 1 goes bankrupt at least once, whereas in this simulation it does not.

e. **All imitation**. In the next simulation, we consider the impact of the idea of imitation of the firms making up the market. If firm 1 can avoid a pathway leading to bankruptcy, then it shows that it is using a 'risk reducing' strategy. Rather than taking the risk of finding out whether the firm's individual strategy will work out, it seems tempting to imitate whichever strategy is making maximum profit. The 'decision-maker' has a role model instead of going it alone, and the imitated strategy is already making more profit than any other. What happens if all the players decide to imitate whoever is making the most profit? The model shows us that all the firms move to the same place in strategy space, and in so doing increase the degree of competition that they each experience. As a result, there are more bankruptcies (9) than in any of the other simulations. What might have been seen as a 'risk averse' strategy turns out to be the opposite! To imitate in a market of imitators is highly risky.

f. **Diverse learning strategies**. In this simulation real micro-diversity is present and there will be a diverse set of strategies being played out in the collective system. This is equivalent to saying that none of them are following some conventional 'Best Practice' but that some firms imitate winners and others hill climb.

While firm 1 does not do particularly well, this simulation actually produced an overall market structure that has been largest in total profits, and which has only suffered 3 bankruptcies. This introduces an interesting point about the different levels at which we can look at market evolution – that of the internal capabilities of firms and of their products, the strategy of one firm relative to the others and finally the overall outcome of the different capabilities and strategies adopted by participating firms. In some ways, for public policy what matters is the level of customer satisfaction and the level of overall profit for the sector. In our accounting for overall costs we need to include that of bankruptcy; every time that it occurs in our model, the social system, other firms and so on lose 10 000 units. In the real world the costs can be more devastating still to those involved and could even lead to a serious limitation on the willingness of actors to innovate.

We can examine the question as to the overall outcomes for the 'industry' of different strategies. In order to look at this, we have calculated the overall profits of the whole market, and we have included the costs of bankruptcies, in which a loser often starts by taking trade away from others in an attempt to keep going, but eventually crashes with debts. In Figure 2.11 we show the overall outcome for four different learning strategies. They are:

- Darwinian (random strategies, no learning)
- Old strategy (if profit less than half average, reduce %)
- Hill climbing
- 3–6 hill climbers, 1–3 imitators

The comparative results for the overall profit profile for the market are shown in Figure 2.11. However, here we have also performed four different runs for different sequences of random numbers, implying simply a different sequence of chance events. The important result that emerges is that in general, hill climbing in profit space is a good strategy, but a system in which some firms also imitate success seems to yield even better outcomes. However, what is really significant is that the particular random sequence that seed 6 provides and that of seed 5 differ remarkably in the overall outcomes. Seed 6 has high values for the collective performance of participants in the sector with all strategies other than pure Darwinian. However, seed 5 only yields value for the whole sector under one strategy. Indeed, using the Darwinian strategy the value of the whole sector is still increasingly negative. This shows us that for the same potential demand, for the same technology, the same strategies and the same interactions, chance can still allow great variation in market structures to emerge, some very favourable and some very unfavourable, and this tells us that the 'structural attractors' of economic markets are diverse and of very different overall efficiency. The invisible hand seems to be highly capricious.

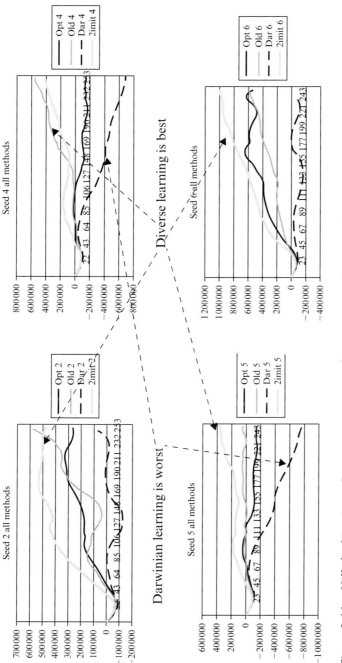

Figure 2.11   Hill climbing in profit space as a strategy by participants has a good outcome for the sector as a whole, but a mix of hill climbing with imitation of success is best. However, luck (the random sequence) can lead to very different market outcomes from highly profitable to only marginally so

Having looked at the level of the marketplace, we can now look at the problem at the level below, inside the competing firms. How do they gain their capacities to produce and deliver products and services sufficiently effectively to survive?

Evolution of Manufacturing Organizations

The previous sections demonstrate theoretically how micro-diversity in character space, tentative trials of novel concepts and activities, will lead to emergent objects and systems. However, it is still true that we cannot predict what they will be. Mathematically we can always solve a given set of equations to find the values of the variables for an optimal performance. But we do not know *which* variables will be present, as we do not know what new 'concept' may lead to a new structural attractor, and therefore we do not know *which* equations to solve or optimize. The changing patterns of practices and routines that are observed in the evolution of firms and organizations can be looked at in exactly the same way as that of 'product' evolution above. We would see a 'cladistic diagram' (a diagram showing evolutionary history) showing the history of successive new practices and innovative ideas in an economic sector. It would generate an evolutionary history of both artefacts and the organizational forms that underlie their production (McKelvey 1982, 1994; McCarthy 1995; McCarthy *et al.* 1997). Let us consider manufacturing organizations in the automobile sector.

With these characteristics (Table 2.2) as our 'dictionary' we can also identify 16 distinct organizational forms:

- Ancient craft system
- Standardized craft system
- Modern craft system
- Neocraft system
- Flexible manufacturing
- Toyota production
- Lean producers
- Agile producers
- Just in time
- Intensive mass producers
- European mass producers
- Modern mass producers
- Pseudo lean producers
- Fordist mass producers
- Large scale producers
- Skilled large scale producers

Table 2.2 Fifty-three characteristics of manufacturing organizations

Standardization of parts	1
Assembly time standards	2
Assembly line layout	3
Reduction of craft skills	4
Automation (Machine paced shops)	5
Pull production system	6
Reduction of lot size	7
Pull procurement planning	8
Operator based machine maintenance	9
Quality circles	10
Employee innovation prizes	11
Job rotation	12
Large volume production	13
Mass sub-contracting by sub-bidding	14
Exchange of workers with suppliers	15
Training through socialization	16
Proactive training programmes	17
Product range reduction	18
Automation (Machine paced shops)	19
Multiple sub-contracting	20
Quality systems	21
Quality philosophy	22
Open book policy with suppliers	23
Flexible multifunctional workforce	24
Set-up time reduction	25
Kaizen change management	26
TQM source	27
100% inspection sampling	28
U-Shape layout	29
Preventive maintenance	30
Individual error correction	31
Sequential dependency of workers	32
Line balancing	33
Team policy	34
Toyota verification of assembly line	35
Group vs. teams	36
Job enrichment	37
Manufacturing cells	38
Concurrent engineering	39
ABC costing	40
Excess capacity	41
Flexible automation of product versions	42
Agile automation for different products	43

Table 2.2   (continued)

In-sourcing	44
Immigrant workforce	45
Dedicated automation	46
Division of labour	47
Employees are system tools	48
Employees are system developers	49
Product focus	50
Parallel processing	51
Dependence on written rules	52
Further intensification of labour	53

The evolutionary tree of Figure 2.12 can be deduced from cladistic theory, and this shows the probable sequence of events that led to the different possible organizational forms. However, in the spirit of complex systems thinking and that of the formation of networks, we want to consider the synergy or conflict that different *pairs of attributes* actually have. Instead of only considering the different list of characteristic features that constitute the different organizational forms, we also look at the pair-wise interactions between each pair of practices, in order to examine the role of 'internal coherence' on the organizational performance. In this 'complex systems' approach, a new practice can only invade an organization if it is not in conflict with the practices that already exist there. In other words, we are looking at 'organizations' not in terms of simply additive features and practices, but as mutually interactive 'complexes' of constituent factors.

From a survey of manufacturers (Baldwin *et al.* 2003) concerning the positive or negative interactions between the different practices, a matrix of pair interaction was constructed allowing us to examine the 'reasons' behind the emergent organizational forms, with successful forms arising from positive mutual interactions of constituent practices. This is shown in Figure 2.13.

We have then been able to develop an evolutionary simulation model, in which a manufacturing firm attempts to incorporate successive new practices at some characteristic rate. There is a very wide range of possible structures that can emerge, however, depending simply on the order in which they are tried. But, each time a new practice is adopted within an organization, it changes the 'assimilation capacity' of the organization for any new innovations in the future. This is an illustration of the 'path dependent evolution' that characterizes organizational change. Successful evolution is about the 'discovery' or 'creation' of highly synergetic structures of interacting practices.

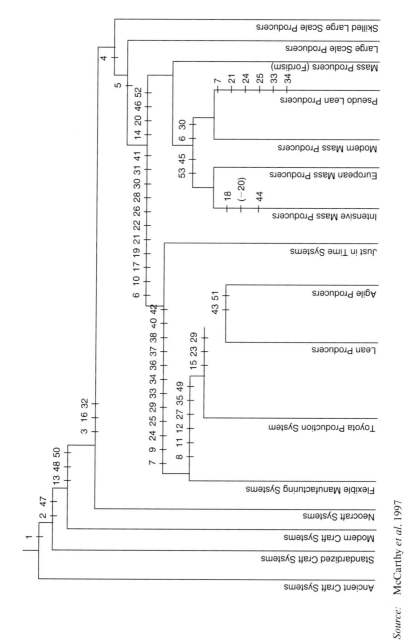

Source: McCarthy *et al.* 1997

Figure 2.12 *The cladistic diagram for automobile manufacturing organizational forms*

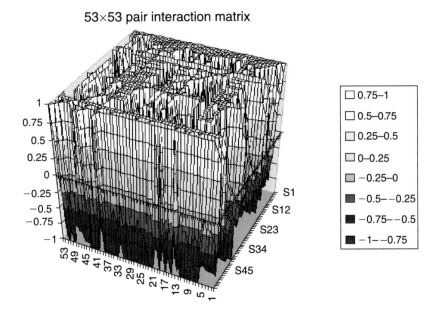

Figure 2.13   *The 53 × 53 matrix of pair interactions of the characteristic*
practices. It allows us to calculate the net attraction or
conflict for any new practice depending on which ones are
present already

In Figure 2.14 we see the changing internal structure of a particular
organization as it attempts to incorporate new practices from those available. In the simulation, the number available start from the ancient craft
practice on the let, and successively add the further 52 practices on the right.
At each moment in time the organization can choose from the practices
available at that time, and its overall performance is a function of the
synergy of the practices that are tried successfully. We see cases where practice 4, for example, is tried several times and simply cannot invade. However,
practice 9 is tried early on and fails, but does successfully invade at a later
date. The particular emergent attributes and capabilities of the organization
are a function of the particular combination of practices that constitute it.

The model starts off from a craft structure. New practices are chosen randomly from those available at the time and are launched as a small 'experimental' value of 5. Sometimes the behaviour declines and disappears, and
sometimes it grows and becomes part of the 'formal' structure that then
conditions which innovative behaviour can invade next.

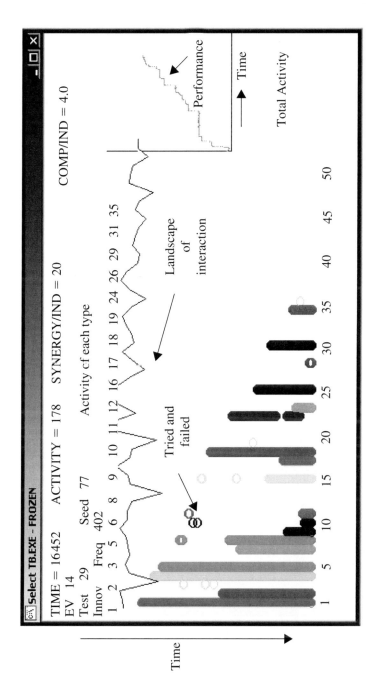

Figure 2.14   An evolutionary model tries to 'launch' possible innovative practices in a random order. If they invade, they change the 'invadability' of the new system

Different simulations lead to different structures, and there are a very large number of possible 'histories'. This demonstrates a key idea in complex systems thinking. The explorations/innovations that are tried out at a given time cannot be logically or rationally deduced because their overall effects cannot be known ahead of time. The very impossibility of prediction gives the system 'choice'. In our simulation we mimic this by using a random number generator to actually choose what to try out, though in practice this would be promoted by someone who believes in this choice, and who will be proved right or wrong by experience, or in this case by our simulation. In real life there will be debate and discussion by different people in favour of one or another choice, and each will cite their own projections about the trade-offs and the overall effect of their choice. However, the actual success that a new practice meets with is pre-determined by the 'fitness landscape' resulting from the practices already present and what the emergent attributes and capabilities encounter in the marketplace. But this landscape will be changed if a new practice does successfully invade the system. The new practice will bring with it its own set of pair interactions, modifying the selection criteria for further change. So, the pattern of what *could* then invade the system (if it were tried) has been changed by what *has already* invaded successfully. This is technically referred to as a 'path dependent' process since the future evolutionary pathway is affected by that of the past.

Our results have already shown, in Figure 2.15, that the evolution through the tree of forms corresponds to a gradual increase in overall 'synergy'. That is, the more modern structures related to 'lean' and to 'agile' organizations contain more 'positive' links and fewer 'negative' links per unit than the ancient craft systems and also the mass-producing side of the tree. In future research we shall also see how many different structures could have emerged and start to reflect on what new practices and innovations may be available today for the future.

Our work also highlights a 'problem' with the acceptance of complex systems thinking for operational use. The theory of complex systems tells us that the future is not completely predictable because the system has some internal autonomy and will undergo path dependent learning. However, this also means that the 'present' (existing data) cannot be proven to be a *necessary* outcome of the past – but only a *possible* outcome. So, there are perhaps so many possible structures for organizations to discover and render functional, that the observed organizational structures may be 16 among several hundred that are possible. In traditional science the assumption was that 'only the optimal survive', and therefore that what we observe is an optimal structure with only a few temporary deviations from average. But, selection is effected through the competitive interactions of the other

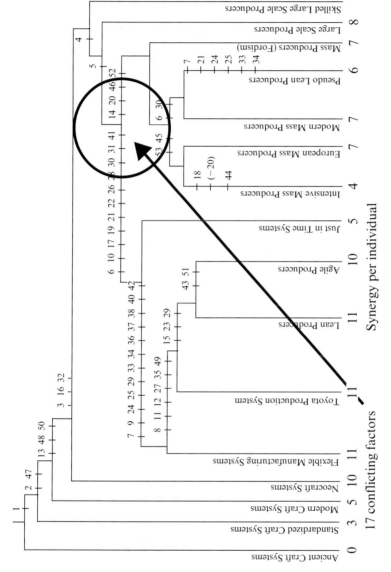

Figure 2.15   Knowledge of the pair matrix for the different characteristics allows us to calculate the synergy/individual in the different organizations

players, and if they are different, catering to a slightly different market, and also sub-optimal at any particular moment, then there is no selection force capable of pruning the burgeoning possibilities to a single, optimal outcome. Complexity tells us that we are freer than we thought, and that the diversity that this freedom allows is the mechanism through which sustainability, adaptability and learning occur.

This picture shows us that evolution is about the discovery and emergence of structural attractors (Allen 2001) that express the natural synergies and conflicts (the non-linearities) of underlying components. Their properties and consequences are difficult to anticipate and therefore require real explorations and experiments to be going on, based in turn on diversity of beliefs, views and experiences of freely acting individuals.

CONCLUSIONS

The evolutionary models described above show us the multi-level nature of socio-economic systems. Individuals with characteristic and developing skills and particularities form groups within companies, generating specific capabilities and also particular receptivities for possible future changes. The products and services that emerge from this are perceived by a segmented and heterogeneous population of potential consumers, who are attracted by the qualities of a particular product or service and the low price at which it is offered. This results in a market share and in changing volumes of activity for different firms. When volume increases, economies of scale occur and allow further price decreases and greater attractiveness for potential customers. However, debts can be cleared more quickly if higher prices are charged, and since there is an interest rate in the model, paying off debt is also a way of reducing costs.

The important result from the multi-agent, complex systems simulations above is that instead of showing us *the* optimal strategy for a firm, it tells us that there is *no such thing*. What will work for a company depends on the strategies being played by the others. The overall lesson is that it is better to be playing in a diverse market ecology than in one involving mainly imitation. So, having a unique identity and product may seem 'risky', but it is better than simply packing into the same strategy as others. Coupled with having an individual product and strategy, it is an advantage to 'learn'. So, exploring the landscape sufficiently to enable 'hill climbing' in terms of profit is generally better than not doing it. However, it does not necessarily solve all problems because the pathway 'up-hill' can be blocked by other firms. In this case a more radical exploration is required with the possibility of a 'big jump' in the product and strategy space. In general then, just as other chapters here discuss the source of ecological and engineering resilience, economic resilience comes from internal diversity.

The lower level evolutionary model of section 5 shows us how firms explore possible functional innovations, and evolve capabilities that lead either to survival or to failure. They describe a divergent evolutionary diffusion into 'possibility space'. Each of these is then either amplified or diminished depending on the 'performance' of the products or services provided, which depends on the internal trade-offs within them, on the synergies and conflicts that it encounters or discovers in its supply networks, retail structures and in the lifestyles of final consumers. As is discussed by Garnsey *et al.* in Chapter 7, the real entrepreneurial process depends on exploration and the ability to understand and interpret developments. Entrepreneurs may decide to innovate by providing new varieties within a technology standard unless the sector is so young that standards have not yet emerged and there is a chance that a completely new variant of technology may become a new dominant standard.

Either way, at the level of the marketplace, firms with different strategies or capabilities also try to 'invade' and remain in the system. Exploratory changes lead to a divergent exploration of possibilities. New elements are amplified or diminished as a result of the dual selection processes operating on one hand 'inside them' in terms of the synergies and conflicts of their internal structures, and also 'outside them', in their revealing of synergy or conflict with their surrounding features in the market. So, a new practice can 'invade' a system if it is synergetic with the existing structure, and this will then either lead to the reinforcement or the decline of that system in its environment if the modified system is synergetic or in conflict with its environment. Because of the difficulty of predicting both the emergent internal and external behaviours of a new action, the pay-off that will result from any given new action can therefore generally not be anticipated. It is this very ignorance that is a key factor in allowing exploration at all. Either the fear of the unknown will stop innovation, or divergent innovations will occur even though the actors concerned do not necessarily intend this. Attempting to imitate another player can lead to quite different outcomes, because either the internal structure or the external context is found to be different.

Throughout the economy, and indeed the social, cultural system of interacting elements and structures we see a generic picture at multiple temporal and spatial scales in which uncertainty about the future *allows* actions that are exploratory and divergent, which are then either amplified or suppressed by the way that this modifies the interaction with their environment. Essentially, this fulfils the early vision of dissipative structures, in that their existence and amplification depend on 'learning' how to access energy and matter in their environment. Can they form a self-reinforcing loop of mutual advantage in which entities and actors in the environment wish to supply the resources required for the growth and maintenance of the system in question? In this way, structures emerge as multi-scalar entities of cooperative, self-reinforcing processes.

What we see is a theoretical framework that encompasses both the evolutionary and the resource-based theory of the firm. This is not only relevant to the firm, but also to the social and economic system as a whole. It is the complex systems dialogue between explorations of possible futures at one level, and the unpredictable effects of this both at the level below and the level above. There is a dialogue between the 'trade-offs' or 'non-linearities' affected inside and outside the particular level of exploration. But it is also true that all levels are exploring. Unless there is an imposition of rigid homogeneity up and down the levels of the system, there will necessarily be behavioural explorations due to internal diversity. In this way, multi-level systems are precisely the structures that can 'shield' the lower levels from instantaneous selection, and allow an exploratory drift to occur, which can generate enough diversity to eventually *discover* a new behaviour that will grow. Without the multiple levels, selection would act instantly, and there would be no chance to build up significant deviations from the previous behaviour. We find that complexity and resilience is about the evolution of 'multi-level' systems, and our fundamental diagram of Figure 2.9 can be seen as operating on the different levels discussed in Chapter 6 by McGlade *et al.* (see Figure 2.16).

The whole system is an (imperfect) evolutionary, learning system in which people learn of different ways that they could spend their time and income, and what this may mean to them. Companies attempt to understand what customers are seeking, and how they can adapt their products and services to capture these needs. They attempt to develop new capabilities and practices to achieve this, and create new products and services as a result. These call on new technologies and materials and cause evolution in the supply networks. Technological innovation, cultural evolution and social pressures all change the opportunities and possibilities that can exist, and also the desires and dreams of consumers and their patterns of choice and of consumption.

This supports and perhaps fills out the view of evolutionary economics driven by 'restless capitalism' as presented by Metcalfe and Ramlogan in Chapter 5 of this book and in Metcalfe (1998, 1999). The successful working of the market requires underlying heterogeneity – both of potential consumers and of the agents on the supply side. Diverse strategies are required, and ones that are maintained even when some other strategy is working better. This chapter presents a view of socio-economic systems as evolving, multi-scale, spatio-temporal structures with emergent functions,

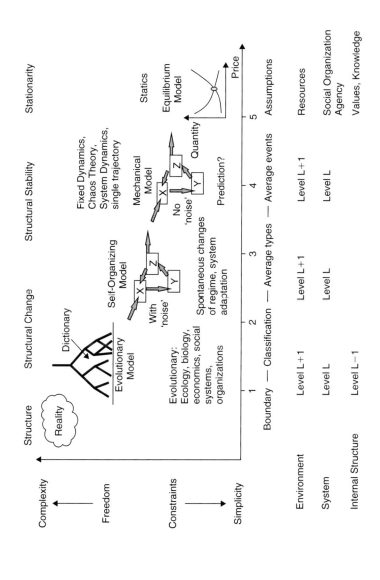

Figure 2.16 The coupled levels of description corresponding to different levels of approximation relating to the discussion of McGlade et al. in Chapter 6

needs and capabilities. Underlying the market model are the capabilities of the firms/agents to produce goods and services of a particular quality at an attractive price. And this comes about because of the creation of productive organizations that have the appropriate capabilities. These capabilities are, however, emergent properties of the constituent components and their pattern of interaction. These organizational forms are emergent over time, as new practices, techniques, technologies and routines are brought into the existing structures. The overall market structure is therefore the result of the interacting strategies of the different competing firms and of their inherent capacities to produce goods and services of appropriate qualities and prices. This is necessarily a multi-level evolutionary process, in which the 'explanation' of the market structure involves an explanation of the internal structures of the firms and vice versa. Sense-making creates knowledge that self-destructs over time when used, since it creates responses both around and inside which change the system. Complexity therefore provides us with a new model of history and of structural change. It tells us that although structure will often increase in complexity and dissipation, it can also collapse. There is no guaranteed steady improvement to better and better worlds. Progress can happen from some points of view, but so can catastrophes. Complexity is for adults in that it means that what we do *matters*; there is no 'optimizing invisible hand' as a back-up. Instead, there are multitudes of branching possibilities with unknown implications and consequences and it is through the risky exploration of these that we can and do discover and create new worlds, with new qualities, both good and bad. Keeping our capacities open for change and for exploration is the key to surviving in this connected and open reality.

APPENDIX 2.1

Consider as an example, the simplest possible ecosystem, a single species growing according to the logistic equation,

$$\frac{dx}{dt} = bx\left(1 - \frac{x}{N}\right) - mx \tag{A2.1}$$

This equation, describing the growth of a species x in a system with limited resources has a stable, stationary state, $x^0 = N(1 - m/b)$.

Let us consider, however, the effect of the arrival in the system of a 'mutant', x', that is different from x. For example, x' competes with x to an extent β for the limiting resource N $(0 < \beta < 1)$. The mutant is characterized by some other birth rate b' and death rate m'. The system equations become:

$$\frac{dx}{dt} = bx\left(1 - \frac{(x + \beta x')}{N}\right) - mx$$

$$\frac{dx'}{dt} = b'x'\left(1 - \frac{(x' + \beta x)}{N}\right) - m'x' \qquad \text{(A2.2)}$$

Can x' invade the system? A simple stability analysis shows that the condition for x' to invade is,

$$N'(1 - m'/b') > \beta(N(1 - m/b)) \qquad \text{(A2.3)}$$

If this condition is fulfilled, x' will grow.

Two cases arise. If the mutation x' were in total competition with x, then $\beta = 1$, and the condition becomes:

$$N'(1 - m'/b') > N(1 - m/b) \qquad \text{(A2.4)}$$

Hence, as a result of random mutations, evolution within a given 'niche' can lead to increased 'exploitation', or increasingly efficient use of the resources.

When overlap is not total, $\beta < 1$, invasion is easier, since the value of $N'(1 - m'/b')$ need not be as high. Over a long time period an initially empty resource spectrum will gradually be *filled* by different populations, each adapted to a certain range of resources.

This can be generalized (Allen 1976). We suppose that n species are interacting according to some dynamic equations,

$$\frac{dx_i}{dt} = G_i(x_1, x_2, \ldots x_n) \qquad \text{(A2.5)}$$

Let us further assume that these n populations have attained a stable, stationary state, $x_1^0, x_2^0, \ldots x_n^0$. If some new populations occur, for example following the appearance of a new allele, then the stability matrix for the expanded system will be: see (A2.6) overleaf.

Because of the zeros in the lower left-hand corner expressing the fact that there is no *systematic* production of the $n + \Delta$ by the n (otherwise the $n + \Delta$ would have already been present) we find:

Stability Matrix of Whole = {Stability Matrix of Old} × {Stability Matrix of New}.

But we had supposed the old system had attained a stable stationary state, so that if an evolutionary step is to occur, then it can result only from the existence of a positive root of the stability matrix for the new populations

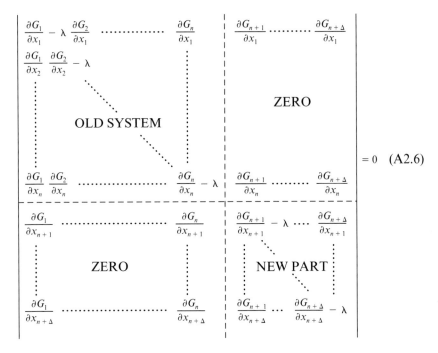

$$= 0 \quad \text{(A2.6)}$$

– evaluated at the existing stationary state, $x_1^0, x_2^0, \ldots x_n^0$ and $x_{n+1}, x_{n+2} \cdots$ $= 0$, that is, there exists a positive λ satisfying:

$$\left| \frac{\partial G_{n+i}}{\partial x_{n+i}} - \lambda \right| = 0, \quad \text{(A2.7)}$$

at $x_1^0, x_2^0, \ldots x_n^0$ and $x_{n+1} = x_{n+2} \ldots x_{n+\Delta} = 0$

This general result has been applied to several different ecological systems (Allen 1975, 1987).

A particularly interesting application of these methods has been to the evolution of 'specialists' or 'generalizes' in ecosystems. Consider a resource base of density c, in which we find a species x, that 'extracts' E units of energy from each particle during a time τ. Each individual of the species x feeds on a certain band of resource type having a width w (a volume in hyperspace),

$$\frac{dx}{dt} = \frac{\alpha Ewc}{1 + \alpha \tau wc} x \left(1 - \frac{x}{N}\right) - mx \quad \text{(A2.8)}$$

Using the evolutionary criterion (11), we see that N will increase, m will decrease and, as a result of random mutation $\alpha Ewc/(1 + \alpha \tau wc)$ will also increase.

However, different ways of increasing this latter term are possible, and according to the prevailing circumstances, some are more effective than others. If the system is 'rich' that is if $c \gg 1/\alpha\tau w$, then,

$$\frac{\alpha E w c}{1 + \alpha\tau w c} \to \frac{E}{\tau} \tag{A2.9}$$

The most effective amplification will occur for those mutations that increase the value of E/τ independently of the width utilized. As there is an inverse relation between the width and the value we can expect for E/τ, it follows that we shall observe an evolution towards *specialization* in these circumstances.

If, on the contrary, we are in a 'poor' system, with $c \ll 1/\alpha\tau w c$, then because

$$\frac{\alpha E w c}{1 + \alpha\tau w c} \to \alpha E w c \tag{A2.10}$$

evolution will tend to increase Ew, and lead to generalists exploiting a resource width that will depend on the precise form of the curve relating E and w.

It is possible to combine our results with those of May (1973) to obtain an expression for the expected morphological diversity. If the number of species is n, and their 'niche' separation d, then we should find that, $d/w = \varepsilon|\sigma^2|$, where σ reflects environmental variability, since $n = L/d$ then

$$n = \frac{L}{\varepsilon\sigma^2 w_s}$$

$$\text{That is } nw_s = \frac{L}{\varepsilon\sigma^2} \tag{A2.11}$$

But the width occupied by a species is given by the variability, v, of the species multiplied by the width occupied by individuals,

$$W_s = vW_i \tag{A2.12}$$

and W_i is inversely related to resource density c. Therefore, we may write,

$$nv = L/(\varepsilon\sigma^2 W_i) = Lc/(\varepsilon\sigma^2) \tag{A2.13}$$

which tells us that morphological diversity (for example of feeding apparatus) should be proportional to resource volume, Lc, and inversely proportional to the degree of environmental fluctuation. This is confirmed by the finch beak diversity in the Galapagos.

ACKNOWLEDGEMENT

This work was supported by the ESRC NEXSUS Priority Network.

REFERENCES

Allen, P.M. (1975), 'Darwinian evolution and a predator–prey ecology', *Bulletin of Mathematical Ecology*, **37**, 389–405.

Allen, P.M. (1976), 'Evolution, population dynamics and stability', *Proceedings National Academy of Science*, USA, **73** (3), 665–8.

Allen, P.M. (1981), 'The evolutionary paradigm of dissipative structures', in E. Jantsch (ed.), *The Evolutionary Vision: Toward a Unifying Paradigm of Physics and the Social Science*, AAAS Chosen Symposia, Boulder, USA: Westview Press.

Allen, P.M. (2001), 'Knowledge, ignorance and the evolution of complex systems', in Foster, J. and J.S. Metcalfe (eds), *Frontiers of Evolutionary Economics*, Cheltenham, UK and Northampton, MA, USA: Edward Elgar.

Allen, P.M. and J.M. McGlade (1987), 'Evolutionary drive: the effect of microscopic diversity, error making and noise', *Foundation of Physics*, **17** (7), 723–8.

Baldwin, J.S., P.M. Allen, B. Winder and K. Ridgway (2003), 'Simulating the complex cladistic evolution of manufacturing', *Innovation: Management, Policy and Practice*, **5** (2–3), 144–56.

Bowman, R. (1961), 'Morphological differentiation and adaptation in the Galapagos finches', Charles Darwin Foundation for the Galapagos Islands – Contribution 1; *University of California Publications in Zoology*, **58**.

Lack, D. (1947), 'Darwin's finches', Cambridge University Press, *Scientific American*, **188** (4): 66–71.

May, R. (1973), 'Complexity in model ecosystems', Princeton, USA: Princeton University Press.

Maynard-Smith, J. (1979), 'Game theory and the evolution of behaviour', *Proceedings. Royal Society London B*. 205: 475–88.

McCarthy, I. (1995), 'Manufacturing classifications: lessons from organisational systematics and biological taxonomy', *Journal of Manufacturing and Technology Management – Integrated Manufacturing Systems*, **6** (6), 37–49

McCarthy, I., M. Leseure, K. Ridgway and N. Fieller (1997), 'Building a manufacturing cladogram', *International Journal of Technology Management*, **13** (3), 2269–96.

McKelvey, B. (1982), 'Organizational systematics', California, USA: University of California Press.

McKelvey, B. (1994), 'Evolution and organizational science' in J. Baum and J. Singh (eds), *Evolutionary Dynamics of Organizations*, Oxford: Oxford University Press, pp. 314–26.

Metcalfe, J.S. (1998), *Evolutionary Economics and Creative Destruction*, London, UK: Routledge.

Metcalfe, J.S (1999), *Restless Capitalism, Returns and Growth in Enterprise Economics*, Manchester, UK: CRIC, University of Manchester.

Prigogine, I. (1981), *From being to becoming*, New York, USA: W.H. Freeman.

3. Cities: continuity, transformation and emergence

Michael Batty, Joana Barros and Sinésio Alves Júnior

HISTORICAL ANTECEDENTS

Cities are never what they seem. Our usual response when faced with trying to understand their form and function is to revert to the almost reflex actions which are instilled into us from an early age whereby we try to make sense of the world by 'adding things up'. With cities in existence before we even begin, we know that this strategy will not work. Our own behaviour is hard to reconcile with the kind of routine order that we see when we observe the ways in which people travel to work, the places where housing estates are built, and the almost mindless flocking that we see when we visit entertainment centres, from sports arenas to large shopping malls. In short, the 'whole is more than the sum of the parts' (Simon 1962). We cannot assemble the whole by simply adding up the parts, for all would agree that there is something more that makes cities function as ordered wholes. Equally, we cannot get at their essence by simply tearing apart the whole and examining the parts; through its reductionist strategy, classical science simply fails us when we try to understand such complexity.

Half a century ago, science began to deal with complexity under the banner of *general system theory* (Bertalanffy 1972). Since then there has been a sea change in many sciences as highly centralized, purist explanations from the top down have been found wanting. The idea that science in its classical form could be used as a basis for such control has been widely discredited, in the West at least, as the move to decentralized government and action has gained ground. This has been dramatically accelerated by the miniaturization of information technologies, which have given much greater power to the individual, and it is no surprise that in such a world, the dominant mode of explanation has shifted to theorizing how systems emerge and are generated from the bottom up. Urban planning, which was first institutionalized as a function of government over one hundred years ago, is focused on making cities more attractive, efficient and equitable places in which to live, but its history has been far from successful. Like all controls which are applied to complex systems, it fails to anticipate change that originates from the bottom up.

The failure of urban planning is as much a consequence of our inability to understand how cities work as it is of any political or ideological reaction against the idea of control and government. Cities are not just the sum of their parts; trying to make them workable by tinkering with their parts is born of a deep misunderstanding as to their nature. In fact, contemporary approaches to general systems under the guise of complexity theory take the gestalt implied by the whole-parts continuum-disjunction even further. For example, Anderson (1972, p. 393) says that 'the whole . . . [is] . . . not only more but very different from the sum of the parts'. It was Jane Jacobs (1961), however, who first raised the notion that cities should be treated as problems of organized complexity. In a series of prescient books and essays, she argued vociferously that diversity was the hallmark of cities and that this was being destroyed by contemporary urban planning. She drew her inspiration for a new science of cities from the speculations of Warren Weaver (1948) who suggested in an address to the Rockefeller Foundation that systems could be classified as being applicable to three kinds of problem: problems of simplicity, problems of disorganized complexity and problems of organized complexity. It is the third category that Weaver argued should form the cutting edge of science, claiming that most problems in science, once they left the controlled conditions of the laboratory, became complex but in an organized sense that required new approaches which treated the systems associated with them as evolving from the bottom up. It was the process of showing how this bottom-up thinking could generate useful theories and applications that represented the all-important quest.

In this chapter, we will illustrate how complexity theory might be applied to cities, showing how changes in urban form and function reveal sometimes bewildering patterns and processes which are often pictured in over-simplistic ways. The trap that many urban theorists trying to explain urban form have fallen into is to assume that the way cities looked in the industrial age – rather ordered ring patterns around their traditional market centre, the core or Central Business District (CBD) as it is now called – could be explained by equivalently simple processes of growth and change. Cities are formed for exchange and the traditional core was the market place where trade took place. Most urban theories explain cities as a trade-off between getting as close as possible to the core, the value of the goods and products exchanged in the core, and the amount of space required for their production. An inadequacy of this model is that it assumes little specialization. It cannot reconcile itself to dealing with more than one core, so competing cores or market places are problematic, and it handles travel and transport in far too simplistic a way in a world now full of alternative communications paths. Little wonder that simulating cities and making decisions based on these kinds of theory leads to unrealistic plans. Furthermore, this type of model is entirely static; it is based on a world in equilibrium. Although at first sight cities look as though they might be in equilibrium, this can never be the case. What might appear to be in equilibrium is their physical artefacts, their structures, buildings and streets; but the economic and social rationale for what goes on inside them is in continual flux. One only has to look at downtown Manhattan or the City of London and think about how different these locales have become over the last half century to know that although nothing appears to have changed physically, everything has changed functionally and behaviourally.

We will explore cities through three related perspectives on change: continuity which contrasts with discontinuity and bifurcation, transformation where forms and functions evolve from one pattern to another, and emergence which concerns the way qualitatively new and novel structures arise. In a sense, these dynamics imply processes operating at different temporal rates and spatial scales, although in cities it is the perspective we take and what we define as relevant to our representation that dictates the kind of change that we focus upon. We will illustrate each of these themes through examples that manifest themselves physically and spatially. One of the key features of cities is that spatial order is never what it seems, for the same kinds of pattern can emerge from very different processes. This means that we need to be careful in illustrating complexity through spatial pattern and in each case we will unpack these to reveal the processes that generate them.

Our first foray into urban evolution will deal with continuity, where we will dwell on how slow and gradual change suddenly but subtly reveals that bifurcation might have occurred. Transformations are another way of looking at such change and here we will show how systems are resilient at certain thresholds. Theories of self-organized criticality are useful in illustrating such change, particularly the conditions under which dramatic transitions occur, propelling the system towards a new state. These perspectives can also be subsumed under the notion of emergence, which John Holland (1998) sums up rather nicely as 'much coming from little' (p. 1), entirely consistent with structures being *different* as well as *more* than the sum of their parts. Our thesis will be illustrated with morphological patterns which characterize the contemporary city: urban sprawl, edge cities, bi- or multipolar CBDs, residentially segregated areas, ghettos of various sorts, and technological changes forced by new transportation, global and world city patterns.

CONTINUITY: RELATIVELY SLOW CHANGE

The process of city growth is intrinsically different from that of urban decline in that growth at some point involves the transformation of land from non-urban to urban, whereas decline does not necessarily imply any such reversibility. Over the very long term, cities have waxed and waned in size but our focus here is on contemporary times where growth is the dominant mode of change. In a world which will be almost entirely urbanized by the end of this century, we may then face a rather different prospect of what constitutes a city and city growth; our discussion is restricted to the growth of cities over the last 200 and the next 100 years. At very fine spatial scales, growth involves individual transitions, which are measured with respect to land use, occupancy and density, and change can be slow or fast, gradual or abrupt. But as we scale up, then this volatility is averaged out and at the level of the whole town or metropolis, the change in spatial pattern appears slow and gradual, notwithstanding the fact that growth of absolute volumes of activity may be proceeding exponentially.

A measure of this slow change is captured in the growth of Las Vegas over the last 100 years, pictured in the movie-like clip which we show in Figure 3.1. The sprawl does not look very different from time period to time period in that the pattern always looks like more of the same. Inside the city, things have changed rather more dramatically as the place has moved from desert oasis and staging post prior to 1950 to the entertainment and gambling capital of the United States in the modern day. Exponential growth of population, employment and tourism is implied by the volume of urban development in Figure 3.1, but the pattern is one of continuing but relatively similar peripheral expansion. The fact that the city has grown in some directions rather than others is largely due to a combination of physical and accidental historical factors; it does not imply any differences in the way growth has occurred from one time period to the next.

This kind of change has convinced many that cities are comparatively simple structures whose urban form and pattern is explicable in general terms that apply to many time periods of their growth. Whether large or small, the same bottom-up development processes are at work, and large structures are correspondingly similar to small. Idealized models where entirely local development rules are operating uniformly across the space to grow a city from a single seed lead to fractal patterns. These patterns are self-similar in form with respect to scale, of the kind observed in real cities. We show the operation of deterministic rules in Figure 3.2, where a cell is developed if there is one and only one cell already developed in its immediate neighbourhood, and how this leads to a growing structure.

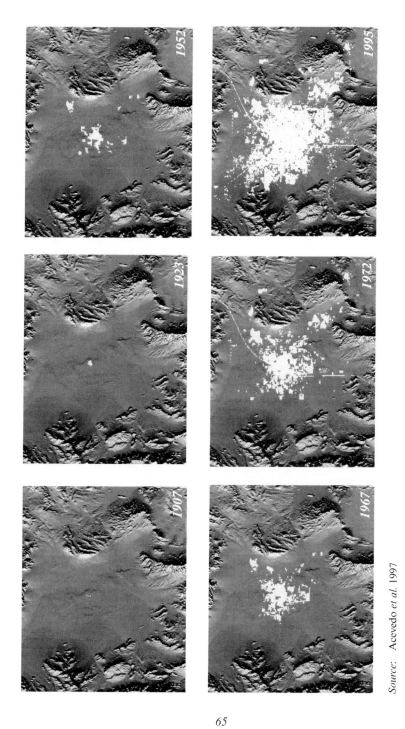

Source: Acevedo et al. 1997

Figure 3.1   The growth of Las Vegas from 1907 to 1995

65

Complexity and co-evolution

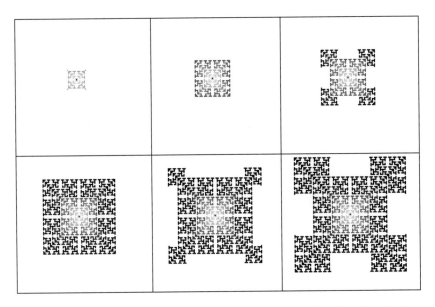

*Figure 3.2   Deterministic growth from the bottom up: based on developing
              cells if one and only one cell is already developed in their 8-cell
              adjacent neighbourhood*

This is a typical example of a modular principle that preserves a certain
level of density and space when development occurs, but that when operated routinely and exhaustively, leads to cellular growth that is regular and
self-similar across scales. Idealistic Renaissance towns were often patterned in this fashion, as templates for an urban utopia based on classical
architectural principles. Adding some noise or error into this structure,
however, and any symmetry is immediately broken. If we relax the
growth rule to one where the probability of the growth of a cell varies
directly with whether or not adjacent cells have already been developed,
then we generate something more like an amorphous mass, a radially-
concentric-like structure closer to that we see in the development of
Las Vegas. We show the resulting patterns in Figure 3.3 where the shape of
the structure is now circular in that development eventually occurs every-
where. The city fills up completely but the order in which this takes place
is a result of development taking place at each time period with random
probability.

If urban growth is modular and scales in the simplistic way that is portrayed in these models of fractal growth, then it is not surprising that there
is a tendency to explain such patterns generically, without regard to growth

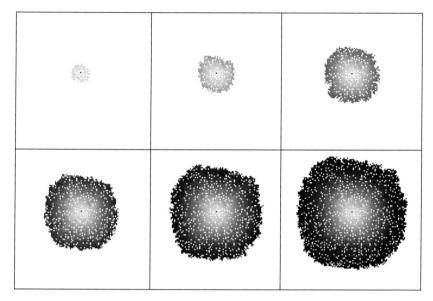

Figure 3.3 Stochastic growth from the bottom up: based on developing a cell if any cell is developed in the adjacent neighbourhood according to a random probability

per se; to study these as if they represent systems with an equilibrium pattern that simply scales through time. But this is a trap that must be avoided. Dig below the surface, examine the processes of growth and the activities that occupy these forms, disaggregate the scale and change the time interval, and this image of an implied stability changes quite radically. During the era pictured in Figure 3.1, technology has changed dramatically. Las Vegas did not acquire its gambling functions until the 1950s, but by then it was already growing fast and the subsequent injection of cash into its local economy, the largest per capita in the western world for those who reside there, did little to change the pattern of explosive growth that followed. The manner in which people moved in the early Las Vegas was by horse and wagon but the city could only grow with the car, the plane and air-conditioning, not to say the incredible information technologies that now dictate how one gambles, wins and loses.

Has a subtle bifurcation occurred during these 100 years of growth? If it has, you cannot see it in its spatial pattern, but bifurcation there has surely been as anyone who knew Las Vegas in 1945 or in 1970, or knows it today could easily attest. Cities are never what they seem.

TRANSFORMATIONS: PERSISTENCE AND SELF-ORGANIZED CRITICALITY

Our six-frame movie of the growth of Las Vegas reveals that the established pattern of adding to the periphery is not the complete story because small blobs of development seem to attach themselves and then are absorbed back into the growing mass as growth catches them up. In this case, this is simply housing being constructed a little beyond the edge due to the mechanics of the development process. In older, more established settlement patterns such as those in Western Europe for example, this might be the absorption of older villages and freestanding towns into the growing sprawl. Consider the picture of population density in London recorded in 1991 and illustrated in Figure 3.4. Here there are many towns and villages that existed long before London grew to embrace them. One kind of dynamics that this picture reveals is the transition to a metropolitan area. Let us define the metropolis as the connected pattern of settlement that fills an entire space where everyone can connect to everybody else either directly or indirectly. Connection in this sense is simply the ability to circumnavi-

Figure 3.4   London: connected villages and towns within the sprawl (as population density on a 200m grid from the 1991 census of population)

gate the system, from one side to another. In the days before the towns and villages in Figure 3.4 were part of the metropolis, such connection was not possible, for one could not proceed across the system in this way without entering empty space, the countryside. Moreover our definition of a metropolis is an urban form where such connection exists in as simple a fashion as possible but not more so.

In Figure 3.4, one could envisage London being connected in this way with a much sparser network of links, while at the other extreme the entire space could be filled. In fact, it would seem that the level of connectivity which has evolved with respect to the density of the space filled is just enough for the city to function as a whole, and it is this morphology and degree of connectivity that marks the fact that the city has reached a level of self-organization that is regarded as critical. If connectivity were greater than this with more space being filled and many more connections in place, then the structure would contain a certain degree of redundancy, making it inefficient. Below this, the system would not be connected at all and it would not function as a metropolis.

Again this is a rather obvious point, but what it serves to show is that cities evolve to a self-organized level and persist at this level until some radical change in technology pushes such systems into another regime. For example, London's form is largely dependent on a mix of transportation technologies, dominated by the car but overlaid on fixed rail lines. Such a system could not exist prior to the 19th century, and the London that was based on walking and the horse and carriage was a very different structure. New transport technologies possibly based on substituting electronic for physical movement would change the form of the city quite radically in that the critical threshold would be breached and activities would probably readjust themselves in space in ways that we find almost impossible to envisage. This kind of technological change does indeed mark different regimes. It is tempting to think of different eras as being based on the evo-lution of resilient systems; when radical change does eventually take place, the system is pushed beyond the threshold, taking it to a new level of criticality in which the processes at work then self-organize to another critical level. Several commentators describe this process as some sort of social phase transition analogous to well defined physical phenomena. For example, Johnson (2001) summarized Iberall and Soodak's (1987) emphatic argument on the role of flows and phase transitions in the evolu-tion of civilizations with a description of the process by which Europe underwent a social phase transition as:

> not unlike that between H_2O molecules changing from the fluid state of water to the crystallized state of ice: for centuries the population is liquid and

unsettled – and then suddenly a network of towns comes into existence, possessing a stable structure that would persist more or less intact until the next great transformation in the nineteenth century during the rise of the industrial metropolis. (Johnson 2001, p. 110)

To give some form to this rather mystical perspective on urban dynamics, it is easy to show how a system self-organizes to the point where it becomes critical but not beyond. Imagine a series of five small villages randomly located and spaced on a regular lattice such as we show in Figure 3.5. We gradually increase the density of these villages, which is equivalent to growing them into larger towns, and as we do this we compute the average distance between all the occupied points. For a long time it is not possible to travel between every occupied point because they are not connected. Suddenly however, we reach a density where around 59 per cent of the lattice is randomly filled so that every occupied point can be linked to every other. At this point, there is an abrupt change as the average distance falls from 'infinity' to a realistic level. If we then continue increasing the density,

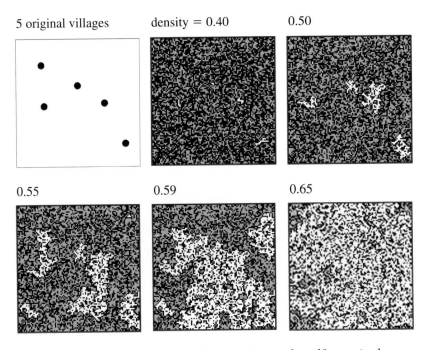

Figure 3.5   Increasing density and connectivity to the self-organized critical threshold

this average distance does not fall much further and little is gained by continuing in this way. In terms of cities, the point of criticality where everything becomes connected marks the emergence of the metropolis in this space, like London, and this only becomes possible when transportation technology reaches a level where it is feasible to realize such connections. In a sense, this is also an oblique way of saying that very large cities of the kind that are now dominant worldwide are only possible with current technologies, not just those of transportation but also those others that enable large-scale urban living. In the ancient world, where one could not travel faster than by chariot, the largest city that could be sustained was Rome, and this did not grow much beyond one million.

In Figure 3.5, we provide a graphic demonstration of the effect of increasing density and connectivity for a hypothetical distribution of settlement in 101×101 grid space where we show how the villages merge into one another when somewhere between 40 and 65 per cent of the lattice is occupied. If we were to plot a graph of the transition to a realistic average distance between all the occupied points to establish the level of criticality, there would be a dramatic change at around 59 per cent; this is known in the physics of porous media as the percolation threshold. At this threshold, average distance falls from infinity to a proper value. By the time the density reaches 65 per cent, this travel distance has stabilized so that rises in the density of the media above this level do not change this distance significantly.

EMERGENCE: QUALITATIVE, SOMETIMES ABRUPT CHANGE

The abruptness of change in cities depends very largely on the scale at which we observe it and the time interval over which it occurs. For example, traffic jams simply build up as density increases with wave effects due to differential acceleration and braking happening over minutes, while stock market crashes usually happen over days and weeks, sometimes months. Booms and busts in the housing market with respect to prices as well as effects on subsequent mobility usually happen over months, rarely over years, while gentrification and related migrations usually take place over years. Sea changes forced by technological innovations happen over centuries or parts thereof, portrayed for example as Kondratieff waves of over half centuries or more. All these events can reveal abrupt change in terms of their measurement if observed at particular scales and time intervals but averaging over time and space certainly smoothes this abruptness. What can appear as abrupt change at one level becomes gradual at another.

All that can be said is that although there may be an ideal scale and time period consistent with the operation of such change, which is usually defined with respect to the purpose of study or application in mind, abrupt change is a relative phenomenon defined with respect to the change before and after it takes place. Moreover it is in the eye of the beholder as to whether such change is meaningful. Abrupt change may not be qualitative change for such changes can take place gradually and only with respect to the past might they reflect some discontinuity whose actual happenstance cannot be dated. For example, the industrial city is clearly now very different from the post-industrial. Compare any 21st century western city that has continued to grow with its form in the 19th in terms of its spread and sprawl, the incomes, occupations, and so on that define each. Yet it might be argued that the contemporary city which we are calling post-industrial is merely a reflection of the outcomes of industrialism – based on the automobile and related technologies – and that we have not yet glimpsed what modern information technologies might do to the future city during the next 100 years. Qualitative change can in fact be pinned down to the invention or emergence of new categories of object, new classifications of the old that only have meaning for the contemporary world. All the great technological innovations that we loosely referred to in the last section – the agricultural revolution which began some 10 000 years BC, the emergence of the modern world from the 12th century onwards, industrialism, perhaps post-Fordism, and the computer revolution – are all candidates for the kind of qualitative change that is clearly manifest in the form of the city.

Without trespassing further on this minefield of definition, we will return to abrupt change and in particular emergence in its narrower context to demonstrate a last example of the way cities can restructure themselves in ways that are surprising. One of the best examples is how different residential neighbourhoods change in their social composition, becoming gentrified or ghettoized due to very mild preferential differences amongst their populations. To avoid any racial connotations, we will in fact assume in more light-hearted fashion that the population is divided equally into those who support the Yemeni soccer team and those who support the Norwegian, which we define as Y and N respectively. Let us array the population on a square grid of dimension 51×51 where we place a Y supporter next to an N supporter in alternate fashion, arranging them in checkerboard style as in Figure 3.6a. The rule for being satisfied with one's locational position vis-à-vis one's own and the other supporters is as follows: supporters of a different team will live quite happily side by side with each other, just as long as there are as many supporters of the same persuasion in their local neighbourhood. The neighbourhood in this instance is the eight cells that surround a supporter on the checkerboard in the N, E, S, W, and NE, SE, SW and NW positions. If however a supporter finds that the supporters of the opposing team outnumber those of their own team, which would occur if there were more than four opposition supporters, then the supporter in question would change their allegiance. In other words, they would switch their support to restore their own equilibrium, which ensures that they are surrounded by at least the same number of their own supporters. There is a version of this model that is a little more realistic in which a supporter would seek another location – move – if this condition were not satisfied rather than change their support, but this is clearly not possible in the completely filled system that we have assumed; we will shortly return to this slightly more realistic model.

In Figure 3.6a, the alternative positioning shown in the checkerboard pattern meets this rule and the locational pattern is in 'equilibrium': that is, no one wants to change their support to another team. However let us suppose that just six supporters out of a total of 2601 (51×51 agents sitting on the checkerboard) who compose about 0.01 per cent of the two populations, change their allegiance. These six changes are easy to see in Figure 3.6a where we assume that four supporters shown by the black colour, the Norwegians say, change in their allegiance to white, to support the Yemeni team, and two Yemenis change the opposite way. What then happens is that the equilibrium is upset in these locations but instead of being quickly restored by local changes, this triggers a mighty unravelling, which quickly changes the locational complexion of the system to one where the Ys are completely and utterly segregated from the Ns. We show this in Figure 3.6b. From a situation where everyone was satisfied and mixed completely, we get dramatic segregation, which is a most unusual consequence. At first sight one would never imagine that such segregation would arise from so mild a balance of preferences. The ultimate pattern implies that Ys will live nowhere near Ns unless they really have to and there is nowhere else to live and vice versa. If a Y or an N would not tolerate more than one person living near them, then such segregation would be understandable but this is not the case: Ys are quite content to live in harmony with Ns as long as the harmony is equality.

This model was first proposed more than 30 years ago by Thomas Schelling (1969, 1978). In fact we can make this a little more realistic if we provide some free space within the system. In this case, we assume that one third of the lattice is empty of supporters of any kind, one third is composed of Ys and one third of Ns, and we mix these randomly as we show in Figure 3.6c. Now the rule is slightly different in that if there are more opposition supporters around a supporter of one persuasion, then that supporter will try to move his or her location to a more preferential position. This sets up a process of shuffling around the checkerboard, but as we show

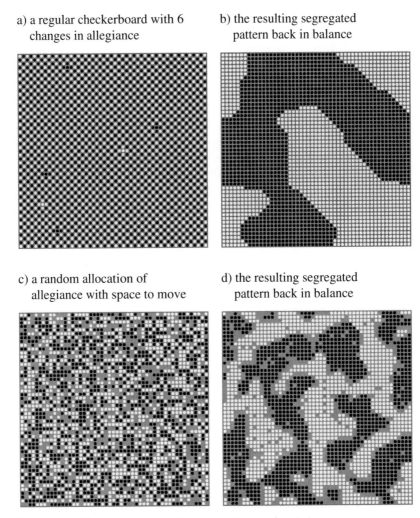

a) a regular checkerboard with 6
   changes in allegiance

b) the resulting segregated
   pattern back in balance

c) a random allocation of
   allegiance with space to move

d) the resulting segregated
   pattern back in balance

Figure 3.6   Emergent segregation: a fragile equality (a) gives way to
segregation (b); a random mix (c) gives way to segregation (d)

in Figure 3.6d, quite dramatic shifts take place in location which leads to
the segregation shown. This is the kind of effect that takes place in residential areas in large cities, where people wish to surround themselves with
neighbours of their own kind. What is surprising about the phenomenon,
what makes it 'emergent' in this sense, is that for very mild preferential bias,
dramatic segregation can take place. Of course if the preferences for like
neighbours are very strong anyway then segregation will take place. But in

reality, such preferences are usually mild rather than strong, and extreme segregation takes place anyway. The conclusion is that cities often look more segregated around racial and social lines than the attitudes of their residents suggest.

It is hard to find clear examples of this process taking place because by the time it is clearly underway, the very segregation is revealed and a detailed chronology becomes impossible to reconstruct. There are many examples of this in western cities; comparisons at the level of census tracts over 10-year periods are easily accessible from the many social atlases of cities that have been constructed in the last decade.

EVER GREATER COMPLEXITY

We have barely scratched the surface of the study of complexity in cities during this short chapter, for at every twist and turn, and from every perspective, there are signals that indicate surprise, novelty, innovation, and emergence in the way cities grow and change. Symmetry is forever being broken and urban processes display a bewildering variety in terms of the reversibility and irreversibility. In all of this, what is very clear is that we cannot take at face value what we observe superficially. If there is one message that complexity theory forces on the social sciences, it is that the search for an understanding in terms of regular pattern must be viewed with suspicion because beneath such patterns there is often volatile change and unstable processes of the most extreme nature. A generation or more ago, our study of cities was dominated by explanations that suggested that cities were rather stable kinds of structure as revealed in the patterning of their land use and transport systems. People mainly worked in the centre, with richer people who could afford better transportation and more space living on the periphery. In fact, we now know that this was never as clear cut as was believed. What we were enticed by was the fact that cities through their built form are rather long-lasting kinds of artefact but that what goes on within that form is subject to quite rapid change. Take a city like London which we illustrated in Figure 3.4. At first sight, it appears strongly monocentric with small towns being absorbed in its growth as it has exploded outwards. But most people do not in fact work in the centre. Cross-movements are substantially greater than any movements from the edge to the core and most 'Londoners' never visit the centre, even to shop or for entertainment. Cities are more complex than this, and complexity theory refocuses our attention on the need for a deeper understanding (Batty 2005).

Our quest in this chapter has been to show that complex systems must be understood from the bottom up and that prior reductionist strategies simply fail to grasp the way such systems work. Process rather than product, function rather than form, time rather than space are all important for a better understanding. Missing from our argument, however, is the notion that cities like many other social systems might be becoming more complex, certainly more complicated as they evolve through time. Some would argue that our theories and models must inevitably adapt to embrace new forms and categories that get invented and which are not intrinsic to the system when we observe it at any one time or even over past time periods. This is a subtle issue that is taken up by others writing in this book, but it is important because it further reinforces the relativism that complexity theory tends to bring to the social sciences. Nevertheless, the issues posed here which involve surprising features of temporal urban processes, and which lead to unexpected spatial patterns, appear to have been a part of cities for a much longer time than we have alluded to here. As we learn more about these through the lens of complexity theory, it is likely that we will gain a much greater understanding of how we might intervene in these processes to effect better cities through their design.

REFERENCES

Acevedo, W., L. Gaydos, J. Tilley, C. Mladinich, J. Buchanan, S. Blauer, K. Kruger, and J. Schubert (1997), *Urban Land Use Change in the Las Vegas Valley, US Geological Survey, Washington DC*, http://geochange.er.usgs.gov/sw/changes/anthropogenic/population/las_vegas, 10 February 2005.

Anderson, P.W. (1972), 'More is different', *Science*, **177** (4047), 393–6.

Batty, Michael (2005), *Cities and Complexity: Understanding Cities with Cellular Automata, Agent-Based Models, and Fractals*, Cambridge, MA: MIT Press.

Bertalanffy, Ludwig von (1972), *General System Theory*, Harmondsworth: Penguin.

Holland, John H. (1998), *Emergence: From Chaos to Order*, Reading, MA: Perseus Books.

Iberall, Arthur and Harold Soodak (1987), 'A physics for studies of civilization', in F. Eugene Yates (ed.), *Self-Organizing Systems: The Emergence of Order*, New York: Plenum Press, pp. 521–40.

Jacobs, Jane (1961), *The Death and Life of Great American Cities*, New York: Random House.

Johnson, Steven (2001), *Emergence: The Connected Lives of Ants, Brains, Cities and Software*, New York: Scribner.

Schelling, T.C. (1969), 'Models of segregation', *American Economic Review, Papers and Proceedings*, **58** (2), 488–93.

Schelling, Thomas C. (1978), *Micromotives and Macrobehavior*, New York: W.W. Norton and Company.

Simon, H.A. (1962), 'The architecture of complexity', *Proceedings of the American Philosophical Society*, **106** (6), 467–82.

Weaver, W. (1948), 'Science and complexity', *American Scientist*, **36**, 536–44.

4. Ecohistorical regimes and *la longue durée*: an approach to mapping long-term societal change

James McGlade

INTRODUCTION

The evolutionary structuring of societal systems is a core concern of the historical sciences and one that has persisted as a constant on the research horizon since the emergence of social science as a distinctive discipline in the 19th century. The reasons for this ubiquity are not difficult to fathom, since they are consistent with the late 19th and 20th century fixation with understanding human evolution and in a sense are testimony to the over-whelming influence that Darwinian ideas have had on intellectual thought generally. Somewhat inevitably, the nascent discipline of archaeology, growing up like a number of other social sciences in the second half of the 19th century, eagerly embraced the implications of the new evolutionary Zeitgeist; in particular, archaeology was transfixed by Lyle's new geo-stratigraphy with its rejection of biblical time and its vision of a new tem-poral chronology. This latter, with its emphasis on linear, progressive evolution, was to form the underpinning of all subsequent theorizing on the nature of social change within the discipline.

One celebrated attempt to go beyond the fixity of such chronological frameworks is due to the work of the *Annales* school founded by Febvre and Bloch in 1929. Their critique of history as a sequence of discrete events in the service of chronology and its attendant cult of detail was to provide the impetus for a manifesto of radical change. An important part of their central thesis was that, by contrast to normative schemes of history based on the primacy of great men or single political events, they proposed to emphasize instead the correspondences and interactions between material, social and mental structures. Following these precedents, it was the work of Braudel that was to provide the key to an alternative understanding of the nature of long-term change. Braudel's central thesis was that social change was a confluence of the intersection of different temporalities and these

were basic to the structuring of the *longue durée*. Not surprisingly, this focus
on the long-term has meant that his work has had a particular resonance
for archaeology, with a number of researchers arguing for the importance
of the Braudelian model, though from divergent perspectives (for example
Hodder 1987; Bintliff 1991; Knapp 1992). Braudel's model is innovative
precisely because it confronts the difficult issue of how to conceptualize the
trajectory of social evolution, and underlines the necessity for a new
reading of the relationship between structure and event. However, its preoccupation with the structural scaffolding of history means that the role of
individual events and of human agency tend to assume an epiphenomenal
role, consigned to the marginalia of history. Individuals are merely the
'foam' cresting momentarily on the waves of history (McGlade 1999).

In an attempt to pursue these temporal issues further, this chapter
focuses on the dynamics of growth and change at the landscape scale and
sets out to examine to what extent the structuring of social space – from a
long-term perspective – can be explained by the existing cultural chronology that gives preference to a series of technological changes as human
societies move through a manifest as 'stone–bronze–iron' sequence of
material culture changes, and one that is seen as being synonymous with
increasing socio-political complexity. More succinctly, we are attempting to
shed light on the thorny question of just what are the respective roles of
structure and agency in the construction of social change. In doing so, we
shall examine the landscape from a specific evolutionary perspective, situ-
ating our discussion within the wider context of issues on order, disorder
and structural stability. Specifically, we shall investigate to what extent it is
useful to invoke the methods and theory of complex systems and the role
of non-linear interactions in generating emergent evolutionary patterns
(McGlade 1990, 1995; McGlade and van der Leeuw 1997).

ARCHAEOLOGY, NARRATIVE AND THE
LONG-TERM

Simply put, the fundamental question being addressed in this chapter is
essentially a narrative one: how are we to conceive of the long-term? Is it
simply the accumulation of a sequence of short-term events strung together
to form a cohesive whole? Additionally, what is the role of contingent
processes and unplanned events in this process? Archaeology, almost by
definition, has been particularly concerned with long-term developmental
sequences in an effort to understand the growth of human societies and the
emergence of civilization and statehood. However, one of the main problems with conventional archaeological explanation is that it has tended to

privilege gradualist explanation, based on the slow accumulation of events (McGlade and van der Leeuw 1997). As with classical approaches to history, there is a tendency to downplay discontinuous change, since it gets in the way of a coherent, progressive narrative that stresses the historical trajectory as a gradualist process of increasing complexity.

Such linear models have come under increasing scrutiny over the past decades, and largely in the wake of a burgeoning post-modern discourse – that is with the variety of critical treatments that have emerged across the social sciences, and frequently lumped together as defining a 'post-modern condition' (for example White 1971; Ermarth 1992). Whether we subscribe to such over-arching labels or not is not at issue here, rather more to the point is that this ongoing 'post-mortem of the modern', has provoked a critical examination of historiography, along with methods of historical reconstruction, and specifically, a concern for the means by which we are to understand the processes which structure social, political and economic change. At its most extreme, these ideas have even manifest themselves as a denial of history as we have come to know it, or at least of the increasingly problematic status of meta-narratives, the grand sweeping models of civilization. Not surprisingly, such debates have gradually moved beyond historiography, and more recently have begun to play a central role in archaeological theory (for example Shanks and Tilley 1987; Hodder 1992; Tilley 1993).

As Hayden White (1971) has pointed out, his deconstructionist reasoning has sought to undermine the writing of history as a single, comfortable trajectory and by implication, one proclaiming the developmental superiority of the contemporary western worldview.

History is essentially a narrative discourse as much imagined or invented – it can lay no legitimate claim to fundamental truths; thus, following Kant, White suggests that we are free to create the kind of history we want. From this it follows that we must pursue a plurality of histories, as the only logical, and indeed valid, alternative to the procession of biased historical constructions that our society feeds on. However, if we are to jettison the idea of global history as promoted by writers such as Engels, Spengler and Toynbee, what are we to put in its place? Does this mean we are faced with the *horror vacui* of relativism, of a world of endless 'thick description' (McGlade 1999)?

Certainly the writing of grand narrative with its implicit model of progress is increasingly contentious, not to say futile – on the other hand, although replacing this model of linear temporality, of episodic accumulation, is decidedly non-trivial, we shall argue that the writing of history – and archaeology's central part in such a project – is eminently feasible. What we shall argue here is that it is a question of recasting the problem and resetting the discourse within another arena, that of complexity theory: one in which we confront an alternative model of causality and thereby create a different reading of time. We shall argue that the success of such a project is dependent on its ability to create a *rapprochement* between the temporal nature of social phenomena and the non-linear temporalities which are resident in and central to the structural dynamics, which articulate historical process.

By invoking complexity issues, what we are suggesting is nothing less than a radical shift in the dominant conception of causality within archaeological theory – one in which the relationship between contingency and determinism is recast, so as to better encompass the temporal nature of the social-historical dialectic as it is acted out both at the local scale and at the level of long-term dynamics. We might reasonably ask what consequences this new reading of time might have on archaeology and, additionally, how it might affect the construction of narrative history. It is to these issues and to the philosophical shift, which they imply – not just for an archaeological epistemology, but rather in providing a basis for a revised ontology – that the remainder of this chapter will concern itself.

ARCHAEOLOGY, COMPLEXITY AND CO-EVOLUTION

As has been demonstrated in Chapter 1, complexity thinking is gradually assuming a prominent place in disciplines such as biology, ecology and especially the physical sciences. On the other hand, it is yet a newcomer to archaeology and for this reason is frequently treated with some suspicion. The triumph of a largely post-modernist perspective in the social and political sciences, and a research community mindful of the positivist excesses of the 'scientism' of the 1960s, has meant that conventional practice is to question any borrowings from the physical sciences. Notwithstanding this caution, as we shall argue here, the oft-repeated rhetoric of 'old wine in new bottles' is wholly unjustified since as we have seen in the first chapter, the conceptual shift implied by adopting a complexity discourse is a radical departure from the causal structures of normal science. Rather more than the addition of new analytical tools, it is nothing less than an epistemological step-change (Hayles 1990; McGlade 2003). Elsewhere (McGlade 1990, 1995; McGlade and van der Leeuw 1997) I have suggested that archaeology has much to gain from an engagement with these issues, in particular its ability to create a much-needed bridge between the relativism of extreme post-modernist positions and the strictures of reductionist science.

While complexity per se has only recently begun to affect archaeological theory (for example Bentley and Maschner 2003), the *idea* of complexity has formed a central research core in archaeology for at least a century. The archaeology of complex societies particularly as expressed in the transition from hunting/gathering to sedentism and the origins of agriculture has assumed a key research preoccupation, as has its relationship to the onset of urbanism and statehood. Essentially, when used in this context, complexity has a rather precise meaning – and one that differs substantially from complex systems thinking and complexity theory. In an archaeological (and anthropological) context, it is generally taken to refer to the degree of organizational elaboration possessed by a particular society, in particular, as a consequence of social and environmental adaptation. More recently however, a number of researchers influenced by work at the Santa Fe Institute have begun to assess the utility of invoking ideas from complex adaptive systems research (for example Kohler 1993; Gummerman and Gell-Mann 1999). While these works are largely in developmental stages, nevertheless they have opened the door to alternative readings of complexity within archaeology, particularly with respect to the emergence of statehood. Indeed, it is the thesis of the present chapter that the application of the tools afforded by complexity thinking, set within a co-evolutionary model of human-environment dynamics, is capable of revealing new insights on the nature of long-term change.

As we have seen from the introductory chapter, the vocabulary associated with complexity presents us with a particular set of concepts that are central to any analysis of complex phenomena. With respect to our present landscape study, we might underline those concepts that will play a central role in the construction of an alternative evolutionary model.

Self-organization

A central aspect of self-organization is that, by contrast to models of structural evolution that focus on top-down centralized control, emphasis is on the ability of uncoordinated, 'bottom-up' dynamics to generate coherent structure. In complex systems, the process of self-organization is a continuous dynamic that defines the adaptive behaviour and search for new attractor 'solutions'.

Attractors

One of the most intriguing outcomes of complexity studies is that the evolution of non-linear complex systems is marked by a sequence of phase transitions, each of which is governed by an attractor that may be said to (temporarily) dominate the system at that time. From a social perspective, we can define an attractor as a societal system that exhibits a collection of behaviours that are coherent and organized, while at the same time being susceptible to abrupt change. The system evolves over time, causing a shift between attracting states. Significantly, by analogy with ecosystems, these shifts are not smooth or continuous – indeed the system frequently 'flips' its organizational state in dramatic ways (Kay *et al.* 1999, p. 725).

Distributed Systems

One of the consequences of viewing landscape from a complexity perspective is that it can usefully be conceived as a *distributed system*. Distributed systems are those systems that are made up of a collection of entities or states wherein decisions are the product – not of a central hierarchical control, but rather spread across system nodes in a heterarchical manner. Descriptions of such systems are frequently made by reference to ant colonies, and the human brain (for example Johnson 2001). Such studies conclude that 'intelligent' global behaviour emerges from local interactions.

Emergence

At a generic level, emergence refers to the appearance of novel and coherent structures, patterns and properties during the process of self-organization in complex systems. Importantly, they are neither predictable nor deducible from lower level system components (Goldstein 1998, pp. 49–50). This unpredictability is a function of the operation of non-linear dynamics and hence the intractability of complex systems. Emergent phenomena may be said to be an intrinsic property of complex social systems.

Co-evolution

A key concept for our understanding of complex socio-natural systems is the role of co-evolutionary dynamics. Elsewhere (McGlade 1995, 1999) I have suggested that at a general level, socio-natural interaction must be conceived as a co-evolutionary process and seen in terms of a model of *human ecodynamics*; that is as a reciprocal set of interactions driven by positive feedback (self-reinforcing) processes. This co-evolutionary perspective argues for a non-functionalist human ecology in which human agency plays a vital role in creating environmental outcomes that are subsequently seen to act back on human societal processes. Thus the reproduction of society is a consequence of this continuous reciprocal dynamic.

Consistent with these ideas is the need to view any co-evolutionary dynamic from a long-term perspective, thus recognizing the importance of history in creating the enabling and constraining conditions within which socio-natural systems co-evolve. Such a research agenda is designed to present a more complete and integrated view of human societal structuring; it thus eschews current developmental evolutionary models, emphasizing in their place, a discontinuous, non-linear perspective, which acknowledges the crucial importance of different temporalities and scale-dependent dynamics in the emergence of societal structure (McGlade 1999).

Broadly speaking, a co-evolutionary perspective focuses on the way that self-organizing processes at work in socio-natural systems act to generate the system's evolutionary character. Finally, a co-evolutionary perspective suggests that if there is something close to a dominant selection criterion in the 'survival' of 'populations' (policies, firms, and so on) this is not efficiency, but 'learning', that is the ability to continuously adapt to the co-changing, and at times unexpected and dramatically altered, conditions (Allen 1994).

Accepting the challenge of a discourse that focuses on the self-organizing behaviours and emergent properties inherent in open hierarchical systems, this chapter will attempt to apply such a perspective to the problem of human settlement evolution viewed as a long-term phenomenon.

THE SETTLEMENT LANDSCAPE AS A DYNAMIC, SOCIO-SPATIAL SYSTEM

In order to address these issues, our chosen focus is at the landscape scale. What we shall argue here is that a landscape focus uniquely allows us to confront the totality of socio-natural interaction and, significantly, as a long-term phenomenon. Our starting premise is that landscapes have a specific 'identity', as a consequence of social-natural evolutionary history. They comprise a historical ensemble of attitudes, actions and choices; a confluence of the intended and unintended consequences of human behaviour. It is for this reason that we must reject any deterministic explanatory frameworks. In essence, a landscape focus provides a platform from which to explore the relationship between historically determined structures and contingent processes that lie at the root of societal change.

Within archaeology, conventionally, descriptive works on landscape have tended to emphasize the locational history of the landscape, that is focusing on landscape as pattern. By contrast, we are interested in the fact that space is not simply a container of human activities; rather, it is a conscious creation – it is above all a socially constructed phenomenon. It is, thus, that we can talk of the long-term *(re)production* of the landscape as a social historical process.

With respect to our current concerns, ultimately, we are interested in gaining insight into the structural stability of the various social-natural configurations that have characterized landscape history as a single trajectory from its formative Neolithic imprint to the socio-political structures that characterize the post-Roman landscapes of Late Antiquity. In essence, we shall attempt to isolate specific 'ecohistorical' constructions of space.

In what follows we shall examine the Empordà landscapes of north-east Spain, as a pertinent example of long-term human occupation characterized by significant socio-political change. In the spirit of a multi-narrative approach to historical change, we shall attempt to add another interpretive layer to the spatio-temporal palimpsest. Our discussion will seek to resituate the nature of the historical trajectory, eschewing conventional linear description in favour of a more punctuated exposition of human-ecodynamic evolution and its expression as territoriality. The ensuing narrative will argue that by constructing a trajectory based on concepts and methods derived from the complexity discourse,[1] it may be possible to generate an alternative framework to account for the non-linear dynamics that are implicated in the emergence of novel structure and the long-term transformation of the social landscape.

AN ALTERNATIVE SPATIO-TEMPORAL STRUCTURATION: *ECOHISTORICAL REGIMES*

As we have already noted, history is essentially concerned with the construction of narrative. For this reason, we must accept the plurality of narrative as a reality and thus preferable to the imposition of any single authoritative or 'received' version of history. It is in this context that we offer the following narrative structure with the intention of presenting a new reading of long-term landscape development.

The essence of the alternative structure we are proposing is its evolutionary context, and specifically its opposition to gradualist developmental schemes and the dominance of chronometric ordering that forms the basis of the archaeological knowledge of the region. In what follows, we shall set out the constituent elements of an alternative reading of the trajectory of long-term change. At the core of this structuration is the concept of an 'ecohistorical regime'.

We shall argue that the long-term history of the landscape under study is punctuated by a series of distinctive human ecodynamic signatures or *ecohistorical regimes* – the biophysical, material, cultural, and social manifestations of specific socio-political organizational forms. These constitute a co-evolutionary constellation of social, economic and environmental factors that define specific 'basins of attraction' in the socio-natural landscape. However, unlike the attracting sets to which conventional dynamical systems converge (that is point attractors, limit cycles and so on), these do not mark the long-term behaviour or final point of a system trajectory. Rather, they are self-organizing entities with emergent properties and are more properly conceived of as *structural attractors*.

Ecohistorical regimes are thus attracting sets or socio-natural mappings embedded in which self-reinforcing relationships link knowledge production, resources and specific relations of production. They represent temporary locations of socio-natural coherence defined by a dominant set of values that frequently manifests as a distinctive ideology.[2]

As with all complex systems, the boundaries are mobile and can be thought of as porous, with no absolute time–space dimension. And as with all complex systems, the existence of non-linearities in socio-natural relations creates a system that is characteristically metastable. What this means is that in company with many physical and ecological systems, the social trajectory moves or 'flips' between a variety of possible attracting states. It is this fact that is responsible for the appearance of emergent behaviour. As we shall see below, new structural attractors evolve when the system bifurcates and is restructured, creating fundamental changes in the nature of power relations. In summary, these structural attractors (qua ecohistorical regimes) represent constellations of power, knowledge and spatiality that define spatio-temporal order. Additionally, they define a complex array of temporalities such as are represented by the slow turnover rates of bio-geophysical processes all the way to the decadal and annual temporal rates inherent in ecological and biological systems. The complex and intricate temporal web we are describing is also overlain by the micro-level temporalities implicated in quotidian domestic activities, in human biological reproduction as well as those responsible for decision-making and cognitive processes.

UNPACKING ECOHISTORICAL REGIMES

Each *ecohistorical regime* (qua structural attractor) can usefully be thought of as comprising intersecting sets of socio-spatial entities that encompass a series of spatio-temporal dimensions:

- *Geo-biophysical space*: boundary conditions represented by the physical and ecological environment

- *Production space*: agricultural/hunting territories, human modification of rivers, littoral, wetlands
- *Communication space*: tracks, roads, rivers, coast
- *Settlement space*: location, topography, population
- *Political space*: territory, property, the space of power and control, the space of conflict
- *Transactional space*: barter exchange, symbolic alliances, market economies
- *Symbolic space*: ritual, burials, cemeteries, monuments, churches, monasteries
- *Cognitive space*: decision space, culturally modified by values, ideology and history

It needs to be pointed out that these dimensions are not discrete entities, that is they are not subsystems (*sensu* systems theory) but sets of interlocking socio-spatial processes that have no fixed point in time and space; rather they are constantly in a state of becoming. What we are stressing here is that societies are not a single unitary entity and hence they cannot be reduced to distinctive functionalist sub-sets such as environmental, social, ideological and so on (Mann 1986; McGlade 1995). Following Mann, we shall argue that 'societies are constituted of multiple, overlapping and intersecting socio-spatial networks of power' (1986, p. 1).

For our present purpose, these multi-level dimensions we have identified can be seen to form the dynamic spatio-temporal context within which human action is situated. What we shall argue here is that these dimensions can usefully be collapsed to form a reduced description of the socio-natural system; one that can be expressed in terms of three primary sets of co-evolutionary interactions. These are *resources*, *agency* and *transactions*, along with the self-reinforcing feedbacks between them. Ultimately, these interactions may be said to characterize fundamental relations of power underpinning each *ecohistorical regime* (see Figure 4.1).

With respect to resources, we shall follow Giddens' useful distinction between two types, allocative and authoritative, acknowledging also that the duality of power is situated in a logic of control over allocative and authoritative resources (Giddens 1979, p. 91).

- *Allocative Resources (material)*: these include raw materials, land, technology, production instruments, goods, and so on. Allocative resources derive from human co-evolution with the natural environment whereas power is derived from human attempts to dominate the environment. Ecohistorical regimes are also defined by specific relations of production.

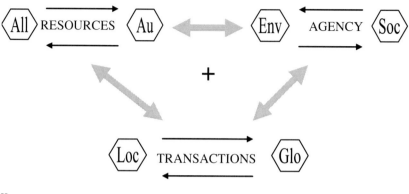

Key:

All = allocative resources   Loc = local transactions (regional)

Au = authoritative resources   Glo = global transactions (Mediterranean)

Env = environmental agency   + = self-reinforcing dynamics (positive feedback)

Soc = social agency

Figure 4.1   A minimal model of an ecohistorical regime *emphasizing co-evolutionary dynamics*

- *Authoritative Resources (ideological)*: these non-material resources involve the possibility for dominion over the social world through the exercise of power over others; thus, some individuals aspire to dominate others and to control information and knowledge in society. Symbolic orders and political and legal institutions comprise authoritative resources.[3]
- *Agency*: here represents two types of action – environmental and social. Environmental agency concerns those natural processes such as climate, weather, geomorphological action as well as potentially catastrophic events such as fire, flood and drought. Social agency, on the other hand, concerns the capacity of individuals and groups to change their environment through the introduction of new technologies and modes of production and to initiate new types of social organization, as well as the means to control and dominate others; in this sense, it is involved with the operation and maintenance of networks of power.
- *Transactions*: the inclusion of transactional processes such as trade and exchange as a separate socio-spatial domain, serves to emphasize their key role in converting resources to power. It is in this sense

that we can speak of the action of exchange networks in terms of 'circuits of power'. An important aspect of trade/exchange systems in pre-industrial economies is their inherent instability as new goods and information constantly probe the system. Non-linear interactions at the heart of these transactional networks may ultimately induce chaotic dynamics (McGlade 1990, 1997).

THE EMPORDÀ: THE TRAJECTORY OF LONG-TERM CHANGE

From a normative perspective the history of the Empordà region would appear to be self-evident. This rich agricultural region lying astride the main inland route linking France with Spain, is at the same time open to the Mediterranean and largely shut off from the interior (see Figure 4.2). Throughout its history, the Empordà has been an area of passage and contact, linking the French plains of Rousillon and Languedoc over the Pyrenees and this has generated a rich archaeological and historical record. This region, over the past six thousand years, spanning the first Neolithic colonizations, through the later Bronze Age, Iberian, Roman and Medieval periods down to the present day, presents a particularly well developed sequence of changes, some coercive and others contingent and underpinned by a variety of processes such as conquest, colonization, and migration at the hands of Greeks, Romans and Visigothic kings.

In essence, we shall argue that the long-term is characterized by a series of major structural transformations in the organization of political space, for example the emergence of urbanization, with the development of the first towns in Iberia such as the Greek city of Emporion and its Iberian counterparts, Ullastret and Mas Castellar de Pontós, the subsequent Romanization of the landscape and with its decline, the implantation of new Visigoth kingdoms. Ultimately, what we have is a historical sequence of extractive economic strategies which have sought to appropriate the land for political and/or economic gain. It is in this sense that the history of the Empordà can be viewed as the history of land use conflict (McGlade and Picazo 1999).

From our current complexity perspective, we shall view the Empordà in terms of a distributed system. As we have seen, this model eschews any concept of the landscape as a single coordinated whole, organized as a coherent hierarchical system; instead, it focuses attention on the landscape as being defined by a series of nodes whose local interactions can generate macro-structures through a process of self-organization. In this heterarchical system, individual and group decisions that underpin the slow

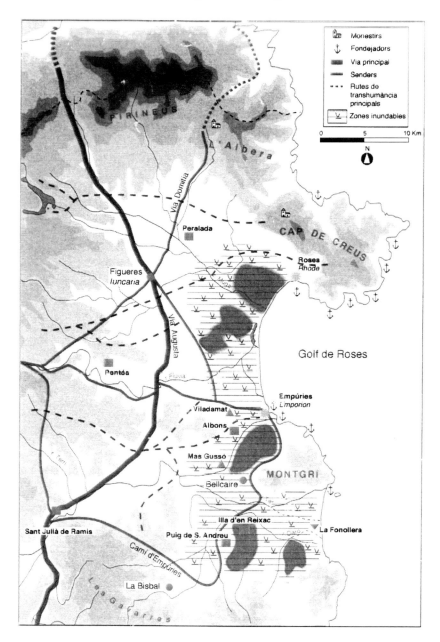

Figure 4.2   A map of the Empordà research area, showing relic wetlands and the primary Roman road system

agglomeration of settlements can evolve to create a single emergent urban structure.[4]

The Empordà: Initial Conditions

Viewed as a dynamical, distributed system, the historical trajectory of the Empordà can be seen to be the product of a particular series of bio-geophysical processes, providing the enabling and constraining features within which human ecodynamic co-evolution takes place. These 'initial conditions', as with all complex systems, have an important bearing on the structuration and future bifurcation history of the landscape; that is, they provide the primary conditions to which all future evolution can be attributed. However, with respect to human adaptations, it needs to be made clear that while the biophysical world, that is climatic regimes, hydrological and geomorphological processes act conjointly to circumscribe human societal activities, and to a degree act to produce determined outcomes, equally, political, social and ideological processes and individual agency are implicated in structural change, often in a contingent way. In essence, human societies are not adapted to any pre-existing niche. Rather humans are opportunistic, able to insert themselves into the ecological dynamic and to construct the type of environmental conditions that will allow them to prosper – at least over the short-term.

What is the justification for creating the specific spatio-temporal boundaries we have selected to represent successive stages of human ecodynamic development? In the first place, each *ecohistorical regime* represents a bifurcation in the biophysical, social and political dimensions that constitute a particular attractor within which the societal system is embedded. A key issue here, is how does this schema relate to the existing archaeological chronology?

Unlike the conventional historical trajectory which divides the long-term into discrete periods of technological – and by implication – societal change, the change from one *ecohistorical regime* to another is not necessarily linked to changes in material culture. Rather we are searching for breaks or interruptions in the structural coherence of societal systems that are driven by shifts in relations of power and the social relations of production.

We are looking for bifurcation points in the social trajectory, moments when the prevailing order or a particular set of embedded traditions are transformed as a result of internal ideological shifts, or as a result of changes wrought by co-evolutionary dynamics. In some cases these are manifest as radical changes in social organization or in the subsistence economy and/or relations of production. In other cases, they represent

Table 4.1   Structural attractors (ecohistorical regimes) and their relationship to conventional archaeological chronology

1st Ecohistorical Regime	(Neolithic–Late Bronze Age: c. 5000BC–1100BC)
2nd Ecohistorical Regime	(Late Bronze Age–Early Iron Age: c. 1100BC–650BC)
3rd Ecohistorical Regime	(Early Iron Age–Late Iberian: c. 650BC–200BC)
4th Ecohistorical Regime	(Late Iberian–Late Roman: c. 200BC–470AD)
5th Ecohistorical Regime	(Late Roman–Late Antiquity: c. 470AD–700AD)

a shift (discontinuity) in the symbolic order – a revisioning of the cognitive 'horizon' within which the societal system is situated. Alternatively, it is represented by the invasion or diffusion of new exchange items as contact is made with new trade networks and/or the society is incorporated into an alternative prestige economy. Most obvious of all are the bifurcations caused by invasion and incorporation, as is the case with the Empordà's appropriation by the Roman empire (see Table 4.1).

AN ALTERNATIVE TRAJECTORY OF CHANGE

We shall now present the human ecodynamic sequence as an evolutionary schema, demonstrating its relationship to the existing archaeological chronology.

1st Ecohistorical Regime (c. 5000BC–1100BC)

This structural attractor is uniquely long-lived in that it persists for almost four millennia. Archaeologically, it covers the various stages of the Neolithic (Early, Middle and Late) as well as the Early and Middle Bronze Age.

Resources
Allocative resources: the attractor that defines this regime is the product of a phase transition. As with the rest of Europe, the onset of the Neolithic in the post-glacial landscape represents a dramatic shift, or discontinuity, in the social, political and economic nature of human society. Coeval with this social transformation was a radical change in biophysical conditions with the onset of a climatic optimum at c. 5000BC, resulting in a significant amelioration of climate to warmer conditions. This facilitated changes in the productive economy with the gradual spread of cereal agriculture complemented by stock rearing and pastoralism, though the

archaeological evidence also testifies to the continued gathering of fruits and plant material (Buxo 1997). In short, what we see is the emergence of a semi-sedentary economy that stands in direct contrast to the preceding Palaeolithic and Mesolithic economies – essentially representing a non-sedentary way of living characterized by hunting, gathering and coastal exploitation strategies. In a sense, this Neolithic 'revolution' increased the 'possibility space' of social action and began a way of life that was to persist for some four millennia, that is until the advent of the Later Bronze Age at c. 1100BC.

By comparison with the succeeding ecohistorical regimes, this regime is represented by a largely extensive mode of production based on stock rearing, cattle ranching and transhumance, along with small-scale, mixed cereal agriculture. In complexity parlance, it represents a significant *phase transition*, as human populations were transformed from a largely passive relationship with the environment to one in which they emerge as a *productive* force (Pons and Tarrus 1987). Population density was low, hence the extent of human impact on the landscape was reduced with no extensive modification of the environment. Archaeological evidence demonstrates that settlement was largely dispersed, occupying caves and a variety of semi-permanent, seasonal locations.

Authoritative resources: visible changes in ideology are witnessed in burial rites dominated by the spread of megalithic structures, particularly on the higher slopes such as in the Albera region. What we see are the first visible signs of collective identity, and by implication the emergence of boundaries and territoriality. Initially, the hedgerow, the course of the river, the mountain peak or the dolmen serve to mark identity and an association with 'place'. Over time, these social signifiers intensify the level of group identity, until by the end of the 2nd millennium and the advent of the Late Bronze Age they evolve to become distinctive territories, signifying the control of both space and resources. It is in this sense that boundaries create new conditions for mutual hostility and conflict (cf. Sack 1986).

Death and burial is another aspect of this regime that must also be considered in terms of *authoritative resources*. That is to say that locational behaviour is never the sole product of ecological determination – it equally belongs to the realms of the social and symbolic. For example, in the Neolithic and early Bronze Age societies being described here, the role of ancestors is pivotal and is reflected in the wide diffusion of megalithic tombs. Since these are, in effect, collective repositories of community identity, knowledge and genaeology, the social geography will tend to reflect this. For example, a wide array of anthropological and archaeological evidence from around the globe demonstrates that specific areas in the environment might be proscribed or categorized as 'other', hence the practice of hunting and/or farming is prohibited. With respect to settlement, too, the landscape is not simply the location of a set of 'available resources' defined in terms of modern economic criteria, rather they must be seen as the locus of a web of material, symbolic and ideological structures.

Agency

Environmental: the role of environmental agency forms an important structuring aspect, since this regime is coeval with a major climate change. Consequently, the soils, hydrology and vegetation that comprised the early Neolithic landscape provided an improved set of circumstances within which sedentary agriculture and attendant population growth could flourish.

Social: from a social perspective, sedentism brings with it a variety of new modes of social organization that emerge as a response to more intensive subsistence patterns. In addition, a more sedentary way of life creates a new attitude to the land – less a mobile, shifting resource, it now becomes synonymous with place and social identity. These ingredients provide the basis for a sense of ownership and property and along with it a sense of territoriality. Significantly, this *ecohistorical regime* sets in motion a growing social inequality that was to find its apogee some centuries later during the Bronze and Iron Ages.

Transactions

The transactional processes that dominate this regime can be said to be driven by the need to accumulate everyday goods such as salt, hides, and meat products. In concert with this quotidian exchange was an alternative sphere dominated by the movement of prestige items. These were generally traded over long distances and in this sense the Iberian peninsula during the Neolithic and Bronze Age was crossed by an elaborate series of trade networks linking the Atlantic with the Mediterranean, as well as the Pyrenees with Andalucia in the south. As was pointed out above, we can see these exchange networks in terms of 'circuits of power'.

Summary

The structural attractor that describes this *1st ecohistorical regime* demonstrates that there is little evidence of any overt control over nature, but rather is characterized by the development of a symbiotic understanding of weather, soils and plant and animal population dynamics, as human societal systems are mapped onto the natural world and its temporal rhythms. These cyclical temporalities testify to the embeddedness of the social with the natural in prehistoric communities and their mapping onto the seasonal rhythms of the landscape, that is their co-evolution. Thus, human ecodynamic structure emerges as a result of the intersection of temporalities, ranging from the slowest geo-tectonic movements, through climatic cycles, all the way to population dynamics and other micro-level phenomena. The social natural landscape is thus comprised of multiple sets of intertemporal dependencies, defining a reciprocal dynamic that maps the social on to the natural and the natural on to the social (McGlade 1999). This symmetry between nature and culture produces a human ecodynamic relationship whose co-evolution demonstrates the highest degree of resilience of any *ecohistorical regime*.

2nd Ecohistorical Regime (c. 1100BC–650BC)

Archaeologically, this attractor spans the period from the onset of the Late Bronze Age until the beginning of the Early Iron Age.

Resources

Allocative resources: the changes in the subsistence economy that were seen to characterize the 1st human ecodynamic attractor, now achieve a radical transformation as the economic system is re-organized to promote high levels of production, with the beginnings of intensive cereal agriculture and increased stock rearing. Archaeological evidence suggests an increase in population, something that is augmented by the new Urnfield immigrations from the southern Alps via southern France. Above all, a new sedentary economy begins to dominate, pushing previous diverse hunting and coastal exploitation strategies to a secondary role. A measure of the new controlling influence on nature is to be seen in the introduction of *sitges* or storage pits by which agricultural surplus could be managed, both as a hedge against poor harvests and to provide surplus for exchange. This regime, thus, witnesses the first dramatic signs of the effects of human modification on the landscape, as the co-evolution of natural agency (climate change) and human adaptive response acted to create an entirely different set of production possibilities. In marked contrast to the preceding regime, population clusters began to develop around larger settlement nuclei and we see the beginnings of the type of intensive agricultural exploitation that marks this regime as a real phase change in the social trajectory.

Authoritative resources: one of the key discontinuities that define this attractor as a legitimate phase transition is that it marks the arrival of the Urnfield populations from across the Pyrenees (c. 1100BC–1000BC). Most radically it represents a discontinuity in pottery traditions, metallurgy production and most significant of all, in funerary ritual (Ruiz Zapatero 1997). The introduction of a new rite of cremation marks a genuine separation from previously embedded traditions of inhumation and suggests a society undergoing a radical change in worldview, as the relationship between the world of the living and that of the dead is reconceptualized.

Agency

Environmental: an important defining characteristic of this attractor is its coincidence with the Sub-boreal climatic phase (c. 1000BC–500AD) and this was to radically affect human ecodynamic evolution of the landscape. Broadly speaking, with the general drying trend, subsistence practices become localized on the plain with the opening up of new spaces formally occupied by wetlands.

Social: growing social inequality first appears as a new attribute of this attractor and is manifest in increasing territorialization of the landscape along with the emergence of overt leadership. What previously was a landscape divided along ancestral lines and organized for the mutual benefit of the population, gives way to a new conception of land ownership and authority. From a geographical perspective, we begin to see the landscape as being divided with a view to controlling the primary river systems and hence the emergence of fortified *oppida* as central places. Moreover, the use of large storage pits, noted above, represents a dramatic change in the control/management of the natural environment; however, it can also be viewed as a significant authoritative device in the sense that it represents the overt control of production by a central authority – in this case the emerging aristocratic elite.

Transactions

Initially, trade/exchange activities are dominated by regional and domestic contexts and follow the embedded traditions practised over millennia. As we have already noted, long distance trade in prestige items was a prominent part of Later Bronze Age exchange systems linking the Atlantic with the Mediterranean as well as the Pyrenees with Andalucia in the south. These 'circuits of power' conferred substantial advantage on those who controlled them.

Summary

Among the key characteristics that define this regime as a discrete attractor, is a quickening pace of change in social, political and economic spheres; thus from a temporal perspective, the structural attractor underpinning this regime encompasses not simply change, but a significant shift in the *rate of change*. The Urnfield migrations with their alternative burial practices and probably cosmology, appear to act as a trigger, flipping the social system towards a new attractor; it is thus that we can clearly identify spatio-temporal discontinuity as one of the signatures of this attractor.

Significantly, this structural attractor represents a major transition phase in the societal trajectory, that is between two contrasting sets of temporalities: the semi-sedentary pastoral economies with their loose-knit structures of power, characteristic of the Neolithic and the new intensive exploitation of territory for economic and political gain that is to become the hallmark of later Iron Age society. Perhaps, above all, the attractor is marked by the seemingly inevitable movement towards a hierarchical society along with its attendant social inequalities.

3rd Ecohistorical Regime (c. 650BC–200BC)

The time range covered by this regime is consistent with the Iron Age/Iberian period and the transition to statehood. It ends with the phase transition represented by Roman conquest and colonization.

Resources

Allocative resources: landscape productivity reaches significant levels, as a growing population expands to work previously marginal zones – something also aided by the profusion of new iron technology, creating demonstrable change in agricultural practice. This regime is characterized by significant innovation at social, political and economic levels. For example, human modification of the environment is apparent from palaeoecological and archaeological material that shows substantial modification of the forest and evidence for managed woodland. Additionally, new types of cereal agriculture are apparent as well as the introduction of grapes and olives. From a complexity perspective, what is of note is the increasing connectivity of the landscape as it becomes more densely populated and formally divided into distinctive territorial units, focused on large scale production – not only for domestic consumption, but for a growing Mediterranean market that was the consequence of the establishment of the Phocaean Greek colonies at Emporion and Rhode.

Authoritative resources: the emergence of an Iberian aristocratic system based on new ideas of agnatic descent is a key social development during this period and is an abrupt rupture with previous community-based societal systems. What we are seeing here is a radical transformation that was – particularly in the south of the peninsula – to lead to the emergence of the Iberian state and the domination by local warrior aristocracies (Ruiz and Molinos 1993, p. 262). With respect to the region under study, the rise of statehood is yet unproven, but we can at least speak of a form of 'proto-statehood', as existing tribal chiefdoms evolved to become aristocracies (Cabrera 1998, p. 203) resident in large *oppida*. By the 5th century BC, the exercise of power is to be seen in the establishment of urban centres, or *oppida*, wielding political and economic control. In some cases, this coincided with the establishment of ethnic territories. By the 4th century BC, it may be possible to define a decentralized state; that is functioning without a dominant central place, but as a distributed system in which roughly equal polities coexisted and indulged in trade exchange relations.[5]

Agency

Environmental: the onset of this regime is coeval with a climate change, as drier conditions lead to the disappearance of many lakes and wetland areas. In turn, this was to open up the landscape for more intensive agriculture. A period of drying such as this promoted the evolution of a new ecological and bio-climatic phase – that is the appearance of *sclerophytic* species typical of the Mediterranean today, for example holm oak, white pine, steppe brushwood and heather. Changes to the local and regional ecology are also to be seen in the presence of riverine species such as poplars, willows, alders, tamarax and elm (Buxo *et al.* 1996).

Social: the nature of human agency in this regime is distinctive for a number of reasons. In the first place, the general trend to inequality and unequal access that characterizes the Iberian Iron Age, severely constrains human activity and practice at the local domestic level. The new territorial *oppida* act not only as central places, but more significantly, as the locus of social control – control of production and consumption, prestige trade items, as well as control of social alliances and all other legal affairs. This exercise of power by an aristocratic elite acts as a severe constraint on independent human action at all levels of society. Thus, for example, within the domestic sphere, human groups have decreasing power to affect their own lives, particularly since domestic production of pottery is now increasingly controlled and geared towards an emerging external market.

Transactions

The Greek colonial establishment of Emporion was close to the ancient basin of the river Fluvia which provided access to the Garrotxa and the Pyrenees zone, since they were rich in mineral resources. But perhaps the most distinctive feature of this regime, setting it apart from the previous two, is in the appearance of a true market economy. From c. 600BC the Empordà plain can be considered an open market as Phoenician, Punic, Etruscan and Greek material constitute primary commercial transactions. The intensification of this trade was largely an indigenous response to the availability of Mediterranean markets and functioned as a self-reinforcing or positive feedback dynamic. What was to emerge from this interaction was the appearance of a more homogeneous material culture – aided particularly by the adoption of wheel thrown ceramic types to feed a growing market. These new commercial opportunities were to have profound effects on Iberian social structure as access and control of prestige goods increased the wealth and power of existing elites, creating an essentially competitive landscape. One of the clearest expressions of this new-found wealth and the burdens that it produced is to be seen in the growth of fortifications in existing *oppida*. Territoriality and its expression was to reach its highest apogee between the 3rd and 2nd centuries BC.

During the 6th century BC the Greek commercial activity slackened off, and penetration into the hinterland was reduced. When the Greeks arrived in the Empordà, the local populations already had commercial relations with the Phoenicians and, on a smaller scale, with the Etruscans. Ultimately, however, Greek commerce was to dominate the coastal zone between the French colony at *Massalia* and *Emporion*. During the 5th–4th centuries BC, Emporion developed an important commercial network that reached the Midi de la France, Rousillon, the entire Catalan littoral, the Levant, as well as the south-east and the Balearic islands. Most of this presence is to be seen from the presence of Greek imports, especially of Attic pottery. It has also been suggested that in return, Emporion exported cereals to Athens and through this connection it was consolidated as a redistribution centre of Attic pottery in the North-East Mediterranean (for example Ruiz de Arbulo 1992).

Summary
From a complexity perspective, what we see across the landscape is a process of self-organization, whereby markets emerge from a distributed network. Thus, the observed global organization is the result of locally interacting individual agents – in this case the individual elites who control the *oppida* centres – and their role in pursuing self-interest. Above all, however, this attractor is defined by the transition to statehood as the Iberian warrior aristocracy evolves to assume absolute control of the entire region. This is not a conventional centralized control of the landscape, but is rather a distributed system whereby individual *oppida* do not compete in a hierarchy of central places. By contrast they assume the position of roughly equal status in a model that seems to fit Renfrew and Cherry's (1986) scheme of 'peer polity interaction'.

4th Ecohistorical Regime (c. 200BC–476AD)

This regime is consistent with the onset and growth of Romanization across the landscape. During the summer of 218BC, a Roman army commanded by the consul Scipio landed in the port of Emporion, an action which marked the start of the Second Punic War and, for the Iberian population, the beginning of a systematic conquest. The imposition of Roman colonization represents a dramatic shift in human ecodynamic relations as the landscape is converted into a centre of production for export to Rome.

Resources

Allocative resources: during the first hundred years of Roman domination there was general continuity in the human occupation of the Empordà landscapes; significantly, we also see the emergence of new sites on the plain and the growth of others, such as Castell de la Fosca at Palamos, Fortim at Sant Feliu de Guixols, and so on. By the end of the 2nd century BC there was a clear change in the situation, related to the arrival of an important number of Italian colonists who seem to have been responsible for changes in the exploitation of the territory, through the introduction of new crops, new technologies, different storage systems, as well as new building methods. Significantly, this process is paralleled by a crisis in the status of the Iberian *oppida*, and marks the point at which most of them were abandoned and eventually, disappeared. Thus, by the advent of the 1st century BC the pace of Romanization accelerated and became fully established; this was the beginning of a radical and distinctive change, marking a new phase of land use practices, settlement pattern and population dynamics in the Empordà.

The process that we refer to as Romanization, meant in the Empordà (as in other areas of Catalunya) the introduction of villa-based agriculture, the construction of a new communication network roads, and the creation or expansion of many small local centres with Iberian–Roman components. The most important development of the Roman colonization of the Empordà was the creation of the villae – rural settlements set far from the urban centres and which constituted the basis upon which subsistence exploitation was to operate and persist over subsequent centuries. Compared to their Italian counterparts, the villae of the Empordà, such as the Tolegassos and Olivet d'en Pujol, were relatively small, and cultivated different crops, so as to maintain a form of economic diversity. In Tolegassos, we know that there were 125 *dolia* (cereal container) with a storage capacity of 40 tons of cereals. Olivet, on the other hand, had 75 *dolia* which represented 22 tons of cereals. From this evidence we can deduce that their respective areas of exploitation were 12–13 ha. and 7.5 ha. respectively.

Sometime between the last centuries of the Roman Republican period and the beginning of the Empire, the traditional practice of cereal cultivation in the Empordà was gradually changed by the introduction of other crops; in particular, grapes and olives were growing in importance. Thus by the end of the 3rd century AD, the villa of Vilauba has extensive technology used for oil production. Additionally, wine production was important too in the Empordà during Imperial times, as is evidenced by excavated remains of workshops for the production of amphorae. The proximity to the coast meant that other important production activities at this time were related with fishing, and we see the construction of factories such as at Roses, for the production of sauces and salt fish products such as *garum* and *salsamenta*.

Authoritative resources: during the first phase of the Roman occupation, Emporion acted as the base of the conqueror's army, from where they quelled the revolt of the indigenous tribes in 197BC. This act resulted in the final demise of the *oppida* as centres of political power and the beginning of Roman hegemony, a process which was to gradually transform both the landscapes and the patterns of land use, ultimately leading to the incorporation of the indigenous Iberian population. Collectively, these changes – and particularly the superimposition of a network of roads centred on the via Augusta – produced a set of constraints upon which the future evolution of the landscape was to be based.

It is likely that opinion was polarized (as in other Roman provinces) between those kings, princes and/or aristocrats who had initially controlled the trade with Etruscans, Phoenicians and Greeks, and who saw nothing but opportunity in the potential development of Romanization, and those tribal leaders further inland who sought to foment resistance, rather than be absorbed by Rome. What is clear is that there was a significant degree of resistance across the landscape, culminating in the revolt of 197BC. The putting down of this revolt and its brutal consequences mark the demise of the *oppida* and the beginning of Roman hegemony. Thus the landscape is transformed from a landscape of resistance to one dominated by a new discourse of power with the indigenous Iberian aristocracy as willing participants in the new order dominated by the Imperial goal to annexe the entire region as a source for production to satisfy the ever-growing city of Rome.

Agency
Environmental: at a global level, the changes in the natural environment must be seen as part of a continuum that is part of the Late Holocene climatic regime – one characterized by a great deal of variability. Recent palaeohydrological and climatic data summarized by Buxo *et al.* (1996) concludes that the period between 4300BC and 1500BC is characterized by long-term cycles of organic lacustrine deposition which define and redefine the changing wetland landscapes of the plain. Significantly, by the end of the Roman period, deposition increased from 3mm/year to 1m/year in the area of the river mouths. However, the combination of palaeohydrological, erosional and climatic phenomena makes it difficult to determine the difference between natural geomorphological processes and those wrought by agricultural intensification during the Roman period.

Social: the process of colonization, apart from the obvious political and military consequences it had for the indigenous population, marks a radical change in the sphere of human action. Not surprisingly, the 'possibility space' within which communities and households could operate was severely constrained by the imposition of what amounts to a new world order. The introduction of the villa system as the basis of economic production created not only a new type of economic landscape, but more significantly it can be seen as constructing new relations within the context of social freedoms and class structure. Thus the widespread use of slavery became the motor of production in the fields and the mines, forming the basis of wealth for the local elite. In this system the *plebs rustica*, or rural peasantry, produced just enough to pay taxes and rents and to provide for their families. However, the uncertainties of climate, added to the constant political pressure to increase production, meant that poverty was a constant threat. While slavery can be accounted as one of the instruments of power of the land owning elite, we must also account for the *liberti*, or freed slaves, who formed an important part of the plebian population. This section of the population enjoyed a degree of social mobility and through the accumulation of wealth, could aspire to become magistrates, although they were prevented from holding public office.

One of the most important aspects of the Roman system with respect to discussions of agency centres on patron–client relations and their central role in Hispano-Roman society. As an expression of power and influence, wealthy citizens gave financial and legal assistance to dependants who, by way of return, performed a variety of services for the patron. Indeed one of the measures of an aristocrat's position in society was the extent of his client network.

Transactions
The transaction space that dominates this fourth structural attractor is basically a combination of the previous regional exchange networks set up virtually since the first peopling of the landscape, overlain with a new market economy linked to expansive Mediterranean trade routes controlled by Imperial Rome. Crucial to the efficient functioning of this market economy was the villa system and its role in the creation of agricultural surplus for exchange. Thus commodities such as grain, olives, olive oil, fish and wine found their way by riverine and sea routes to Rome as well as to other parts of the Iberian peninsula. Not all villas were involved in agriculture, and archaeological evidence demonstrates that some of the coastal villas were centres of production for pottery and other materials. A key to the efficient functioning of the villa system was the communication network based on the primary river systems (Ter, Fluvia and Muga) and

the Roman road system. For example, the via Augusta provided a north–south artery, while the via Capsacosta linked Emporion to the mineral areas of the sub-Pyrenees zone.

Summary

This structural attractor is above all defined by the hyper-connectivity of the landscape, based on a network of roads connecting villas and urban centres alike. In addition, all available land was brought into production to cater for the demands of a growing empire as well as the increasing needs of Rome itself. One significant difference separating this *ecohistorical regime* from those preceding it, is that it sees the emergence of a true market economy because the effects of colonization and Romanization effected a radical change, transforming legal, political, social and economic realms. By contrast to the sparsely connected landscapes of the first attractor (ER1), this attractor can be described in terms of 'hyper-connectance'; thus in company with the general behaviour of all complex systems, as the number of information connections increases, the system becomes densely connected and brittle and is subject to collapse.

5th Ecohistorical Regime (Early–Late Antiquity: c. 476AD–700AD)

The final regime is consistent with the end of the Roman world and the transition to medieval society. The invasions and movements of Germanic peoples in Iberia between the early and late 5th century AD served to separate late Roman from early medieval Iberia in political terms. In 415AD, the Visigoths crossed into eastern Tarraconensis at the invitation of Rome, in an attempt to bring the provinces back under Roman control. This was the first phase in the long and confusing process whereby Rome gradually lost all influence in Iberia. However, Tarraco, the capital of the province, remained in Roman hands until the invasion of Tarraconensis by the Visigothic King Euric between 470 and 475AD, just before the dissolution of the western Roman Empire.

Resources

Allocative resources: the onset of Gothic political dominion did not cause a radical disruption and was represented by continuity of land structure and settlement patterns, with most of the towns and villages continuing in use, for example Ametllers, Pla de Palol, Camp de la Gruta, Roses, Puig Rodon, and Vilauba. Although the land was not settled as densely as it had been in previous periods, it is possible to point out two new facts: firstly, there is new evidence for the sporadic occupation of caves as settlement places and shelter areas; secondly, the emergence of a fortified *oppidum* on

an isolated altitude, far from the main routes and dominating the surrounding territory. This site, Puig de les Muralles, in Puig Rom (Roses) was
founded around the end of the 6th century AD and was subsequently abandoned around 780AD, probably as a consequence of the Saracen invasions.
These two phenomena are clearly related to the upheavals of the long and
confusing process whereby Rome gradually lost all influence in Iberia,
immediately preceding the dissolution of the western Roman Empire. The
renewed importance of the old Greek colony at Roses is also to be seen in
the construction of a factory for the production of salted fish that lasted
until the 6th century AD. By this time we see new patterns of settlement
emerge, along with a decrease in the importance of cereal agriculture and
an increase in stock-breeding and exploitation of forest resources.
Palynological evidence shows substantial deforestation to create new pas-
tures. It is also significant that during this period there was a substantial
restructuring of territory as the old Roman systems of centuriation were
remodelled and/or destroyed to make way for the increasing needs of a
pastoral economy (Palet i Martinez 1997). Coeval with this latter, is the
evidence for transhumance and the temporary occupation of caves in the
lower Pyrenees. Significant changes also occurred in the villa system, with
many being transformed to accommodate small industries and olive
presses, and kilns for glass and ceramics (Arce 1977, p. 31).

Authoritative resources: as a consequence of the dissolution of Roman
imperial power, a new authority imposed itself on the Empordà; as with the
rest of Catalunya, it became part of the kingdom of the Goths. The disintegration of the Roman administrative system during Late Antiquity was
coeval with a reduction in the power of the local aristocracy. It was at this
juncture that the church became the focus of judicial and political authority and was organized by aristocrats who made up the clerical class. Locally,
control was exercised by clergy at the parish level who assumed the role of
educator, protector and confessor – above all, the earthly intermediary
responsible for salvation. These ideological changes are also evident in the
transformation of some villas as Christian basilicas often with nearby
cemeteries (Arce 1997).

Agency

Environmental: a number of changes in the physical landscape are
apparent, particularly the enlargement of the primary river deltas. It is
likely that this process was a consequence of human induced erosion
through deforestation. This attractor above all sees a number of significant
biophysical changes that over two centuries (5th–7th) create major transformations in the vegetation and soil structure. These changes, rather than
being the manifest results of human engagement with the environment, are

essentially the unplanned outcome of a variety of non-linear interactions that make up the social–natural system.

Social: the collapse of Roman hegemony removed a variety of political and administrative constraints on the rural population, resulting in the emergence of new forms of self-sufficiency (Gurt 1998). This process seems to be coeval with the transformation of a number of villae that appear to become centres of olive oil and wine production. Most importantly, the landscape and its population becomes more dispersed, less centralized than previously, with the emergence of distinctive parishes and their churches as the focus of rural life in a new Christianized worldview – one in which individual freedom was conceded to the church.

Transactions
The arrival of Visigothic political rule did not signify any abrupt change in Mediterranean trade/exchange transactions; thus the Empordà region still had access to goods from the central and eastern Mediterranean as well as North Africa. At a regional level, the nature of commercial trade in Late Antiquity is to be understood with reference to the importance of markets and their urban and peri-urban contexts (Gurt 1998). Archaeological evidence suggests a clear continuity of commercial activity in those urban centres (for example Rhode and Emporion) that had dominated trade during the period of Romanization. Transactions may be divided in terms of interregional exchange of domestic and agricultural products as well as coastal maritime trade based on cabotage. This latter is probably the route by which the abundance of North African goods – especially ceramics and tableware – arrived in the north-east.

Summary
The definitive end of the ancient world, that is its politico-military break-down, was accelerated by the plundering raids of Saracens, ushering in a period of instability. Most of the rural sites decayed or were abandoned, and the various changes produced during the previous centuries reached their logical conclusion. Archaeological evidence seems to show the end of a phase that had begun during the 3rd century AD, and the beginning of another – what we have come to refer to as the Early Medieval period. Thus the colonization of the frontier territories (such as the Empordà) characterized the 5th–7th centuries AD and transformed, at least partially, the organization of property and land tenure and, in consequence, the demographic patterns of the region. From an ideological perspective, this attractor is dominated by an emerging Christianity that signals new relationships between people, the land and the clergy – effectively redefining man's place in the universe.

SYNTHESIS: RESILIENCE VERSUS CONNECTIVITY

Having outlined the descriptive properties of each *ecohistorical regime* and suggested the co-evolutionary dynamics underpinning them, we shall now evaluate the relative merits of each regime by assessing their relationship to core complexity criteria; that is their role in maintaining structural stability in terms of two distinct attributes: i) resilience and ii) connectance.

i) *Resilience*: What we are arguing is that the persistence of socio-economic systems over the long-term is a function of their inherent resilience, in the sense that they are able to *incorporate* change and perturbation without experiencing major structural transformation or collapse (cf. Chapter 6). Importantly, this capacity to absorb and accommodate new conditions – be they natural, social or political – is itself a measure of the 'elasticity' of socio-economic organization and above all, the historical trajectory along which the system has developed. As was argued previously, historical precedent plays a crucial role, in the sense that a particular regime that has historically been exposed to constant, periodic disturbance, will develop an adaptive capacity to absorb periodic change, whereas this will not be the case with a system which experiences extreme events on an infrequent, irregular basis.

ii) *Connectance*: With respect to complexity, we can say that for any system, the higher the degree of connectedness, the lower is the probability of system stability. Conversely, if a system is underconnected, its cohesion is destroyed and it can become so fragmented that its resilience is reduced (Klomp and Green 1996). For example, monoculture practices in agriculture are highly dependent on constant inputs of artificial fertilizer, and this makes them prone to a variety of pest infestations. The spatial homogeneity of these types of systems stands in direct contrast to pre-industrial (and prehistoric) systems, which were based on an intuitive understanding of intercropping and spatial patchiness. Significantly, the lower connectivity of these subsistence systems and their embeddedness within the natural vegetation cycles renders them more resilient to perturbation.

Turning to our Empordà example, it is apparent from our previous discussion that in a number of cases the loss of resilience acted to push the dominant socio-economic system towards uncertainty and increasing instability, causing it to flip to a new (temporary) attractor state. Here we see the essential difference between an equilibrium-centred view and a metastable view of reality. For example, an equilibrium focus emphasizes, not only constancy in time, but also spatial homogeneity and linear causation. In such a model, instability is viewed as detrimental – something to be countered and controlled. By contrast, a metastable view emphasizes the existence of more than one stable state; here, instability, rather than being considered as a system pathology, is seen as maintaining the resilience of the system. Notably, it emphasizes variability, spatial heterogeneity and nonlinear causation. Above all, this property of metastability is the key to understanding the functioning and persistence of all socio-economic systems.

By way of illustration, Figure 4.3 shows a snapshot of the Empordà landscape as just such a metastable trajectory, focusing on the relationship between the two fundamental complexity concepts, resilience and connectivity. Here, resilience is calculated as a measure of longevity (persistence) of settlement occupation, while connectivity is calculated as a measure of the number of nearest neighbour settlements divided by the occupation space for each period.

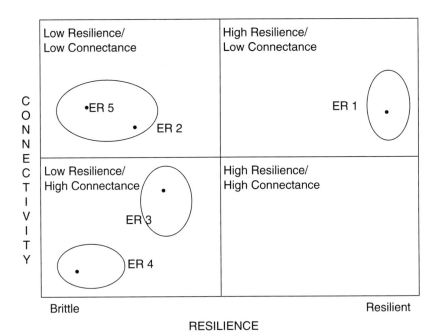

Figure 4.3   *Relationship between ecohistorical regimes and complexity*
                criteria, connectance and resilience. The figure shows the
                abrupt discontinuity between regimes, emphasizing their
                discontinuous nature

The identification of the initial structural attractor (ER1) provides us with an example of the most resilient human ecodynamic regime – one that persists for almost five millennia. It is also characterized by low connectance since there are relatively few sedentary settlements. The bifurcation that results in a move to ER2 presents a rapid and discontinuous change governed by an entirely new set of values brought in by an emergent immigrant population. This socio-political regime is in turn superseded by an entirely different attractor – one governed by intensive agriculture and increasing socio-political inequality. These types of relationships are further pronounced during the Romanization process that forms the basis of ER4. Now the densely packed settlement landscape is highly connected to the point of being 'brittle'. By analogy with ecological systems, this means that the social system is in danger of 'hyper-coherence' or the kind of over-connectance that is frequently the hallmark of collapse in complex systems. This brittle hierarchical regime does collapse and we see in our final attractor (ER5) a rapid shift to a previous state of low connectance across a more sparsely populated landscape.

Historical Path dependence

The five structural attractors that we have enumerated also reveal another aspect of complex systems behaviour: *path dependence*. One of the most important aspects of adopting a long-term perspective is that it stresses the importance of understanding the role of preceding events (qua initial conditions) and their long-term effects on the subsequent development of the system. In our present context, this emphasizes the fact that decisions made in the past inevitably form the initial conditions of what are later perceived as 'current' crises. It is in this sense that apparently arbitrary or unintended features emerge to determine subsequent political and social pathways. Arthur (1988a, 1988b) has discussed the role of historical path dependence as a process which emphasizes the critical role of both chance and necessity in directing the evolution of economic structures and urban agglomerations. In describing the historical evolution of urbanism, he uses a genetic analogy to suggest that chance events act to 'select' the pattern that becomes fixed, and that regions that are economically attractive have an intrinsic 'selectional advantage' and hence a better chance of achieving economic dominance. The main point here is that contingent factors acting upon historical events can generate conjunctions in an *unplanned* way and as a consequence, create inevitable and irreversible historical outcomes. This appears to us as an unintended consequence (McGlade 1999).

In our present case, we can see how aspects of landscape structuring and territoriality emerging in the 1st ecohistorical regime have exerted a primary influence on all subsequent spatial organization of the Empordà. This spatial structuring of territory is particularly pronounced by the advent of ER3 during the pre-Roman Iberian period, when the politico-administrative boundaries become 'locked in' in such a way that they determined the character of socio-spatial interaction for the ensuing two and a half millennia up to the present day. Thus, what began in the Neolithic (ER1) as symbolic identifiers, dividing the landscape into tribal and ethnic territories, act as the basis for subsequent socio-political and administrative demarcations during the later Roman, medieval and modern periods.

The construction of the Roman road network is a revealing example of the long-term persistence of 'initial conditions'. The establishment of the via Augusta as the principal north–south axis linking the province of Hispania with Italy, represents a major bifurcation in the structuring of social space. Indeed it can be seen as one of the key discontinuities marking the transition from ER3 to ER4. The superimposition of this road along with the cadastral field system, symbolizes a major transformation in the political, economic and eventually the cultural life of the region; this new north–south axis supplanting the previous east–west orientation represented by the river systems of the Empordà – a system that had remained unchanged for 4000 years, that is from the beginning of our 1st ecohistorical regime, ER1. The construction of the via Augusta, the spine along which Rome was to achieve the conquest of Hispania, produced a 'lock-in' effect, defining the possibility space of all subsequent social, economic and political interaction; indeed, the dominance exerted by this axis of passage persists to the present day, with the Roman road transformed into the modern autopista route connecting the Iberian peninsula with France and the rest of Europe (McGlade and Picazo 1999).

Finally, perhaps what Figure 4.3 demonstrates most clearly, is that we must be wary of subscribing to simplistic models of adaptive evolution, particularly with respect to societal change. By contrast, we see that social change has no inherent directionality, but is represented – at least in our case – by a series of transitions that are essentially contingent.

NARRATING THE BIFURCATION HISTORY OF THE LANDSCAPE

Returning to our initial discussion on history and narrative, what we can say is that the landscapes of the Empordà are an assorted palimpsest of relict 'signatures' – residual traces of human engagement with the landscape. As we have argued, this is first and foremost a co-evolutionary relationship in which the social is implicated in the natural and the natural in the social, to form a recursive socio-natural system. The model of complexity we have suggested for the Empordà landscapes has enabled us to interpret the long-term, not as a single linear trajectory of increasing social, political and economic organization, but rather as one punctuated by a sequence of discontinuous shifts or phase transitions. Significantly, these bifurcations have no intrinsic direction but are a consequence of the conjunction of contingent events and historical processes driving the societal system – neither forwards nor backwards – but along a variety of exploratory pathways.

We might usefully summarize the principal outcomes of our exploration into the long-term:

- *Long-term evolution*: social systems are usefully described as complex dynamic systems and underline the importance of history in understanding the evolutionary trajectory. The Empordà landscapes can profitably be viewed as a sequence of topological transformations brought about by the interaction of determined and contingent processes. The long-term is punctuated by distinctive human ecodynamic 'signatures' that define a metastable landscape comprising a series of structural attractors. These are conceived as discrete spatio-temporal entities, or *ecohistorical regimes*.

- *Organizational structure*: societal systems do not necessarily learn from history, for example from past failures or successes. This, ironically, is the real lesson of history. Human socio-natural systems are subject to unanticipated outcomes on account of inherent non-linearities; this is the source of emergent behaviour.

- *Co-evolution*: ecohistorical regimes are driven by co-evolutionary processes, linking knowledge structures, resources and power. These dimensions form a variety of non-linear couplings that generate self-organizing dynamics. The role of contingent events (political, social and cultural) means that, unlike 'fitness landscapes', *ecohistorical regimes* do not seek to maximize any stated 'evolutionary potential', but rather follow a trajectory that is essentially contingent.

- *Adaptation*: with respect to human adaptations it needs to be made clear that while the biophysical world, that is climatic regimes, hydrological and geomorphological processes, act conjointly to circumscribe human societal activities, and to a degree act to produce determined outcomes, equally, political, social and ideological processes and individual agency are implicated in structural change. In essence, human societies are not adapted to any pre-existing niche. Rather humans are opportunistic, able to insert themselves into the ecological dynamic and to construct the type of environmental conditions that will allow them to prosper – at least over the short-term.

- *Temporalities*: human ecodynamic structure emerges as a result of the intersection of temporalities, ranging from the slowest processes such as tectonic movements (10^7), climatic cycles (10^5), all the way to population dynamics (10^2) and other micro-level phenomena (10^{-1}). Importantly, these temporalities represent differential rates of change. Thus we have slow, cumulative rates represented by glacial and tectonic movements, coupled with soil or vegetational dynamics which display rapid turnover. Research on a number of ecological systems shows that discontinuity – and frequently catastrophic outcomes – can be the result of the conjuncture of 'fast' and 'slow' variables (Holling 1986). Such complexity is further enhanced by the superimposition of human social, political and economic systems. What we have ultimately are sets of intertemporal dependencies, defining a reciprocal dynamic that maps the social on to the natural and the natural on to the social.

- *Resilience*: the resilience of each *ecohistorical regime* depends crucially on the ability to enhance the stocks of knowledge, thus increasing adaptive potential. Landscape is thus viewed as a species of distributed learning environment. From an evolutionary perspective, this can lead to non-linear transformations (regime switches) analogous to phase changes in physical systems. Thus, the slow accumulation of knowledge can be followed by a discontinuous change and movement to a new structural attractor.

CONCLUSION: READING *LA LONGUE DURÉE*

From semi-nomadic settlement to urbanism, statehood, conquest and colonization, we have traced the history of the Empordà over almost six millennia of human ecodynamic co-evolution. In recognizing that history is a multi-braided fabric, our aim has been to construct a plausible evolutionary trajectory for understanding long-term societal change. Thus, our narrative has sought to isolate a sequence of discrete, discontinuous phases in the historical trajectory, so as to underline critical transitions or phase changes in socio-natural evolution. As we have seen, this 'bifurcation history' eschews strict adherence to the conventional linear chronology with its emphasis on the long-term as a series of technological developments and attendant social changes. By contrast, we have argued that technological innovations in material culture, such as the diffusion and exploitation of metallurgy or innovations in ceramic technology are not, of themselves, the drivers of change. Rather, we have attempted to demonstrate that societal change proceeds in a non-linear and contingent fashion – a consequence of specific sets of human ecodynamic relationships. Central to such a model is the assertion that human societal evolution does not follow a path of inevitable increasing complexity.

Significantly, unlike a variety of models that focus on the centrality of environmental factors, such as Braudel's preference for the role of geophysical processes in historical evolution, our conception of the *longue durée* does not view environmental conditions as having a determining influence on societal adaptations. By contrast, we have sought to emphasize the essential co-evolutionary dynamics that underpin social, political and economic interdependencies and the way these self-reinforcing processes are implicated in resource transitions and the maintenance of power. What is clear from our emphasis on the long-term is that the emergent phenomena that act to drive societal systems in a particular direction are contextually specific in the sense that each ecohistorical regime evolves through a unique set of social, political and ecological interactions. Thus, the dimensions that may be said to govern the structural attractor during the period dominated by Neolithic and Bronze Age technologies are qualitatively different from those that form the core of the structural attractor that defines the period of Romanization. For these reasons, it is unhelpful to simply view societal evolution as a sequence of changing economic strategies and productive forces. Indeed, the notion of isolating that which is 'economic' from other aspects of society, for example ideological, political or cultural will always produce a misreading of the complexity of human–social interaction. In a sense, one of the real advantages of invoking the ideas at the heart of the complexity discourse is that, by focusing on the holistic nature of human–environmental interaction, it renders systemic approaches and their reductionist methods as wholly inadequate. The nature of human ecodynamic adaptation is an altogether different fabric – one that resists reduction to sets of singular, easily identifiable threads.

NOTES

1. This chapter deliberately avoids terminology such as 'complexity theory', since it is associated with a specific set of mathematical and computational approaches developed by the Santa Fe Institute. Instead, the broader, more inclusive term 'discourse' describes better the wide range of research currently under way under the rubric of complexity.
2. The discrete nature of successive *ecohistorical regimes* is also consistent with the anti-evolutionist position advocated by Giddens (1979, p. 23) when he supports a model of social change in terms of 'episodic transitions'; that is, 'processes of social

change that have definite direction and form, and in which definite structural transformations occur'.
3. It is important to stress here that power is not itself a resource; *resources* are the media through which power is exercised (Giddens 1979, p. 91).
4. Just such a process of rapid urbanization can be observed, for example in the rise of American cities during the 20th century, where the transition from slow to rapid growth occurs as a discontinuous event – a phase change in physics terminology.
5. This is comparable to Renfrew and Cherry's (1986) idea of peer polity interaction.

REFERENCES

Allen, Peter M. (1994), 'Evolutionary complex systems: models of technology change', in Loet Leydesdorff and Peter Van den Besselaar (eds), *Chaos and Economic Theory*, London: Pinter, pp. 1–17.

Arce, Javier (1997), '*Otium et negotium*: the great estates, 4th–7th centuries', in Leslie Webster and Michelle P. Brown (eds), *The Transformation of the Roman World, AD 400–900*, London: British Museum Press, pp. 19–32.

Arthur, W. Brian (1988a), 'Self-reinforcing mechanisms in economics', in Phillip W. Anderson, Kenneth J. Arrow and David Pines (eds), *The Economy as an Evolving Complex System*, Redwood City: Addison-Wesley, pp. 9–31.

Arthur, W. Brian (1988b), 'Urban systems and historical path dependence', in Jesse H. Ausubel and Robert Herman (eds), *Cities and Their Vital Systems Infrastructure: Past, Present, and Future*, Washington DC: National Academy Press, pp. 76–91.

Bentley, R. Alexander and Herbert D.G. Maschner (eds) (2003), *Complex Systems and Archaeology: Empirical and Theoretical Applications*, Salt Lake City: University of Utah Press.

Bintliff, John L. (1991), 'The contribution of an Annaliste/structural history approach to archaeology', in John L. Bintliff (ed.), *The Annales School and Archaeology*, New York: New York University Press, pp. 1–33.

Buxó, Ramon (1997), *Arqueologia de las Plantas*, Barcelona: Critica.

Buxó, Ramon, Narcís Carulla and James McGlade (1999), 'Human ecodynamic evolution: palaeohydrological, climatic, palaeoecological and societal interactions', in James McGlade and Marina Picazo (eds), *Human Ecodynamics and Land-Use Conflict in the Empordà region of north-east Spain*, ARCHAEOMEDES II final report, DGXII Environment and Climate Programme, Brussels: Commission of the European Communities pp. 50–102.

Cabrera, Paloma (1998), 'Greek trade in Iberia: the extent of interaction', *Oxford Journal of Archaeology*, **17**(2), 191–206.

Ermarth, Elizabeth D. (1992), *Sequel to History: Postmodernism and the Crisis of Historical Time*, Princeton: Princeton University Press.

Giddens, Anthony (1979), *A Contemporary Critique of Historical Materialism*, Cambridge: Cambridge University Press.

Goldstein, Jeffrey (1998), 'Emergence as a construct: History and Issues', *Emergence*, **1**(1), 49–72.

Gummerman, George J. and Murray Gell-Mann (eds) (1999), *Understanding Complexity in the Prehistoric Southwest*, Santa Fe Institute Studies in the Science of Complexity Proceedings, 16, Reading, MA: Addison-Wesley.

Gurt, Josep Maria (1998), 'Pervivències i canvis estructurals Durant l'antiguitat tardiana en el nord-est de la Peninsula Iberica', *Comerc i Vies de Comunicació* (*1000BC–700AD*), XI Colloqui Internacional d'Arqueología de Puigcerdà, pp. 313–26.

Hayles, N. Katherine (1990), *Chaos Bound: Orderly Disorder in Contemporary Literature and Science*, Ithaca: Cornell University Press.

Hodder, Ian (1987), 'The contribution of the long term', in Ian Hodder (ed.), *Archaeology as Long Term History*, Cambridge: Cambridge University Press, pp. 1–8.

Hodder, Ian (1992), *Theory and Practice in Archaeology*, London: Routledge.

Holling, Crawford S. (1986), 'The resilience of ecosystems: local surprise and global change', in William C. Clark and Robert E. Munn (eds), *Sustainable Development of the Biosphere*, Cambridge: Cambridge University Press, pp. 292–317.

Johnson, Steven (2001), *Emergence: The Connected Lives of Ants, Brains, Cities and Software*, London: Penguin.

Kay, James J., Hennry A. Regier, Michelle Boyle and George Francis (1999), 'An ecosystem approach for sustainability: addressing the challenge of complexity', *Futures*, **31**(1), 721–42.

Klomp, Nicholas I. and David G. Green (1996), 'Complexity and connectivity in ecosystems', *Complexity International*, **3**, 1–23.

Knapp, Arthur B. (ed.) (1992), *Archaeology, Annales and Ethnohistory*, Cambridge: Cambridge University Press.

Kohler, Timothy (1993), 'News from the North American Southwest: prehistory on the edge of chaos', *Journal of Archaeological Research*, **1**, 267–321.

Mann, Michael (1986), *The Sources of Social Power*, Cambridge: Cambridge University Press.

McGlade, James (1990), 'The emergence of structure: social transformation in later Prehistoric Wessex', unpublished PhD dissertation, University of Cambridge.

McGlade, J. (1995), 'Archaeology and the ecodynamics of human-modified landscapes', *Antiquity*, **69**, 113–32.

McGlade, J. (1997), 'The limits of social control: coherence and chaos in a prestige-goods economy', in Sander E. van der Leeuw and James McGlade (eds), *Archaeology: Time and Structured Transformation*, London: Routledge, pp. 299–330.

McGlade, James (1999), 'The times of history: archaeology, narrative and nonlinear causality', in Tim Murray (ed.), *Time and Archaeology*, London: Routledge, pp. 139–63.

McGlade, James (2003), 'The map is not the territory: complexity, complication and representation', in R. Alexander Bentley and Herbert D.G. Maschner (eds), *Complex Systems and Archaeology: Empirical and Theoretical Applications*, Salt Lake City: University of Utah Press, pp. 111–19.

McGlade, James and Sander E. van der Leeuw (1997), 'Introduction: archaeology and non-linear dynamics – new approaches to long-term change', in Sander E. van der Leeuw and James McGlade (eds), *Time, Process and Structured Transformation in Archaeology*, London: Routledge, pp. 1–32.

McGlade, James and Marina Picazo (1999), 'Synthesis: some reflections on the *longue durée*', in James McGlade and Marina Picazo (eds), *Human Ecodynamics and Land-Use Conflict: Monitoring Degradation-sensitive Environments in the Empordà, North-east Spain*, ARCHAEOMEDES II Final Report, DGXII Environment and Climate Programme, Brussels: Commission of the European Communities.

McGlade, James and Sander E. van der Leeuw (1987), 'Introduction: Archaeology and nonlinear dynamics – new approaches to long-term change', in Sander E. van der Leeuw and James McGlade (eds), *Time, Process and Structured Transformation in Archaeology*, London: Routledge, pp. 1–32.

Palet i Martinez, Josep Maria (1997), 'Estudi territorial del pla de Barcelona', unpublished PhD Dissertation, Universidad de Barcelona.

Pons, Enrigueta and Josep Tarrus (1987), 'Les primers comunitats ramaderes, agricoles i metal lurgiques', *Jornades d'Historia de l'Empordà: Homenatge a J. Pella i Fargas*, pp. 35–65.

Renfrew, Colin and John F. Cherry (1986), *Peer Polity Interaction and Sociopolitical Change*, Cambridge: Cambridge University Press.

Ruiz, Arturo and Manuel Molinos (1993), *Los Iberos*, Barcelona: Critica.

Ruiz de Arbulo, J. (1992), 'Emporion. Ciudad y territorio (s. VI-I a.C.). Algunas reflexiones preliminaries', *Revista de Ponent*, **2**, 59–74.

Ruiz Zapatero, Gonzalo (1997), 'Migrations revisited: urnfields in Iberia', in Margarita Díaz Andreu and Simon Keay (eds), *The Archaeology of Iberia*, London: Routledge, pp. 158–74.

Sack, Robert D. (1986), *Human Territoriality: its Theory and History*, Cambridge: Cambridge University Press.

Shanks, Michael and Christopher Tilley (1987), *Social Theory and Archaeology*, Cambridge: Cambridge University Press.

Tilley, Christopher (ed.) (1993), *Interpretative Archaeology*, Oxford: Berg.

White, Hayden V. (1971), *Metahistory: the Historical Imagination in Nineteenth-century Europe*, Baltimore: Johns Hopkins University Press.

5. Restless capitalism: a complexity perspective on modern capitalist economies

Ronnie Ramlogan and J. Stanley Metcalfe

The solution of the economic problem of society . . . is always a voyage of exploration into the unknown, an attempt to discover new ways of doing things better than they have been done before. This must always be so as long as there are any economic problems to be solved at all, because all economic problems are created by unforeseen changes which require adaptation. Only what we have not foreseen and provided for requires new decision. If no such adaptations were required, if at any moment we knew that all change had stopped and things would forever go on exactly as they are now, there would be no more questions of the use of resources to be solved. (Hayek 1948, p.101)

INTRODUCTION

In this chapter we explore the idea that economies are complex adaptive systems, that they are strongly ordered to produce their structural properties, and that this order is always changing from within. The problem of economic growth and its relation with the growth of knowledge provides a natural focus for this discussion and we turn to this topic presently, together with a complementary complexity perspective on the firm, entrepreneurship and market processes. The core of the argument is that complexity requires change from within, and change from within depends on the emergence of new knowledge. A non-complex world would be a world of invariant beliefs, a world of the stationary state in which irrespective of its scale the structure of the economy is invariant over time. This is a world without development in which there are no reasons to change the nature of economic activity, for if beliefs are stationary we can only conclude that knowledge is stationary too. Such a world, the world of the timeless circular flow, might be extremely complicated but it cannot be complex. A complex world is not only self-organizing it is also self-transforming; and it is this latter characteristic that forms the signature of economic complexity. It can never be a world in equilibrium, as the word equilibrium is normally intended. Hence, we argue that complexity is a problem in dynamics that transcends the complicated nature of the economic world, while recognizing that all economies are complicated in the sense that they are multi-dimensional and beyond the comprehension of a single mind. One of the most surprising aspects of capitalism from the 18th century onwards is how relatively few individuals have led the process of self-transformation; the crucial changes in beliefs are not initiated in a widespread fashion, a fact which points to the central importance of entrepreneurial activity and economic leadership to the complexity perspective (Witt 2000). Just as a few scientists make the crucial breakthroughs in our understanding of the natural world, so it is in relation to enterprise and the economic world. Complexity analysis cannot avoid recognizing the role of individuals in the economic process, and the only purpose of introducing individuals is to recognize their different beliefs and states of knowing.

Although the analysis of systemic complexity opens up a rich agenda for formal modelling and computer simulation, this is not the direction that we follow here (Allen 2001; Ziman 2000). Rather we explore the deeper foundations of the view that capitalist economies are complex systems. Thus our core argument is that a complexity perspective on the economy requires that we treat the growth of knowledge, the development of the instituted framework of the system, and changes in the beliefs that stimulate action in a co-evolutionary manner. This is why economic history is open-ended and the economic future is unpredictable; this is why there is the close connection between complexity and the emergence of new knowledge.

While there is no single agreed definition of complexity[1] (Horgan 1995; Manson 2001), we take the view that the study of complexity is inherently concerned with the operation of systems defined as sets of components interacting within boundaries. Since economies are systems of interacting elements it is natural to think that economics, market processes and complexity would be closely connected. Yet this is not so. The dominant ideas in economic theory make no non-trivial connection whatsoever with complexity thinking (Colander 2000a, 2000b). For them to do so we must abandon the idea of economies as equilibrium constructs and recognize the significance of the claim that all economies are knowledge based and that knowledge based economies are processes. It is an understanding of the evolution of knowledge; we use the term broadly to cover all rationalizations of private or public action, which provides the key to integrating complexity into economic explanation. Moreover complexity equates to a problem of the emergence of order and within that order the occurrence of phenomena that are quite unexpected (Sole and Goodwin 2000). The idea of the unanticipated and the unintended consequences, the corollary of the inability to predict the future, goes back a long way in the social sciences but the point is that these features are systemic and relate to the interaction between components within boundaries such that the whole cannot be explained by reference to the properties of the individual parts.

Evolutionary explanation is based on the triad of variation, selection and development of new variations (innovations) and it is naturally growth oriented. Indeed its central concept, fitness, is concerned with the differential growth of entities in a population and differential growth naturally leads to structural change and the changing relative importance of the relevant entities. Unfortunately, selection processes, of which economic competition is a leading example, destroy the variety that supports evolution. For the evolutionary process to be renewed we must have processes that replenish variety; development processes that produce innovation and novelty and which are intimately connected to the growth of new knowledge somewhere in the system. This is why entrepreneurship, research, design and development in the technological sense, and the formation of new businesses are essential to the working of modern capitalism. It is an evolving system, one that continually discovers new ways of utilizing resources and, indeed, discovers additions to the set of economically valuable resources. Consequently, the Western economy of today bears little resemblance to the economy of a half-century ago and a fortiori, to the economy of a century ago (Mokyr 1991; Landes 1998). The modern knowledge based economy is continually becoming something different, qualitatively as well as quantitatively, and the fundamental reason for this lies in the evolution and development of new knowledge through processes of variation, selection and development. To perceive fully the implications of this perspective, it is necessary to look at an economy as a system for generating economic experiments, and to identify the processes that generate and spread novelty in the system, processes that add new dimensions to the space of activities.

However, since all economies are knowledge based, and could not be otherwise, it is necessary to treat with care the meaning of knowledge and the particular institutional contexts that distinguish one knowledge economy from another, and to pay particular attention to the co-evolution of knowledge and economic activity.[2] At this point we cannot avoid the discussion taking a more philosophical turn. By knowledge we refer to individual states of mind that bear a specific relationship to some feature of the external world (Plotkin 1994) and which are the foundations for rational beliefs about cause–effect relationships. Knowledge of this kind is essential to economic action and the beliefs that generate economic action, although, as we shall see, not all beliefs can be grounded in objective knowledge, and this is a precondition for the emergence of novelties. If all economies are necessarily knowledge economies, what is it about the modern economy that makes it distinctive in this regard? Even the most primitive societies, if they are to survive, must depend on a systematic and sophisticated understanding of their material environment, an understanding that is reproduced without significant variation from generation to generation. The characteristic of a modern knowledge based society is that knowledge in general, and practical knowledge in particular, is more transient and subject to revision; the certainties of tradition are replaced by the restless search for new beliefs in pursuit of economic advantage. Moreover, these aspects of modern knowledge society are reflected in the instituted processes and organizational ecologies that shape the accumulation, storage and transmission of new knowledge.

To anticipate the following discussion, we claim that since knowledge is never in equilibrium, then, neither can beliefs nor actions nor an economy ever be in equilibrium. A knowledge based economy generally is highly structured and patterned, but structure and pattern reflect order, not equilibrium. Furthermore, if knowledge ever did reach an equilibrium state then all economic change and development would necessarily cease. Here we must face a paradox: order depends on a very high degree of commonality of understanding at different levels of economic action, yet progress and the transformation of an economy depend on the breakdown of that commonality of understanding. If beliefs are too fluid, order will descend into chaos; if beliefs are too rigid, then order descends into lifeless equilibrium. Capitalism, we conjecture, has evolved an institutional structure, which establishes sufficient order for the individuals within it to imagine how the present constellation of activities can evolve into a new constellation without the system breaking down into chaos. These innovations emerge on a small scale in local contexts but at least some have the capacity to stimulate widespread adoption and large-scale transformation. This is perhaps capitalism's most remarkable feature; in Nelson's words, that it constitutes an engine of progress (Nelson 1990; Metcalfe 2001).

Complexity is an antidote to more simple-minded versions of methodological individualism, or the extreme reductionism that is expressed in terms of the methodological atomism, so prevalent in modern economics. As we shall see, individualism remains a central tenet in any adaptive evolutionary account of an economy but it is a heavily nuanced version of individualism, one that places the individual and what she knows in systemic contexts. This is the idea of embeddedness and, of course, markets and social institutions are embedded systems par excellence. A serious treatment of complexity therefore requires an understanding of the process that generates the components of an economy/society and the process that generates their interconnections, so that at a deeper level we understand how complexity is itself created and renewed by economic and social processes. It is these processes of organizing complexity that lead us to a co-evolutionary account of the ongoing development of knowledge and the development of the economy. We believe that an evolutionary adaptive model of development, in which the emergence of macro structure arises from micro diversity and which recognized explicitly the co-ordinating properties of markets, can explain best the dynamic features of modern capitalism, in relation to novelty, innovation and structural change (Dopfer and Potts 2004).

COMPLEX, COMPLICATED OR BOTH?

It is an elementary fact that economic theory has developed very sophisticated accounts of economies as large-scale systems of interacting parts, including for-profit firms, consumers and other public and private agencies. Indeed, the market mechanism is precisely a metaphor for dispersed interaction between such agencies from which prices and the allocation of resources are reluctant properties. That is to say, they are the outcomes of interaction processes at multiple scales. Economists have been dealing with complicated systems since the earliest days of the discipline but this does not mean they have dealt with complexity. Input–output analysis and general equilibrium theory provide two important examples of this complicated but non-complex perspective. The former traces the consequences of industries being connected together such that the outputs of one, say steel, form an input into other industries, say automobiles and machine tools, with the consequence that the relative outputs of the different industries, given technical conditions, must stand in a determinate relation to one another, if a particular pattern of final output is to be sustained. The latter provides an account of how a relative price system can be identified that enables the decisions to buy or sell of many economic actors trading in many markets to be rendered individually harmonious, so that all decisions to buy are, in the aggregate, matched by decisions to sell. The prices which make this possible, will, in certain circumstances, also have remarkable efficiency properties in that they are a guide to the most productive allocation of resources (Nelson 1990). These are constructs of great power and intellectual elegance but even a casual acquaintance with these ideas suggests that they relate to model economies that are complicated, in the sense of being difficult to comprehend in their entirety. However, they are not complex economies in the sense of generating unexplained behaviours or novel events, indeed their properties are closed and fully predictable, given knowledge of the framing axioms.

What then is needed to turn complicated systems into complex systems? First, it involves a shift of mind-set from the characterization of equilibria to the specification of dynamic processes. Brock (2000b) for example, carefully distinguishes chaotic dynamics from complex dynamics. In the former, unpredictable behaviour follows from the dynamics of simple non-linear systems, in the latter it follows from the interactions within large-scale complicated dynamic systems. The signature of complexity is found in the statistical distribution of the size of events generated by that system, which are almost invariably found to follow a Pareto-Levy scaling law within which individual events remain unpredictable in timing and scale (Bak 1997; Mandelbrot 1997; Krugman 1996). This view provides only one window on complexity where we observe the generation pattern of similar, commensurable events, such as the daily change in price in a given financial market. There is more to complexity than this. In his recent survey of non-linear economic theories, Brock (2000a), building on Arthur, Durlauf and Lane (1997) suggests that the foundations of complexity involve dispersed interactions, self-organization without a guiding hand, the interlinking of hierarchies at different levels, perpetual novelty, continual adaptation, and, out of equilibrium dynamics. The first three of these are contained within input–output and general equilibrium economics and have a long tradition in economic analysis more generally, but the latter three raise quite different issues, precisely the issues that turn a complicated economy into a complex economy. They map closely onto the more traditional evolutionary principles of variation and selection. Perpetual novelty relates to the generation of variety and keeps selection processes far from equilibrium. Continual adaptation is another way of defining the consequences of a selection process, and out of equilibrium dynamics points to the open-ended, unpredictable nature of evolutionary economic processes from which patterns of order emerge but are not imposed from on high. Moreover, interacting hierarchies capture the point that selection (and development) can occur at multiple interdependent levels.

Therefore, it seems that one of the most important insights that complexity analysis brings to the study of social phenomena is that complex economic systems must be understood as adaptive, evolving processes, in which adaptation of the economy is only possible because of the adaptation of knowledge. The crucial point here is that complex systems are evolving systems in which the components, ultimately the individual actors, change their behavioural properties because of their becoming more knowledgeable. This view contrasts sharply with the standard economic approach of considering the equilibrium or steady state behaviour of the system, which presupposes an unchanging state of knowledge. Indeed, as Durlauf (1997) has emphasized, the conceptualization of a social, economic or political system as a complex dynamic process involving the interrelationships of many actors with limited information about the intentions of others implies that the behaviour of such a system cannot be understood by asking whether it has any steady states. More crucially, the structural and developmental changes we observe in any economy are generated from within the system. It is an elementary but obvious point that for any equilibrium system, all internal sources of novelty and change have been exhausted and all that is possible in terms of change must be imposed from outside the system and cannot therefore be part of the explanation of the order of that system. An understanding of complexity, therefore, gives a different, dynamic characterization of the economy, not one that is deterministic, predictable and mechanistic, but one that is process-dependent, organic and endogenous (Arthur 1999). Built into this view is another deep evolutionary issue, namely that the components of an evolving system are different, they are individuals in the proper sense of their distinctive properties, among which what they know as individuals is of paramount importance. This is why, as hinted above, methodological individualism requires a sophisticated interpretation in the context of evolution and complexity. Moreover, evolutionary change is impossible without variation, and variation captures the element of individuality located within populations of other individuals.

An important dimension of this perspective is the emphasis on the restless nature of modern capitalist economies. They are organized, indeed self-organized, but they also self-transform as the loci of activity are redistributed within and between firms, economic sectors and countries (Foster 1993). Change arises as the consequence of the operation of the system, it is not imposed from outside; capitalism is a system for promoting change from within, as Schumpeter (1911, 1944) always emphasized. The idea of a capitalism that does not exhibit these properties is surely a contradiction in terms despite the frequent use in economic theory of the benchmark stationary or static state.[3] In fact, the economic process is an unceasing struggle with new activities emerging to compete with older more established rivals, displacing them in the process and ultimately succumbing to competitive pressures themselves. The generation of novelty plays a central part in this dynamic process and this provides the important connections with innovation in capitalism and the fact that adapting to innovation requires a decline in some activities as well as growth in others. Capitalist economies never expand in a uniform fashion in which the growth of all activities is equi-proportional and time reversible. Furthermore, self-transformation is not to be confused with transition. The latter defines a move from initial state A to final state B, with neither state influenced by the process of going between. Hence, transitions are reversible in principle and can take place in logical time. Transformations, by contrast, are open-ended; what is being transformed is a set of possible states that are created in the process of transformation and that take place in historic time. The process alters the end point and the beginning point because the process generates new knowledge and so renders the change irreversible. Economic transformations are a species of far-from-equilibrium process and what keeps them far from equilibrium is the particular set of knowledge-generating and application processes that define a modern economy. Crucial among these processes is the particular mix of market and non-market mechanisms for stimulating and adapting to economic change. They constitute an instituted system for adapting to innovations in technique, product, service and organization that arise within the system. Thus, we suggest, complexity in economics rests on the interaction between processes for generating novelty and processes for adapting to that novelty. It is only because we ignore the knowledge dimensions of an economy that it is possible to treat economic systems in a non-complex, time reversible fashion. We explore these ideas below in terms of three familiar economic ideas: growth, markets and firms. Before we do so, we need to develop more fully the idea that it is the processes of knowledge generation and application that make economies complex systems.

THE KNOWLEDGE DIMENSION

Few scholars would deny that economic and social evolution are contingent on the continued growth of knowledge but precisely who is said to know more when we link the growth of knowledge to the growth of the economy? Our answer is that only individuals can possess knowledge, that all changes in knowledge require changes in the state of individual minds and that the correlation of knowledge across minds underpins the shared understandings necessary for co-ordinated economic and social action.

Knowledge is always private and unarticulated. Consequently, the total of what is known can at best only mean the union of the vectors of the knowledge held by every individual within the relevant domain. From this perspective knowledge is the consequence of life, it is the dominant characteristic of human living. What is articulated is information; and information, data open to sensory perception, is not knowledge, it is a representation of knowledge transmitted via the sensory apparatus. It is information that lies in the public domain, and it is the transmission of information that is essential to the correlation of knowledge across individual minds. Yet, information can only be an imperfect representation of individual knowledge, depending on the respective capacities to encode and decode the implicit messages. There is always a tacit background to everything that we seek to express and interpret; as Polanyi (1966) insisted, we always know more than we can communicate through the senses. Strictly speaking, knowledge itself is never codified, it is only its imperfect representation as information that can so be dignified. Codification can be in terms of sounds or symbols, but the dominant kind of codification that has engaged modern scholars is the written, storable symbolic codification associated with language and mathematics. Moreover, what is codified is, in part, an economic decision dependent on the scale at which the information is intended to be used (Cowan *et al.* 2000; Johnson *et al.* 2002). How does this relate to a complexity view of the economy?

The most distinctive evolutionary property of complex capitalist economic systems is that they are knowledge based and that the primary interactions within them require exchanges of information. It is because of this that capitalism is necessarily restless, for the exchange of information communicated within the market process is a stimulus for individuals to develop further what they know. This positive feedback process leads us to complexity and results in the co-evolution of knowledge and economic action. As Marshall in 1919, and Popper much more recently (1996), recognized, economic activity changes knowledge directly and indirectly, and every change in knowledge opens up the conditions for changes in activity and thus further changes in knowledge ad infinitum. Like any autocatalytic process, the output of knowledge becomes the input into new knowledge and one idea results in another although the connection may only become transparent after the event.

In capitalist economies, much new knowledge results from the conduct of the market process as suppliers and customers interact and learn what to produce and from whom to buy. To this extent, economically valuable knowledge is a product of co-ordination and can be expected to accumulate differently in different co-ordination systems.[4] It follows that every position of temporary economic order creates within it the conditions to change that order, and this is especially true of knowledge accumulated in the pursuit of innovation. This argument is reinforced when we recognize that all economic processes take place in real time, not the clockwork time of the textbooks, and that the mere passage of time means experiencing new events and thus gaining new information. It is an essential feature of human agency that the passage of time, the process of living itself, results in the formulation of new knowledge. Consequently, it is not possible to hold knowledge constant while allowing human economic activity to occur, and to construct our analysis on this premise hides more than it illuminates about the dynamic nature of capitalism. On both these counts it is particularly problematic if we try to posit some equilibrium economic state that is invariant to the motion towards it, for this is tantamount to holding knowledge (and the real time of human experience) constant while we get to equilibrium. This makes no sense to us other than as a formal way to avoid the problem. In short when economies are out of equilibrium they stay out of equilibrium (Robinson 1974). Nevertheless, they always exhibit order and that order reflects, and might be measured in terms of, processes of interaction and the patterns of co-ordination that ensue. Notice that this point runs much deeper than that of path dependence of outcomes in the presence of positive feedback processes. It is the point made by Kaldor (1934); one cannot have economic activity without a change of knowledge and changes of knowledge are irreversible – they are the most significant of positive feedbacks.

In the modern economy, of course, this is reinforced by the practice of allocating a non-trivial portion of the economy's resources to the acquisition of knowledge and the dissemination of information, together with its embodiment in the population via processes of education and training. One of the major steps in the evolution of capitalism, a step that makes the transition to complexity more apparent, has been the purposeful allocation of resources to research and development activities conducted independently from day-to-day experience of production, distribution and consumption activities (Mowery and Rosenberg 1998). This was a key institutional development that enabled society to allocate its resources to the purposeful exploration of the unknown, which has had a profound effect on the conduct of economic life for it builds into the system a further powerful source of novelties. With the passage of time, an increasingly refined division of labour has emerged in the production and application of laboratory based knowledge. New fields of knowledge have emerged together with a complex skein of systemic interrelation between laboratories in firms, their customers and suppliers, universities and other public and private research organizations. In recent theoretical and empirical work on innovation, the idea of innovation systems has justifiably occupied a position of prominence (Freeman 1987; Nelson 1993; Carlsson 1995; Edquist 1997). These ideas are traceable back, of course, to Adam Smith and his powerful insight that the production of knowledge reflects mental specialization and a consequent division of labour. This process is not a reflection of conscious design but rather reflects an ongoing process of the self-organization of knowledge that is deeply dependent on the market process. As individuals, we know a great deal about very little, and we are faced with the difficulty that many problems require multiple kinds of knowledge for their solution and this in turn requires the co-operation of different minds. In modern innovation systems, this is reflected in an increasingly roundabout process of producing practically useful knowledge in which there is specialization of institution, specialization of discipline and the combination of an increasingly wide range of knowledge types to the solution of practical problems. Taken together the two broad modes of knowledge generation, within and without the market process, constitute the basis of the adaptive evolution of a restless capitalism. Innovations in product technique and organization are the principal kind of novelty; they are based on the development of new knowledge that is itself embedded in the economic system. Knowledge in this context means more than the formal knowledge associated with scientific theory and technological practice; it must also include knowledge of market and consumer behaviour and knowledge of organization. Much of this business knowledge may lack the formal, theoretical dimension of science and technology but these elements are no less significant for the conduct of innovation and the entrepreneurial approach to economic change.

Knowledge and economy co-evolve and the orders within both are interdependent and are continually redefined in entirely unpredictable and open-ended ways. All we know about the future is that it will be different from the past and that history is fashioned continually. Modern, orthodox growth theorists recognize this when they point to the endogeneity of knowledge generation (Jones 1995; Aghion and Howitt 1992) but they err greatly in thinking of the growth of knowledge as a public good that follows steady state equilibrium accumulation paths just like physical capital (Steedman 2003). As we have suggested above, systems in steady state equilibrium do not evolve; by contrast, capitalism is a developmental, experimenting system par excellence. Under capitalist rules of the game, every economic position is open to challenge but in an entirely unpredictable way, and the generation of novelty is an essential part of this process.

THE CORRELATION OF KNOWLEDGE

The essential point about methodological individualism, the point that underpins the adaptive evolution of the economy, is that only individuals can know, and what they know depends on perceptions, introspection, memory and inference, in short, experience allied with reason (Audi 1998). Individual knowledge is thus shaped, refined and continually moulded by the activities individuals engage in during their lifetime and by the contexts that frame these activities. What we know arises and develops partly in the context of our innate curiosity as human beings and partly via the stimuli provided by everyday experience of interaction with others all within the context of the limited mental capacities of each individual. All these forms of knowledge are in the subconscious recesses of the mind; they are essentially a matter of electrochemical responses in the human brain, with the consequence that the mind is a store of latent potentialities. Indeed, we

are conscious of knowing only when confronted by a problem or discontinuity in our sense of the outside world. Personal knowledge is from this
viewpoint a conversation with oneself, which is, perhaps, substantially
unconscious. What we hold in our conscious mind at any point in time is
knowledge of organizing principles, templates and reference points from
which to interrogate the subconscious when confronted by questions that
capture attention. It is our private and necessarily individual way of
making sense of the world, of distinguishing facts, of grouping related phenomena, of finding connections and of establishing cause and effect. As
Arthur (1994, 2000) expresses the point, information has no intrinsic
meaning; meanings are provided by individual minds through mental
processes of association. Private knowledge is thus our ever-changing
frame of reference for interaction with the wider world. As such, it is always
incomplete and it is only because of this that learning and creative thought
become possible. We can of course only conjecture a difference in knowledge against some existing frame of reference.

Quite crucially for the following argument, these private states of mind
are not accessible by any other individual, and this carries with it an
implication of great importance, an implication that is a natural, unavoidable consequence of the limited mental capacity of all individuals.
This implication is that those processes, by which we come to know, are
augmented greatly by social processes that permit exchanges of information, representations of knowledge communicated between individuals
such that they can lay claim to common understanding or social knowledge. Through sense experiences of the actions of others, that is to say
through the communication of information, our individual states of
knowledge become interdependent. In this way, private knowledge of any
individual is correlated with but not identical with the private knowledge
of others. The correlation of knowledge is the necessary condition for the
extensive spread of knowledge and thus for the effectiveness of any activities that require individuals to act in concert. It is also essential for the
growth of knowledge in the intensive sense in which any individual comes
to know more. Thus, we are suggesting that what is known is private, and
what is understood socially is necessarily systemic and emergent and, like
all knowledge, continually evolving. This leaves open the question of
whether knowledge within individual minds is also systemic and evolving
in an adaptive sense, but this is a step we need not take here.

This extended reliance upon the testimony of others is one of the key
factors in comprehending understanding as a complex system predicated
on the knowledge of individuals and indeed in comprehending the nature
of capitalism as a knowledge based system. For it leads us directly to one
of the most powerful of the ideas derived from Adam Smith, namely the

division of labour in the production as well as in the use of knowledge. Every economist is familiar with the 'Wealth of Nations' and the story of the pin factory and the detailed specialization within that work process. Yet within a few pages of this famous example, Smith turns to a far more powerful case, the case that underpins modern economies and indeed forms the test for a modern economy. For Smith applies the division of labour to the growth of knowledge, pointing to the role of those specialized philosophers and men of speculation, 'whose trade is not to do any thing, but to observe everything; and who, upon that account, are often capable of combining together the powers of the most distant and dissimilar objects' (Smith 1776, p. 11). Moreover, because the division of labour also applies to the philosophers, 'Each individual becomes more expert in his own peculiar branch, more work is done upon the whole, and the quantity of science is considerably increased by it' (p. 11). In this way Smith reaches the core of the matter, identifying capitalism as a self-exciting system that has caused new methods of inventing novelties to evolve and continue to evolve. What matters here is that the growth of knowledge and the growth of the market are mutually reinforcing. It is this that makes possible an edge of modernity as a persistent feature of capitalism, a system in which fundamental changes are always in train – fundamental changes that arise from within the system. What Smith does not develop is how this growth of knowledge is to be co-ordinated, and how individual knowledge is to be shared in the wider social context, because this will determine how individual knowledge will grow. What is the instituted process that achieves for knowledge activities what markets achieve for conventional productive activities?

To answer this question it is necessary to develop in more detail the distinction between personal knowledge and shared, interactive understanding. What Smith drew attention to is the individually idiosyncratic, specialized nature of personal knowledge; the corollary to this is that not only the use of knowledge, but also the growth of knowledge embedded is in a social process and co-ordinated through appropriate patterns of social interaction. The problem here is that if knowledge remains private it can inform private action but not social action, and, fundamentally, private action is contingent on social action. Some knowledge must be held in common to make possible any economic action. For the framing social action to be possible, for actions to be mutually supporting and collaborative, it is necessary that private knowledge becomes shared, public understanding to the requisite degree. The transmission of private knowledge into shared understanding is a socially distributed process, and this process must depend on institutions for the sharing and common interpretation of flows of information. We can never say two individuals have the same knowledge, nor devise a way of establishing what they know. We can say instead that as individuals they have the same understanding, so far as they provide indistinguishable, or at least closely correlated answers to the same question, or if they respond in indistinguishable, or closely correlated ways to the same instructions.[5]

If information flow is to convey personal knowledge with sufficient accuracy to achieve commonality of understanding, there must be vehicles of communication and common standards of communication, language or other forms of symbolic representation, and agreed standards for the justification of that which can be said to be known. Moreover there must also be shared interpretive frames; theoretical schema to judge the content of information, otherwise private knowledge cannot develop into collective understanding. We must have shared grounds to agree what the facts are, and what facts are relevant to the issue in hand. As Nelson puts it, there must be 'social technologies' to make testimony possible (Nelson 1999). In this regard, institutions and information technologies matter in three fundamental ways in relation to the connection between knowledge and understanding. First, they constitute the means to store and communicate information in general and the means to support particular patterns of interaction, 'who talks to whom with what frequency and with what authority', in a society. This is the question of language, commensuration and symbolic representation in general. Different patterns of interconnection imply different distributed patterns of understanding and thus different paths for the adaptive evolution of knowledge. Nor are the patterns of interconnection given, they are to be explained as a process of institutionalization; whom we communicate with naturally changes as our individual knowledge develops; the networks and modes of intercommunication are themselves emergent properties of our kinds of knowledge based economy. Secondly, institutions embody the rules, the standards of socially agreed belief, that are the means to accumulate justifiably true knowledge in relation to science, technology, as well as organization and social discourse. It is the institution of understanding in common that makes economic and social life possible while simultaneously constituting a powerful engine for the differential growth of personal knowledge. North (1990) is correct in arguing that institutional rules constrain behaviour by facilitating the growth of common understanding. However, these same rules are to a degree enabling and facilitating in that the spread of understanding opens up opportunities for the further growth of private knowledge. Thirdly, and equally crucial, has been the invention and adoption of instituted standards or norms to distinguish reliable from less reliable knowledge. The process of establishing error, of identifying mistakes through criteria for falsification and rejection have provided the critical edge that combats the problem of superfecundity, the problem of being unable to distinguish which of the too numerous rival courses of action to follow (Mokyr 2002). Concerning science, we enquire of the truth of the relation between conjecture and natural fact. Concerning technology, we enquire whether the device works in the environment in which it is intended to achieve the desired effect. Concerning business, we ask whether the plan achieves the profitability required to justify its adoption and continuation. Without these instituted and thus shared winnowing processes, it is not at all clear how knowledge and understanding can grow. Thus, all knowledge and all understanding reflect multiple processes of trial and error of variation and selection (Ziman 2000). We would agree with Campbell (1960) when he argues that all growth of knowledge is predicated upon a process of blind variation and subsequent selection. It should be noted that 'blind' does not mean 'random', rather it means that the validity of new knowledge can never be known in advance which is, of course, an aspect of complexity.

From this viewpoint, it is important not to forget the role of personal creativity in the growth of understanding. Inventive genius associated with individuals, working alone or in teams, is crucial to the progress of knowledge in all its forms; this is the importance of an individualist perspective. Yet, individual creativity alone is not sufficient. What is personal at source must be capable of being placed in and spread within the public domain and here the development of information and communication technologies has been of paramount importance in permitting the creation, storage and transmission of symbolic records. In turn, this fundamental change in the nature of the processes of knowledge generation has greatly enhanced the basis for social testimony to shape what is understood. Indeed, perhaps the distinguishing feature of a traditional (non-complex?) society is that testimony depends almost exclusively on direct, immediate social contact, whereas in advanced knowledge based societies, communication is much more impersonal and at a distance; and, we may note, the impersonality undoubtedly helps soften the bounds of tradition. Consequently, whether we realize it or not, our daily lives in modern capitalism rely upon the information provided by many individuals whom we never meet. This is the impact of the long sequence of novel technologies that begins with printing and trade in books and newspapers, and leads on to the Internet and wireless communication. Exchanges of information are thereby quicker, denser and broader, so changing fundamentally the generation of social testimony. In turn, this changes the information stimuli and their distribution across individuals, so reshaping the emergence of understanding and the development of private knowledge. This is why understanding is the product of a complex information network system, in which every new thought is a novelty opening up potential new dimensions of economic and social behaviour. Modern science is the canonical example of this process, with the academic journal and conference providing the instituted vehicles to transmit information and correlate understanding, but the point applies far more generally, particularly to economic entrepreneurship.

To summarize thus far, human interaction generates directly and indirectly a flow of information between individuals who, at best, treat that information as a representation of the knowledge of others, and interpret it through confrontation and association with their own sense of knowing. In the process, the disjunctures that arise are a powerful stimulus to new thoughts. Information flow may change the knowledge states of the recipients but there can be no expectation that the change of knowledge will be complete, that it will be identical for all recipients, or that it will be accepted. Indeed, it is the fact that information is not interpreted in uniform fashion that there is disagreement, which is essential to the continued growth of knowledge and thus understanding. Knowledge cannot be completely correlated or nothing new will be known. Oddly enough, in science, invention and entrepreneurship, the big prizes go to those who have disagreed most fundamentally with prevailing patterns of understanding. A world in which all private knowledge was identical, would be a world in which the problem of knowledge had ceased to exist, and the individual had ceased to exist also; such a world would not be complex. This is why the growth of knowledge depends on individual differences and why it is a variation selection process. In regard to disagreements, it is important to recognize that they may have no grounding in the current state of understanding. The ability to imagine and conjecture in advance of a supporting base of evidence is the human characteristic par excellence that most directly leads to the generation of novelty, innovation and thus complexity.

As with individual knowledge, shared understanding is an open system; it is emergent, it can grow combinatorially fast, at least in local domains, and it has no rest points or stable, invariant attractors. It can undergo subtle changes as information percolates across networks of relationships or it can undergo sweeping changes that take understanding into entirely new dimensions. To this degree understanding is unstable. Yet the kinds of understanding we develop and share are not unconstrained. The path of understanding is, we suggest, chreodic; it is channelled primarily by the particular nature of the social and institutional context. The conventions as to which information is made public and in relation to who could communicate with whom about what, are deeply important for the growth of knowledge. Institutions, conventions, social standards, the system shapers, can suppress the generation of understanding just as they can enable it. We can find here the unpredictability of knowledge accumulation, the uneven nature of knowledge accumulation, and the corollary, the unpredictability of the surface forms of capitalism in terms of what is produced and consumed.

These considerations tell us a great deal about the unique properties of capitalism as a complex knowledge based system. It is a system for generating business experiments based on the accumulation of scientific, technical, organizational and market knowledge. Business conjectures create sequences of new problems to be solved, give meaning to entrepreneurship, and give to the firm as organization the unique role of combining the multiple knowledge elements that are needed to innovate successfully. In being a problem solving system, any organization such as a firm is necessarily a problem generating system.[6] Hence the restless nature of firms and whole economies: capitalism can never be at rest because understanding and knowledge are never at rest and never can be given the rules of the game; equilibrium of knowledge is an oxymoron. By this notion of restlessness, we intend to convey two separate meanings: first that economic actors are to a degree ill-at-ease, they can never be sure that their position will not be challenged; and second, that they are always searching for new situations, and the route to these is the growth of knowledge. Of course, it is important to emphasize that the growth of understanding cannot be random without further processes to focus that randomness to good effect. Random systems do not evolve, they drift. We make rapid economic progress precisely because the underlying processes of variation are guided, in the sense discussed above, and explore only limited regions of the space of possibilities. Nor can the growth of understanding be entirely deterministic, for it involves choice, judgement, and creativity in the sense of the expansion of thought and action into new dimensions and spaces. For this reason alone genuine uncertainty is an unavoidable element in the complexity picture, for only when the space of possibilities is closed can probability judgement and its formal calculus be entertained[7] (Shackle 1958). Not only are the winnowing processes referred to above crucial to knowledge evolution but the possibility of the recombination of ideas and concepts is essential to the cumulative growth of personal knowledge and shared understanding, because combinatorial processes build on memory and thus upon experience. Only then is it possible to entertain the idea of cumulative learning and cultural transmission. What seems to be unique about capitalism as a knowledge based system is that it has caused a system of knowing and understanding to evolve that is in reality a system for standing on the shoulders of giants.

We have drawn a distinction between private knowledge and social understanding and suggested that shared understanding is an emergent, self-transforming, complex system predicated on processes and institutions for generating social testimony, that is to say for correlating private knowledge. Understanding at multiple levels is the necessary condition for an economy to operate, and the operation of the economy stimulates the growth of new knowledge and thus the emergence of new understandings. This is a system, therefore, in which neither the component parts, the knowledgeable individuals, nor their patterns of intercommunication, the social relations, are given. The point about the complex knowledge system is that it is evolving in parts and connections, it is always becoming something else but not in a way that anyone can predict. That the knowledge system is complex and the fact that any economy is knowledge based suggests that the degree of complexity of the former, largely shapes the degree of complexity of the latter. We can now explore this suggestion in terms of three important economic problems beginning with the matter of economic growth.

COMPLEXITY AND ECONOMIC GROWTH

Understanding processes of economic growth, development and transformation seriously challenges the explanatory power of any theory of economic growth conducted in terms of the analysis of a uniformly expanding economy. A uniformly expanding economy rules out structural change and the reallocation of resources, and it makes no allowance for the emergence of new and the disappearance of old activities. It makes no connection with history as we know it (Metcalfe *et al.* 2005). Only recently, in the guise of endogenous growth theory, have attempts been made to close this loop but not, from a complexity perspective, in a satisfactory way. Why is this so?

First, the dynamics of self-transformation and the rules of economic co-ordination are hidden by the focus on and measurement of the growth of aggregate gross domestic product or indeed any aggregate of economic activity such as a city. While there is nothing intrinsically wrong in constructing and measuring macro indices, these are not natural measures related to actual agency; as macro phenomena, they are necessarily constructed statistics and have no existence beyond their reflection in the underlying structure of the ensemble of activities in the system. Indeed, the most fundamental flaw of macro measurement is that in aggregation, evidence of micro and meso evolutionary processes is averaged away. These are the very processes that we need to study if we wish to enrich our understanding of the growth of knowledge based economies (Dopfer and Potts 2004). This is not at all a statistical matter of eliminating unnecessary detail to get to the essentials. Rather it is the micro-diversity of behaviours, together with the co-ordination process in specific market contexts, which defines the transformation process from which growth is a consequence. In short, the consequences are not the problem, to obscure the process generating them is. Indeed, any aggregate approach, by construction, precludes the study of emergent phenomena. Furthermore, the fact that macro aggregates vary slowly over time does not imply that the underlying micro components also change slowly. Growth does not occur without the continual emergence of innovation and the persistent changes in the relative importance of products, methods of production, firms, industries, regions and whole economies, that adaptation to innovation implies, and these changes in structure are a consequence of and a cause of the growth of knowledge. In the process, entirely new activities and kinds of resources appear and old established ones disappear so that the sets of goods produced and activities undertaken become increasingly different over time. In the aggregate framework, we lose sight of the central fact that growth of some activities requires the decline of others, that the aggregate growth that we observe is based on microeconomic turmoil, the mirror image of new knowledge and understanding.

There are a number of deeper implications of this evolutionary adaptive stance. A first casualty is the resort to expressing arguments in terms of representative agents, or more precisely uniform firms and households (Kirman 1992), for this is tantamount to excluding any notion of individuality from the analysis. Without individuality, there can be no effective understanding of the growth of knowledge. Leaving aside the difficulty of how innovation is to be discussed without destroying the uniformity of behaviour, the fundamental point is that behaviours that are representative in a statistical sense are emergent properties. Emergent properties are the behavioural consequences that arise from the interactions between agents, and such interactions cannot be properties of the individual agents (Langlois 1983; Blume and Durlaf 2000). What is representative behaviour in a statistical sense must be a product of the analysis, not an assumption underpinning it.

A second casualty involves the claim that the idea of economic equilibrium be abandoned, and this is rather more difficult to handle, because equilibrium has been central to all orthodox explanations of growth and mainstream economics more generally (Samuels 1997; Setterfield 1997; Currie and Steedman 1990). It involves the claim that in a complex economy there are no attracting states to which the economy is converging over an indeterminate long-run. Several fundamental issues need to be unravelled here. The first is that the dominant issue in economic organization is that of co-ordination, the way in which a market process can be said to impose degrees of consistency on plans to buy and sell, with reference to a particular time period. There is nothing wrong in referring to this as a temporary equilibrium providing we realize its transient nature. However, it is far better to refer to it as a temporary order, for that is what co-ordination leads to, order rather than equilibrium (Loasby 1999). Order is a recognizable structure to the pattern of activity, a structure dependent on the prevailing rules of the game. Indeed co-ordination is central to the problem of emergence of order, interpreted as the evolution of economic structure from within the system itself (Dooley and Corman 2000). Why is this so? It is because the process of establishing order is a process of problem solving and, in the process of finding solutions to those problems, expectations are falsified, and new, creative thoughts are generated.[8] The fundamental reason why an economy cannot be in equilibrium as a system is that its operation leads to new knowledge and the definition of new problems from within. It is the fact that the solving of problems is not a mechanical sequential activity but involves genuine imagination that makes the process truly historical and not describable in terms of the constraint of initial conditions allied to equations of motion. Knowledge dependent systems necessarily operate with meaningful histories, and no less an authority than Hahn (1987) has suggested that consideration of the foundations of economic belief mean that we cannot satisfactorily pursue a history-free economics (p. 325), that an economic equilibrium must be an equilibrium of beliefs and that, consequentially it is history- or path-dependent (p. 327). With these sentiments we can only agree, but not with the conclusion that Hahn and many other economists draw. A concern to preserve a notion of equilibrium, in a world where knowledge, information and beliefs are paramount, leads inexorably to a view incompatible with the idea of an economy as complex adaptive system, for in equilibrium, history has come to a stop. That is to say, there are no longer internally generated reasons for beliefs and therefore knowledge to change. This is precisely to place equilibrium out of the time and out of human experience, as if the constituent actors are unimaginative automata (Langlois 1990). Whatever this relates to, it surely cannot be capitalism and the actors surely cannot be sentient individuals. How strange to say that history matters in an essential way and yet to organize the theoretical system around a central analytic device that is inherently ahistorical. Like all Utopias, equilibrium is a fiction, at best a satire, a state of perfection within which 'all is still and immutable and eternal' (Berlin 1991, p. 22). It also follows that history versus equilibrium is a false dichotomy; the changing economic order writes history and leads to history dependence without any resort to equilibrium.[9] From a practical modelling direction this suggests a Marshallian methodology; everything changes but does so at sufficiently diverse rates that, in regard to carefully chosen problems, some slower moving elements may be locked, provisionally, in 'the pound of *ceteris paribus*' (Setterfield 1997). Unfortunately, if the problem in hand is that of growth and development, knowledge is not to be so treated (Metcalfe 2001). There are no determinate, equilibrium solutions to the development problem, for economic development is a set of problems that is never fully solved. Consequently, an evolutionary, complexity based approach to economic growth must treat seriously the dynamics of knowledge and this requires that due attention be given to the individual in the context of the firm and the entrepreneur.

COMPLEXITY, THE FIRM AND THE ENTREPRENEUR

The traditional economic view of the firm is of a locus of production, adjusting the rate of its output and input to signals generated in the product and factor markets in which it operates. Typically, the firm chooses a technology to maximize its economic efficiency and generally orders its affairs to maximize its profits over some time horizon. In all of these dimensions its choices presuppose knowledge and this has raised two traditional challenges to this conception of the firm's agency. The first is an argument based on complication, that the guiding minds cannot know all the circumstances relevant to the maximization of profits in a global sense of mastering all relevant options. Olympian rationality is rightly ruled out on the basis of the complicated nature of the requisite decisions, and this line of reasoning leads directly to the boundedly rational approach to choice, and to the rule-based model of firms proposed by evolutionary economists (Nelson and Winter 1984; Dosi *et al.* 2000). Firms can surely be presumed to do the best they can within their available understanding but what is best is naturally contingent on what the firm can be said to know. What matters here is not the meaning of rational behaviour but rather that firms are different in what they understand; it is the differences that matter to the evolutionary adaptive viewpoint and these differences are generated naturally by the very operation of the firm as a transforming unit of production. The active, sentient firm is continually developing its knowledge to generate sustainable competitive advantage, and embodies this new knowledge in its capabilities. This perspective raises three sub-issues for the treatment of complexity. The first is that to generate competitive advantages through innovation the firm requires much more than knowledge of science and technology, it must also comprehend the market opportunities, be capable of organizing to exploit the innovations through its organization and through access to inputs. Thus the unique characteristic of the firm among all knowledge-generating institutions is its combinatorial character, reflected in the need to bring together multiple kinds of knowledge for profitable purposes. Secondly, and following directly, much of the relevant knowledge lies outside the firm in the minds of individuals who are not members of it. The firm is only one of many knowledge based organizations and the development of what it understands is contingent upon its connections with a wider distributed innovation system. The ability of a firm to change its knowledge depends on the information networks in which its members are embedded, and what these are is a reflection of choices made by the firm. In line with the view of knowledge and understanding expressed above, what a firm understands in relation to its productive and market opportunities depends on its processes for combining the specialized knowledge of its members and for accessing the knowledge of outsiders. Thus the firm's organization is an operator that correlates the knowledge of individuals into the collective and hierarchical understanding that uniquely defines each firm. Here we find the importance of the firm's organization as a co-ordination system that combines internal and external information flows into a holistic sense of understanding. Thirdly, like any system of understanding, the internal operator permits knowledge and understanding to progress in some directions but not others; it gives to the firm's innovative activities a strongly guided character and acts as a filter for external information, often with disastrous effects for the viability of the firm. The distinctive nature of the organization operator is thrown into relief more sharply when different firms seek to merge their activities, for then the distinct operators have to be combined and this may not be possible because of their systemic, holistic nature (Allen *et al.* 2002). Similarly, in regard to business leadership, the same individuals may work to very different effect in different firms because their effectiveness depends on the knowledge system in which they operate; no surer sign exists of the unanticipated effects of complexity.

The second broad challenge arising from this approach is that, because a firm is a knowledge based system, its evolution is adaptive and premised on internal variation and selection to generate complex behaviours. The most obvious evidence for this claim lies with the firm as the locus for generation of economic novelty through innovation, its most distinctive role in restless capitalism. All innovation implies the development of new knowledge and its correlation into understanding on which the firm can act. This naturally raises the question of the entrepreneur who is essential to a complex view of the economy. Entrepreneurship is the agency, in existing or new firms, that initiates economic experiments and serves to de-correlate the prevailing level of understanding and to challenge the existing ways of allocating resources. New patterns of economic understanding arise in the process of adjusting to novelty and this is a recursive process of successive trial and error as ideas are applied and selected for or against. From a complexity perspective, this raises further issues. Since individual creativity implies free time to think, the possibility of novelty depends on elements of redundancy in resource allocation in the firm and in the market. There must be space to make economic experiments free from the pressures of immediate activity and processes to channel resources to those experiments. Here we see the importance of two of the vital institutions of a restless capitalism to the rate of business experimentation: namely, venture capital and corporate venturing as sources of risk capital, and the market for corporate control in relation to the possibility of combining and recombining specific business units in the pursuit of superior combinations.

The perspective we have taken on the interleaving of complexity and the evolution of knowledge comes together in the idea of the entrepreneur, and, in so doing, creates a paradox. Economic action depends on co-ordination and teamwork, whether in organizations or markets, and this requires an appropriate degree of correlation of knowledge if entrepreneurial action is to be significant. Yet the role of the entrepreneur as agent of innovation is precisely to de-correlate knowledge; to suggest that there are new, superior understandings in relation to the allocation of resources. We highlight the individuality of entrepreneurs because of the 'disagreeable and disruptive' character of their individuality in relation to what they claim to know and conjecture. Moreover, since entrepreneurs are agents of change they cannot exist in equilibrium; the rewards they earn depend on the emergence of novel behaviours and on the economy being disordered. Clearly, an evolutionary, adaptive account of the economy must give entrepreneurship and enterprise a special place in its analysis. Indeed the notion of entrepreneurial behaviour is, we believe, an unavoidable component of any complexity-based approach to the economy. Yet entrepreneurship is impossible to conceive of without a further institution of the restless market economy, the market system.

COMPLEXITY, MARKETS AND INSTITUTIONS

From a complexity perspective, a key attribute of restless capitalism is the embedded nature of knowledge-generating processes within market institutions; institutions that create incentives to search for new production and market possibilities while simultaneously permitting and stimulating economic adaptation to these new possibilities. This is the double dynamic of knowledge based market capitalism. It has evolved into a system for creating and adapting to the opportunities associated with pervasive innovative activity. Markets are central to this process, yet market phenomena have been understood principally in terms of equilibrium models differing in sophistication, and ranging from the simplest perfectly competitive model for a single commodity to the more complicated general equilibrium models *à la* Arrow–Debreu. The drawbacks of such timeless models are irrefutable. First, there is no need for markets in an Arrow–Debreu economy in equilibrium; once equilibrium is established the market becomes redundant, because the problem it helps solve is no more. Their sole purpose in this framework serves only to arrive at a set of contracts that supports a consistent pattern of production and exchange; once this has been agreed for every date and every contingency, then markets are no longer needed (Loasby 2000, p. 300). Second, and equally cogent, is that these kinds of models cannot account for historical time, for proper uncertainty, for emergent novelty and adaptation to innovation, nor can they account for the institutions within which the economy is embedded (Boettke and Prychitko 1998, p. xvi). We have argued earlier that the evolution of economic systems depends on variation between economic agents: individuals, organizations and firms, (constrained by) institutional arrangements. Markets create a selection environment within which this variety is resolved into economic development. Citing Dubuisson (1998), Loasby (2000) suggests that the market is not an arena for the co-ordination of predetermined supply and demand functions, but an institutional setting for the cognitive processes by which supply and demand are continually reshaped. Experiments with innovation, new products or new methods of production or marketing are tested against the responses of consumers. Additionally, markets provide access to information on which to base these experiments. Each firm draws on the institutional context within which it operates as it develops its own idiosyncratic internal organization and its particular market niche. Each develops, through a combination of strategic choice and as a consequence of its daily interactions, rules and conventions with which it co-ordinates its activities with those of its suppliers and customers. The consequence for businesses that fail to create an appropriate set of institutional responses is their disappearance.

A complexity viewpoint admits a more sophisticated understanding of markets and their evolution, that is, markets as process involving continuous change.[10] The focus of market process theories is on adjustments to changing circumstances. As such they generally recognize entrepreneurship as a dis-ordering phenomenon and place entrepreneurs, innovation and technological discovery at the centre of the analytical framework (Boettke and Prychitko 1998). The various strands of market process theories all attempt to identify market forces, understand the dynamic of market activities and focus on the mechanisms that drive dis-equilibrium processes (Foss 1998). However, any theory purporting to understand change in a market economy must resolve two complementary issues. First, it must explain the underlying forces that cause such an economy to be in a perpetual state of dis-equilibrium and secondly, how such economies can also be characterized by orderly co-ordination. Austrian economists in particular have explored these issues to great effect in their treatments of entrepreneurial processes (Kirzner 1973, 1992, 1994, 1997) and spontaneous market order (Hayek 1973). Indeed, some authors (for example, see Vaughn 1999; Montgomery 1999; Kilpatrick 2001; Vriend 2002) have noted the remarkable similarity between Hayek's notion of spontaneous order and the more modern complexity ideas, although these different schools of thought differ quite fundamentally on the question of policy intervention.[11]

In Hayek (1973), spontaneous orders, social patterns that emerge as a product of human action but not human design, are created when elements of a system adapt themselves to situations and circumstances that only directly affect some of them. As adaptation occurs, it gives rise to unexpected or unanticipated outcomes at the global level and the principal source of adaptation is the new knowledge and understanding generated within the process. When it is said that an economy adapts, in truth it means that knowledge adapts.

Evolutionary spontaneous order was the analytical tool (of the complexity variety) used by Hayek to tackle fundamental problems of economics – the use of knowledge in society, and the way knowledge is acquired and transmitted through social interaction. The problem of explaining order at the aggregate or global level requires a specification of the mechanism through which the interlinking of plans and expectations of different individuals whose knowledge is fragmented, local and specific, could occur. The answer is that a self-organizing order is premised on exchanges of information of which market prices and transactions are particularly important categories. However, this is only part of the answer. The process of self-organization does not take place in the context of a given state and distribution of knowledge. Rather engagement in the market process changes knowledge directly and stimulates individuals to imagine different, and more profitable, economic worlds. Self-transformation is the necessary corollary of self-organization which is the restless nature of capitalism. Thus in a large world, agents are constantly exploring, learning and adapting in a mutually reinforcing, compound fashion. This is a world in which there is a continual process of prediction, a world of variation and novelty as adaptive strategies of some agents open up niches for others to explore, a world that does not, and cannot, settle down in deterministic fashion to any equilibrium. No general equilibrium model can capture these processes as long as it treats agents as atoms rather than sentient individuals, for atoms do not interact in the sense of conveying information to one another, and since no information is conveyed, no change in beliefs can be expected.

In Hayek's framework, markets provide the context in which business information and knowledge of all kinds are accumulated. This is exactly why market processes do not produce equilibrium, since the path to every notional position changes the knowledge and beliefs on which those positions are premised. The crucial point about markets therefore, and the market society in which they are instituted, is that they provide the opportunities and incentives to develop and apply new knowledge in the process of search for economic advantage. In this regard, they permit the simultaneous self-organization and the self-transformation of economic activity, and as Hayek (1948) observed, by concentrating solely on equilibrium rather than process, economists effectively rule out any effective treatment of competition. In the process, knowledge, understanding and the nature, scale and composition of economic activity co-evolve.

By contrast, in Kirzner's exposition, market evolution, market co-ordination and market dynamic emerge out of a systematic, error-correcting sequence of entrepreneurial discovery inspired by the search for profit opportunities. Rather than be tempted to impose an equilibrium configuration, his theory speaks of the order-imposing tendencies of the market process where powerful forces configure and constrain the market but are never so complete as to bring to a premature end the process of market activity via the attainment of equilibrium (Kirzner 1992). Instead, they exercise a dynamic of their own by continually modifying the subsequent realities, and these in turn set off further waves of changes in knowledge and economic order (Kirzner 1973). The competitive process assumes a pivotal role in this explanation marrying the Misean insights of the daring, imaginative and speculative actions of entrepreneurs with that of Hayek in which the order-creating process is one where market participants acquire better information about the plans of fellow market participants. Always we live with the tension between order and its transformation, as new knowledge keeps the economy in permanent transition. It is in this light that entrepreneurs are cast as discoverers, continually scanning the horizon to discover new products, new combinations of resource use, and new possibilities for market arbitrage (Kirzner 1997).

The standards by which a market system can be appraised, look very different from our adaptive evolutionary perspective. Such a system is to be judged, not only by its efficiency at an instant in time, but by its adaptability and creativity with the passage of time, and the search for maximum efficiency at a point in time may limit the ability to generate novelty on which the growth of efficiency ultimately depends. What makes capitalism restless is that markets are open institutions in which experiments can take place to challenge established positions.

CONCLUDING THOUGHTS

In this chapter we have explored the phenomenon of restless capitalism against the backdrop of complexity thinking. We have argued that a complexity framework facilitates a co-evolutionary exposition of the growth of knowledge, changes in economic beliefs and the development of the economy. From an economic perspective, integrating the endogenous growth of knowledge in standard economic models has proven to be a formidable methodological challenge and we have suggested that in order to understand the ongoing transformation of modern Western capitalist economies we need to abandon the idea of economies as equilibrium constructs and recognize the significance of the claim that they are knowledge based. Since knowledge cannot be in equilibrium, a knowledge based economy cannot be in equilibrium. Yet within this dynamic of continual change such economies exhibit order and are highly structured and patterned.

We have explored at length the issue of knowledge and understanding and the importance of its correlation and de-correlation that underlie change. Knowledge-generating activities, entrepreneurial processes and market co-ordination are among the distinctive features that generate restless capitalism, an economic system is which dynamics is not an optional extra. Capitalism is an experimental system, a system for the creation and testing of business conjectures. That conjecture and refutation are as important in business as they are in the practice of science indicates how important the knowledge perspective is to an understanding of modern capitalism. It is the unceasing and unremitting formation of new business hypotheses and their exploration in a trial and error fashion that makes capitalism what it is.

Clearly, the institutional framework of the economy is extremely important for the communication of information and the growth and application of new knowledge. Selection processes in capitalism are essentially market-based processes and the role of markets is to co-ordinate different activities, and at the same time, to value them. Prices are formed through co-ordination, and these prices determine the profitability of the underlying theories of business. But prices alone are not sufficient to capture the qualitative dimensions of the experimental nature of capitalist economies. Thus as Loasby (2000, p. 304) puts it: 'It is no accident that theories of atomistic markets, which lack institutional features, provide an inadequate basis for analysing product innovation.' Moreover, the institutions of the market cannot be taken as naturally given. Markets are costly to establish and operate, they operate by sets of rules in relation to standards and conventions for doing business and they are regulated either by law, by administrative procedure or by informal practice. Most markets reflect the interaction between public and private interest. Other institutions are equally relevant for the development process. The growth of scientific and technological knowledge, in particular, depends on the interaction between organizations in the public and private domains that jointly form systems of knowledge generation and dissemination. These systems reflect the division of labour in the growth and application of knowledge between organizations and disciplines and, within these distributed processes of innovation, firms play the unique role of gathering and combining multiple kinds of knowledge from multiple sources. These higher order institutions and organizations may also be said to evolve by processes of variation selection and development so that the transformation of the economy involves evolution within its institutional structure and evolution of that structure. Only by approaching economic growth in this manner can we begin to unravel the interaction between different levels of evolution in the economy.

NOTES

1. Complexity thinking has emerged in the past half-century as a radically different perspective on the world, and there has been an increasing recognition across the social sciences that complexity offers a novel, integrated framework for the analysis of the hidden dynamics of the socio-economic world. Among the more recent publications see, for example, Stacey et al. (2000) and Colander (2000a). Auyang (1998) provides a valuable summary of the core ideas.
2. For very interesting commentary on varieties of capitalism from a knowledge-generation perspective, see Whitley (2002).
3. An economy expanding in all respects at a uniform rate is in effect a stationary state, a state defined by proportional dynamics.
4. It is this fact which links evolutionary explanation with some Austrian approaches to economic evolution as a discovery process, a matter we treat further below.
5. The rules in relation to the use of roads provide an example, one of many, where correlation is better if it is perfect.
6. The firm is to be interpreted broadly as the entity organizing the production of a good or service. It includes non-profit as well as for-profit organizations.
7. This resonates closely with the point raised by Littlechild (1986) who essentially argues that modelling uncertainty and novelty poses formidable mathematical challenges.
8. Reflect on the fact that a business makes a profit to the extent that it operates with expectations that are different from those of its rivals, and are evaluated by the market as superior expectations.
9. One might conjecture that a world without equilibrium is also a world without disequilibrium and equilibration, *pace* Samuels (1997). Disorder and ordering would seem to be the appropriate concepts. The implications for the notion of far-from-equilibrium economic states, appear equally negative.
10. See Metcalfe (1998) and Metcalfe et al. (2006) for formal models of market dynamics.
11. Whereas modern complexity theorists argue that positive feedback may sometimes result in undesirable effects such as inferior technology choices and thus admit welfare enhancing policies, Austrians hold passionately to the benevolence of the spontaneous

order of market processes, believing that a more efficient system cannot be devised by human beings.

REFERENCES

Aghion, P. and P. Howitt (1992), 'A model of growth through creative destruction', *Econometrica*, **60**, 323–51.

Allen, Peter M. (2001), 'Knowledge, ignorance and the evolution of complex systems' in J. Foster and J.S. Metcalfe (eds), *Frontiers of Evolutionary Economics*, Cheltenham, UK and Northampton, MA, USA: Edward Elgar, pp. 313–50.

Allen, Peter, M., R. Ramlogan and S. Randles (2002), 'Complexity and the merger process', *Technology Analysis and Strategic Management*, **14**(3), 315–30.

Arthur, W.B. (1994), 'Inductive reasoning and bounded rationality', *American Economic Review* (Papers and Proceedings), **84**, 406–11.

Arthur, W.B. (1999), 'Complexity and the economy', *Science*, **284**, 107–109.

Arthur, W. Brian (2000), 'Cognition: the black box of economics', in D. Colander (ed.), *The Complexity Vision and the Teaching of Economics*, Cheltenham, UK and Northampton, MA, USA: Edward Elgar, pp. 19–28.

Arthur, W. Brian, S. Durlauf and D. Lane (eds) (1997), *The Economy as a Complex Adaptive System*, II, Reading, MA: Perseus Books.

Audi, Robert (1998), *Epistemology*, London: Routledge.

Auyang, Sunny, Y. (1998), *Foundations of Complex-System Theories in Economics, Evolutionary Biology and Statistical Physics*, Cambridge: Cambridge University Press.

Bak, Per (1997), *How Nature Works: The Science of Self Organized Criticality*, Oxford: Oxford University Press.

Berlin, Isaiah (1991), *The Crooked Timber of Humanity*, London: Fontana.

Blume, Lawerence E. and S. Durlauf (2000), 'The interactions based approach to socioeconomic behaviour', mimeo, Cornell University.

Boettke, Peter and D. Prychitko (eds) (1998), *Market Process Theories*, Vols. I and II, Cheltenham, UK and Lyme, USA: Edward Elgar.

Brock, W.A. (2000a), 'Whither nonlinear', *Journal of Economic Dynamics and Control*, **24**(5–7), 663–78.

Brock, W.A. (2000b), 'Some Santa Fe scenery', in David Colander (ed.), *The Complexity Vision and the Teaching of Economics*, Cheltenham, UK and Northampton, MA, USA: Edward Elgar, pp. 29–50.

Campbell, D.T. (1960), 'Blind variation and selective retention in creative thought as in other knowledge generating processes', *Psychological Review*, **67**(6), 380–400.

Carlsson, Bo (ed.) (1995), *Technological Systems and Economic Performance*, Boston: Kluwer.

Colander, David (ed.) (2000a), *The Complexity Vision and the Teaching of Economics*, Cheltenham, UK and Northampton, MA, USA: Edward Elgar.

Colander, David (2000b), *Complexity and the History of Economic Thought*, London: Routledge.

Cowan, R., P.A. David and D. Foray (2000), 'The economics of codification and the diffusion of knowledge', *Industrial and Corporate Change*, **9**(2), 211–53.

Currie, Martin and I. Steedman (1990), *Wrestling with Time: Problems in Economic Theory*, Ann Arbor: The University of Michigan Press.

Dooley, Kevin and S. Corman (2000), 'Agent-based genetic and emergent computational models for complex systems', *mimeo*, LOCKS, University of Arizona.

Dopfer, Kurt and J. Potts (2004), 'Evolutionary foundations of economics', in J. Foster and J.S. Metcalfe (eds), *Evolution and Economic Complexity*, Cheltenham, UK and Northampton, MA, USA: Edward Elgar, pp. 3–23.

Dosi, Giovanni, Richard R. Nelson and Sidney G. Winter (2000), *The Nature and Dynamics of Organizational Capabilities*, Oxford: Oxford University Press.

Dubuisson, S. (1998), 'Codification et ajustement: deux moyens pour l'elaboration d'une memoire de l'organisation, le cas d'une activité de service', *Revue Internationale de Systemique*, **12**, 83–98.

Durlauf, S. (1997), 'What policy makers should know about economic complexity', *Santa Fe Working Papers*, No. 97-10-080, Santa Fe Institute, New Mexico.

Edquist, Charles (1997), *Systems of Innovation: Technologies, Institutions and Organizations* (Science, Technology and the International Political Economy Series), London: Thompson Learning.

Foss, N. (1998), 'Market process economics and the theory of the firm', *Copenhagen Business School Working Paper*, No.98-6.

Foster, J. (1993), 'Economics and the self-organization approach: Alfred Marshall revisited', *Economic Journal*, **103**(419), 975–91.

Freeman, Christopher (1987), *Technology Policy and Economic Performance*, London: Pinter.

Hahn, F. (1987), 'Information dynamics and equilibrium', *Scottish Journal of Political Economy*, **34**(4), 321–34.

Hayek, Friedrich A. (1948), 'The meaning of competition' in Friedrich A. Hayek, *Individualism and Economic Order*, University of Chicago Press, pp. 92–106.

Hayek, Friedrich A. (1973), *Law, Legislation and Liberty*, London: Routledge and Kegan.

Horgan, J. (1995), 'From complexity to perplexity', *Scientific American*, **272**(6), 104–9.

Johnson, B., E. Lorenz and B.A. Lundvall (2002), 'Why all this fuss about codified and tacit knowledge?', *Industrial and Corporate Change*, **11**(2), 245–62.

Jones, C.I. (1995), 'R and D-based models of economic growth', *Journal of Political Economy*, **103**(4), 759–84.

Kaldor, N. (1934), 'A classificatory note on the determinateness of equilibrium', *Review of Economic Studies*, **1**, 122–36.

Kilpatrick (Jr), H. (2001), 'Complexity, spontaneous order', *Complexity*, **6**(3), 16–20.

Kirman, A.P. (1992), 'Whom or what does the representative individual represent?', *Journal of Economic Perspectives*, **6**(2), 117–36.

Kirzner, Israel, M. (1973), *Competition and Entrepreneurship*, Chicago: University of Chicago Press.

Kirzner, Israel, M. (1992), *The Meaning of the Market Process*, London: Routledge.

Kirzner, I.M. (1994), 'Entrepreneurship' in P. Boettke (ed.), *The Elgar Companion to Austrian Economics*, Aldershot, UK and Brookfield, USA: Edward Elgar, pp. 103–10.

Kirzner, I.M. (1997), 'Entrepreneurial discovery and the competitive market process: an Austrian approach', *Journal of Economic Literature*, **35**(1), 60–85.

Krugman, Paul (1996), *The Self-Organising Economy*, Oxford: Basil Blackwell.

Landes, David (1998), *The Wealth and Poverty of Nations*, New York: Little, Brown and Company.

Langlois, Richard N. (1983), 'Systems theory, knowledge and the social sciences', in F. Machlup and U. Mansfield (eds), *The Study of Information*, New York: Wiley, pp. 581–600.

Langlois, R.N. (1990), 'Bounded rationality and behaviourism: a clarification and a critique', *Journal of Institutional and Theoretical Economics*, **146**(4), 691–5.

Littlechild, Stephen (1986), 'Three types of market process', in R. Langlois (ed.), *Economics as a Process: Essays in New Institutional Economics*, Cambridge: Cambridge University Press, pp. 27–39.

Loasby, Brian J. (1999), *Knowledge, Institutions and Evolution in Economics*, London: Routledge.

Loasby, B.J. (2000), 'Markets and economic evolution', *Journal of Evolutionary Economics*, **10**(3), 297–309.

Mandelbrot, Benoit B. (1997), *Fractals and Scaling in Finance*, New York: Springer-Verlag.

Manson, S.M. (2001), 'Simplifying complexity: a review of complexity theory', *Geoforum*, **32**(3), 405–14.

Marshall, Alfred (1919), *Industry and Trade*, London: Macmillan.

Metcalfe, J. Stanley (1998), *Evolutionary Economics and Creative Destruction*, London: Routledge.

Metcalfe, J.S. (2001), 'Institutions and progress', *Industrial and Corporate Change*, **10**(3), 561–86.

Metcalfe, J.S., J. Foster and R. Ramlogan (2006), 'Adaptive economic growth', *Cambridge Journal of Economics*, **30**(7), 7–32.

Mokyr, Joel (1991), *The Lever of Riches*, Oxford: Oxford University Press.

Mokyr, Joel (2002), *Gifts of Athena: Historical Origins of the Knowledge Economy*, Princeton University Press.

Montgomery, Michael R. (1999), 'Complexity theory: an "Austrian" perspective', in David Colander (ed.), *Complexity Theory and the History of Economic Thought*, Routledge Press, pp. 227–40.

Mowery, David C. and N. Rosenberg (1998), *Paths of Innovation: Technological Change in 20th Century America*, Cambridge: Cambridge University Press.

Nelson, R.R. (1990), 'Capitalism as an engine of progress', *Research Policy*, **19**(3), 193–214.

Nelson, Richard R. (ed.) (1993), *National Innovation Systems: A Comparative Study*, Oxford: Oxford University Press.

Nelson, R.R. (1999), 'On the uneven evolution of human know-how', mimeo, Columbia University.

Nelson, Richard R. and S. Winter (1984), *An Evolutionary Theory of Economic Change*, Belknap: Harvard University Press.

North, Douglas C. (1990), *Institutions, Institutional Change and Economic Performance*, Cambridge: Cambridge University Press.

Plotkin, Henry C. (1994), *The Nature of Knowledge*, Harmondsworth: Penguin.

Polanyi, Michael (1966), *The Tacit Dimension*, London: Routledge & Kegan Paul.

Popper, Karl (1996), *In Search of a Better World*, London: Routledge.

Robinson, Joan V. (1974), *History Versus Equilibrium*, Thames Papers in Political Economy, Thames Polytechnic, London.

Samuels, W.J. (1997), 'On the nature and utility of the concept of equilibrium', *Journal of Post Keynesian Economics*, **20**(1), 77–88.

Schumpeter, Joseph A. (1911, in German; tr. 1934), *The Theory of Economic Development*, Oxford: Oxford University Press.

Schumpeter, Joseph A. (1944), *Capitalism, Socialism and Democracy*, London: George Allen and Unwin.

Setterfield, M. (1997), 'Should economists dispense with the notion of equilibrium?', *Journal of Post Keynesian Economics*, **20**(1), 89–101.

Shackle, George L.S. (1958), *Decision, Order and Time In Human Affairs*, Cambridge: Cambridge University Press.

Smith, Adam (1776), *An Enquiry into the Nature and Causes of the Wealth of Nations*, (Cannan edition 1904), New York: The Modern Library.

Sole, Richard and B. Goodwin (2000), *Signs of Life: How Complexity Pervades Biology*, New York: Basic Books.

Stacey, Ralph, D. Griffin and P. Shaw (2000), *Complexity and Management*, London: Routledge.

Steedman, I. (2003), 'On "measuring" knowledge in new (endogenous) growth theory', in N. Salvadori (ed.), *Old and New Growth Theories: An Assessment*, Cheltenham, UK and Northampton, MA, USA: Edward Elgar, pp. 127–33.

Vaughn, K. (1999), 'Hayek's theory of the market order as an instance of the theory of complex, adaptive systems', *Journal des Economistes et des Etudes Humaines*, **9**(2/3), 241–56.

Vriend, N.J. (2002), 'Was Hayek an ace?', *Southern Economic Journal*, **68**(4), 811–40.

Whitley, R. (2002), 'Developing innovative competences: the role of institutional frameworks', *Industrial and Corporate Change*, **11**(3), 497–528.

Witt, U. (2000), 'Evolutionary economics: an interpretative survey', in K. Dopfer (ed.), *Evolutionary Economics: Program and Scope*, Boston: Kluwer.

Ziman, John (ed.) (2000), *Technological Evolution as an Evolutionary Process*, Cambridge: Cambridge University Press.

6. Industrial resilience and decline: a co-evolutionary framework

James McGlade, Robert Murray, James Baldwin, Keith Ridgway and Belinda Winder

INTRODUCTION: PROBLEMS IN UNDERSTANDING EVOLUTIONARY SOCIAL SYSTEMS

Ever since the advent of the social sciences in the 18th century, a key preoccupation has been the understanding of change and the evolution of social structures. However, such research is complicated by the fact that the processes ultimately responsible for structuring long run societal dynamics are both elusive and inherently unpredictable. At root this problem is concerned with the nature of causality and its solution lies in the difficult task of unravelling the complex array of micro–macro interactions linking individual purposive action to the larger scale collective processes that produce societal change (van der Leeuw and McGlade 1997).

From this it follows that the central issue in understanding socioeconomic dynamics concerns the problem of emergence; that is, the role of phenomena such as collective action or the spontaneous generation of new innovations. In our present context this would include the propensity for social institutions and industries to generate options that are the result of unplanned outcomes. Thus any attempt to deal with the transformative aspects of social and industrial systems must acknowledge the important role played by initially seemingly trivial or marginal events or decisions and their propensity to produce unintended outcomes over the long-term. It is in this sense that we can speak of the need for an understanding of history if we are to have any appreciation of socio-economic evolution.

The natural and social worlds we inhabit are replete with examples of the way that essentially arbitrary or unintended features emerge to determine subsequent historical pathways. As Arthur (1989) has pointed out, the evolution of technologies provides us with a number of examples where the role of chance elements creates entirely new irreversible evolutionary trajectories. For example the first typewriter keyboard systems emerged in a competitive market with the eventual dominance of the current QWERTY system being due more to the action of chance rather than strict technological advantage; in fact this system was inferior to at least one other of its rivals. In another example Arthur discusses the role of *historical path dependence* and points to the importance of the role of both chance and necessity in directing the evolution of urban agglomerations. In explaining the historical evolution of urbanism at the regional level he uses an analogy from genetics; that is, chance events act to 'select' the pattern that becomes fixed but regions that are economically attractive have an intrinsic 'selectional advantage', and thus have a higher probability of achieving dominance. These examples cited by Arthur might collectively be described as conforming to the 'QWERTY principle of history': historical events that come together in an *unplanned* way create inevitable and irreversible historical outcomes.

What is clear from these examples is that the nature of socio-economic change is far from trivial and is poorly understood by recourse to developmental evolutionist models that are predicated on notions of progressive unfolding (cf. Giddens 1979). Indeed it should be noted that all societal systems are characterized by highly nonlinear interactions, and recent discoveries of chaotic trajectories at the heart of many biological, ecological and environmental systems have caused a revision of our long-held assumptions on the nature of order/disorder and by implication, causality itself. Perhaps the most important aspect of this theoretical realignment is that in underlining the essentially nonlinear nature of socio-economic relations, it foregrounds the importance of *instability* and *discontinuity* not as aberrant processes, but rather as key concepts for understanding the nature of social systems. Chapter 3 demonstrates the inadequacy of a reductionist strategy in understanding how cities evolve and discusses the concept of continuity with reference to *perceived* persistence of urban form and changing function, illustrating the non-equilibrial nature of social and economic processes. In what follows we shall attempt to demonstrate the importance of such a perspective for socio-economic systems generally and more specifically in order to gain new insight into the evolutionary dynamics traced by the South Yorkshire coal industry, viewed as a complex co-evolutionary system.

Complexity and Sustainability

It is something of a paradox that despite the wide coverage and prominence of the theme, 'sustainability' still remains an exceedingly ambiguous term, occupying a territory in which it appears to be 'all things to all people'. Any survey of the literature necessarily must conclude that sustainability is best described as having an 'elastic' meaning, eminently malleable and infinitely variable in usage. Thus it can be invoked to support a variety of positions depending, for example, on our valuation of natural and man-made capital (for example Faucheux *et al.* 1998).

While the search for a comprehensive definition of sustainability is destined to remain elusive, what is clear is that an important distinction must be made as to what kind of sustainability we are dealing with – be it environmental, economic or social – since each has a distinctive meaning as well as being relative to a specific spatio-temporal domain. Beyond the terminological confusion and slack usage however, there are more fundamental problems which need to be addressed; for example, regardless of whether we are discussing resources, economies or societal systems, sustainability must not only be temporally and spatially defined, but most importantly it must be contextualized with respect to specific political, ethical and social parameters (McGlade 2002). Perhaps most imperative if we are to come to terms with sustainable outcomes from a complexity perspective, is to situate such issues within an evolutionary framework. This will allow us to focus on one of the key aspects of sustainable systems in general; that is, their resilience.

Resilience and Stability

Despite its frequent usage by ecologists, economists and some social scientists, resilience is not a unitary concept with a precise and unambiguous definition. In the ecological literature for example, it has two distinct meanings. The first emphasizes stability, control and constancy (*engineering resilience*) – attributes of a desire for optimal performance – while the second by contrast, focuses on persistence, adaptedness and unpredictability (*ecological resilience*) – attributes of an evolutionary perspective. Research using a model of engineering resilience deals with stability near an equilibrium state and is concerned with resistance to disturbance and speed of return to equilibrium (for example De Angelis *et al.* 1980; Pimm 1984; Tilman and Downing 1994). By contrast, ecological resilience focuses on conditions far from equilibrium and is concerned with the role of instabilities in pushing the system beyond a threshold or bifurcation point to a new stability domain. Here, resilience is measured by the magnitude of disturbance that can be absorbed before the system changes structure (Holling 1973). A wide variety of applications exploring ecological resilience now exists spanning resource ecology, wildlife management, fisheries, animal ecology and plant-vegetation dynamics (Holling *et al.* 1977; Walker *et al.* 1981; Walters 1986; Sinclair *et al.* 1990; Dublin *et al.* 1990).

Studies such as these have been instrumental in shifting the ecological debate from an evolutionary model based on the maintenance of stability, to one dominated by a sequence of interacting adaptive cycles based on a developmental sequence defined by four functions: exploitation, conservation, release and re-organization (Holling 1986). More recently these ideas have been extended to encompass the idea of *panarchy*, which emphasizes the evolutionary nature of nested adaptive cycles, with each level going through the cycle of growth, maturation, destruction and renewal (Gunderson *et al.* 1995). A key emphasis in this model is that periods of gradual growth and rapid transformation not only coexist, but act to complement one another (see also Günther and Folke 1993).

Resilience and Societal Systems

All socio-economic systems that can be seen to persist – particularly over long time periods – can be described as being characteristically resilient, in the sense that they are able to *incorporate* change and perturbation without collapsing. This ability to absorb changing circumstances as defined by environmental, social, political or cultural fluctuations is itself a function both of the flexibility of structural organization and system history. The role of history is of crucial importance, in the sense that a particular regime that has been exposed to regular, periodic disturbance, will be more adapted to periodic change than a system which is visited by perturbation and/or extreme events on an irregular basis.

Any loss of resilience will move a particular socio-economic system closer to unstable thresholds causing it to flip from one attractor state to another (metastability); thus for example, exploitation to extinction of a particular resource will have an effect on the local ecosystem inducing system transformation and an irreversible change to an alternative state. Resilience can be said to be one of the primary properties of nonlinear, non-equilibrium systems and needs to be understood more fully if we are to come to terms with sustainable social–natural systems.

A major problem that we are faced with in pursuit of a model of resilience within the context of industrial development is that this cannot be deduced from conventional equilibrium approaches. However, neither can it be derived by the simple superimposition of Holling's (1986) resilience cycle for ecological dynamics. This general theory of ecosystem function – incorporating insights from hierarchy theory (Allen and Starr 1982; O'Neill *et al.* 1986) – has been argued as an appropriate basis for understanding the generic evolutionary behaviour underpinning ecological, economic and societal dynamics (for example Gunderson *et al.* 1995; Berkes and Folke 1998; Peterson 2000).

Notwithstanding the important insights that Holling's evolutionary model provides, its essentially 'organic' nature is an inappropriate model for capturing the complexity of socio-economic systems, in part because social systems are more than simply functional entities – they are defined by symbolic and cognitive attributes. Importantly, Giddens (1979, 1984) provides a robust argument against the idea that societies 'adapt' to anything, since they are not equivalent to biological organisms (1979, p. 21). Instead, social change is seen as non-teleological – a set of contingent, discontinuous transitions which have no inherent developmental logic or pattern.

An additional problem in utilizing ecological resilience as an analogy for societal systems, is that human systems are not neutral; they are a historical product of specific social, political and cultural relations: a factor running all the way from local relations of production to larger scale regional, national and global levels of interaction. Thus, if we are to attempt to isolate the important driving forces of irreversible change which represent a non-sustainable option for society – then we must situate such goals within a milieu that recognizes (1) that all socio-natural systems (*sic* environment) are embedded in webs of power relations and (2) that these networks of power act to both enable and constrain human aspirations and desires. It is in the exercise of such power that the moral and ethical universe within which humans are situated is subject to substantial modification and even destruction.

In summary, what we can say from the perspective of our focus on industrial dynamics, is that while resilience is a useful concept for understanding the long-term evolution of human-modified environments, it needs to be reconfigured to take account of the specific human and socio-political contexts that drive system transformation and change. In essence, we might summarize the main attributes of resilience from a socio-economic perspective as having the following characteristics:

- The amount of re-organization and change a social system can undergo while still retaining the basic institutional and socio-economic structures.
- The degree to which the system structure is capable of self-repair and self-organization.

This implies:

- Institutional flexibility.
- The conscious use of historical knowledge.
- The desire to increase the capacity for knowledge production and learning.
- Conscious management of change to incorporate uncertainty and unintended consequences.

THE RESILIENCE OF INDUSTRIAL SYSTEMS: COMPARING THE DECLINE OF THE UK AND GERMAN COAL MINING INDUSTRIES

The concept of resilience is presented as a particularly useful tool in categorizing different patterns of behaviour and change observed in industrial systems. An interesting and insightful comparison can be made in looking at the different circumstances surrounding the decline of both the British and German coal mining industries. A crucial distinction has already been made between engineering and ecological resilience. This is key to understanding how two very similar industrial systems dealt with change, and the extent to which this change was eventually managed. As with any discussion of the process of decline within the UK coal mining industry, it is of crucial importance to consider its history and in doing so to unearth some of the catalysts, political and otherwise, of the immense changes the industry has endured and the subsequent effects experienced by the communities and individuals who relied on this sole source of purpose and prosperity.

In considering the nature of decline apparent in the UK coal industry, the question arises as to whether different government interventions could have prevented the spectacular decline experienced by former mining communities. As a comparable power, Germany also faced an enforced run-down of its coal industry as costs of domestic coal production increased and other alternative sources of energy became an option. The transition was marked by co-operation and dialogue between the government, employers and union. The result has been a far greater degree of planning in advance of the closure decisions and government money to facilitate transition provided in advance. Co-operation, incidentally, has led to a larger proportion of the German coal industry surviving compared to its UK counterpart (Schubert and Bräutigam 1995). Critcher also notes that although there are doubts about detail in terms of the success of the German approach, it had significant advantages over that adopted in the UK, as far greater levels of planning provided the foundation for a more effective management of change:

> In Germany there was an attempt to plan everything: the annual production of coal, the closure of pits, the training of miners, the reclamation of land, the regeneration of the local economy . . . Symptomatic of the improvised and incremental nature of the British trajectory was the reaction of Secretary of State, Michael Heseltine to widespread political opposition to the wave of proposed pit closures originally announced in October 1992. Seventy-five million pounds of special aid was subsequently made available; it was to be channelled through the Training and Enterprise Councils (by no stretch of the imagination representative bodies); they were to be given two weeks to submit proposals to

the Government. In such a context, any kind of serious planning is not viable. (Critcher *et al.* 1995, pp. 183–4)

The levels of adaptive behaviour displayed by the German mining industry and its active management of change, coupled with its preparedness and communication with government, is characteristic of the concept of ecological resilience – particularly the ability to absorb perturbations and potential problems through co-operative dialogue (Figure 6.1). This is in contrast to the more reactive/retroactive activity observed in the British mining industry's approach, which has been accompanied by a far greater resistance to structural change. Throughout its evolution the British coal industry has been subject to technological development as increased levels of mechanization were introduced. This inevitably required a degree of new knowledge acquisition on the part of the workforce, though importantly the system's structure was largely unaffected and resistance in this respect was minimized. Such significant developments improved the efficiency of the extraction process and were on the whole readily accepted. This unilateral drive for optimization is a typical characteristic of systems based on a form of engineering resilience. Arguably such strategies lead to the development of 'brittle' systems that have no 'slack' or inbuilt flexibility.

Historically, the region's mining sector typically experienced few changes in social organization, environment and culture (influences which remain constant to this day), and had developed a confidence in its ability to 'weather the storm' of political influence. This preoccupation with control and constancy, again indicative of a more engineering form of resilience, meant the industry was ill-equipped and poorly prepared to deal with unpredictable changes. The institutional flexibility, will to learn and conscious appraisal and management of change – features of ecological resilience – were simply not present in the industry when new demands were placed upon it. In fact, the knowledge held from previous encounters between the National Union of Mineworkers and the Conservative Heath government in 1973 led the majority of miners to believe that once more their interests would be protected. This self-belief and ignorance of the true nature of change, developing global markets and the threat of alternative power sources severely weakened their hand initially and later their power to negotiate. It should be made clear however, that in dealing with issues of socio-economic transition, time is a crucial element which should be acknowledged when considering the relative 'success' of adaptation. The length of time made available to the industry to accommodate and prepare for change was doubtless confounded by breakdowns in negotiations and consequent strike action.

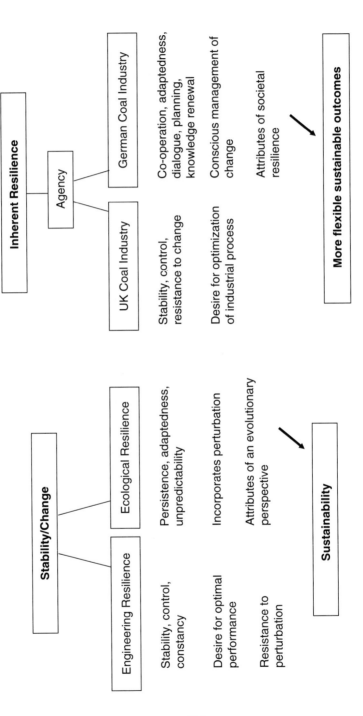

Figure 6.1   Resilience, strategy and outcomes

Generally speaking, the main shortcomings represented by inflexibility and embedded traditional knowledge and practices thus conspired to produce a classic case of systemic collapse (cf. Tainter 1988). Such a scenario was not inevitable, and by way of contrast, we shall attempt to outline the elements of a framework based on the co-evolution of social, cultural and economic processes that is based on the promotion of resilience in socio-economic transformation.

Towards a Co-evolutionary Framework

So far we have argued the need to understand industrial systems from a complexity perspective, in order to emphasize their non-equilibrial, evolutionary nature. Such an approach emphasizes the capacity of small, unanticipated (contingent) events to generate structural transformation and, importantly the role played by co-evolutionary dynamics in affecting discontinuous change. Elsewhere (McGlade 1995, 1999a, 1999b) we have suggested that human–environment interaction seen in terms of a model of *human ecodynamics*, of necessity must be conceived of as a reciprocal set of interactions driven by positive feedback processes. This co-evolutionary perspective argues for a non-functionalist human ecology in which human agency plays a vital role in creating environmental outcomes that are subsequently seen to act back on human societal processes. Thus the reproduction of society is a consequence of this continuous reciprocal dynamic.[1] Consistent with these ideas is the need to view any co-evolutionary dynamic from a long-term perspective, thus recognizing the importance of history in creating the enabling and constraining conditions within which socio-economic systems co-evolve. Such a research agenda is designed to present a more complete and integrated view of human societal structuring; it thus eschews current developmental evolutionary models emphasizing in their place a discontinuous, nonlinear perspective, which acknowledges the crucial importance of different temporalities and scale-dependent dynamics in the emergence of societal structure (McGlade 1999b).

Generally speaking, a co-evolutionary perspective focuses on the way that self-organizing processes at work in socio-economic systems act to generate the system's evolutionary character. In an important contribution to these concepts, Norgaard (1984, 1994) has presented a co-evolutionary model based on the mutual feedbacks and nonlinearities between values, knowledge, social organization, technology and environment. The most significant aspect of Norgaard's model is that it contains no external relations; everything is 'symmetrically' related. All component processes are involved in a co-evolutionary dynamic that is constantly changing in ways that are not necessarily predictable. Each of the defined 'subsystems' (values, knowledge, organization, technology and environment) is composed of different types of ways of valuing, knowing, organizing and doing things (Norgaard 1994, p. 35). The metaphor of biological fitness is employed to explain the co-evolutionary process; that is, selective pressures determine subsystem survival. In this sense, values and beliefs that enhance the co-evolutionary process survive and multiply, while less 'fit' ones disappear. From a developmental perspective, there is no implied teleology in co-evolutionary development; thus:

> knowledge, technologies and social organization merely change, rather than advance, and the 'betterness' of each is only relative to how well it fits with the others and values. Change in the co-evolutionary explanation, rather than a process of rational design and improvement, is a process of experimentation, partly conscious, and selection by whether things work or not. (ibid. p. 37)

What is being argued is that the environment acts as a determinant in the way people behave as guided by knowledge, social organization and technologies, while at the same time, 'how people know, organize and use tools determine the fitness of characteristics of an evolving environment' (ibid. p. 46).

However, there are a number of aspects of Norgaard's model that require scrutiny. First the notion that socio-economic dynamics can be reduced to discrete subsystems is problematic as it suggests that societies can be neatly partitioned into functional categories and thereby analysed from a cybernetic perspective. There is also a 'fearful' symmetry in the relationships between the subsystems, such that the causal linkages are defined as being equal. In reality the relationship between such linkages – comprising a variety of weak and strong links – is constantly changing, since socio-economic systems are perforce, *evolutionary* systems. Moreover, in reality the so-called 'subsystems' evolve at different rates.

A key component missing from Norgaard's framework is an expression of the central role exercised by power and authority and their various manifestations in articulating societal systems. Curiously, while making the astute comment that environmental problems are essentially problems of 'social organization' (as opposed to seeing them in terms of the need for purely technological solutions), no mention is made of the crucial role of the circuits of power and authority that articulate all social and political structures.

A Co-evolutionary Model for Industrial and Societal Transformation

In an effort to promote an alternative model of co-evolution – one that encompasses some of the structural issues described above, particularly the interdependence between agency and structure – Figure 6.2 presents a revised schema based on the mutual interaction of values, knowledge, agency, social organization and resources. In contrast to Norgaard's model, each of the five domains are not considered as subsystems but rather as the locus of *processes* that are connected to each other through self-organizing dynamics driven by nonlinearities. Importantly the connectivities involved are periodically weak and strong as expansion and contraction take place continuously. Some domains are more tightly coupled, and this is dependent on the capacity of a single domain or cluster to dominate or exercise control on the evolutionary trajectory of the socio-economic system. Discontinuous change, collapse, transformation and re-constitution comprise the 'normal' co-evolutionary behaviour of the socio-economic system.

While the manifest complexities underpinning co-evolutionary dynamics are daunting, we can usefully summarize the main attributes of the processes involved thus:

- **Values:** These assume a key role since values, philosophies and beliefs comprise the cultural knowledge of a society that ultimately finds expression in ideology. This is a critical domain for it comprises the

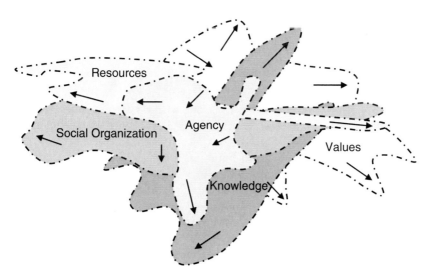

Figure 6.2   A topological 'rubber sheet' (co-evolutionary) model for socio-economic systems, with a variety of possible stretching and folding capabilities as it is 'pushed' and 'pulled' in a number of directions over time

engine of socio-economic systems, responsible for both its practical goals and its highest aspirations. Moreover, it stands in opposition to instrumentalist perspectives that view entities such as agriculture and irrigation as simply material technologies. By contrast, we are arguing that technologies are expressions of value systems.

- **Knowledge:** Knowledge is here conceived as four mutually inter-dependent but semi-autonomous communities comprising: scientific, institutional, technical and local knowledge categories. Our definition of societal resilience was based on the capacity of a society to continuously renew its stocks of knowledge and discard those that are perceived to be redundant; in fact, failure to allow knowledge exchange in this way can lead to fossilization and possible collapse. Co-evolution can therefore be thought of as a 'knowledge intensive' process.

- **Agency:** Actions are here viewed as human interventions in the system. These may be purposive or contingent and given the nonline-arities structuring socio-economic processes, they can result in wholly unintended consequences. Agency is intrinsically related to the application of 'means' to achieve 'outcomes'; thus, it is intimately related to power. The distinction separating 'power over' from 'power to' is an important structuring principal, for it recognizes the capa-city of human agency to engage in either exploitative relations or alternatively, to empower people.

- **Resources:** Resources follow Giddens' (1979, 1984) distinction between *allocative resources* (those involving control over nature) and *authoritative resources* (those involving control over social interac-tions). Allocative resources thus comprise the material features of the environment (raw materials) as well as the instruments of produc-tion, technology and their products. By contrast, authoritative resources comprise the organizational elements of human spatial interaction as well as the communication and information content defining human social interaction. Crucially, it is the specific inter-relationship between these two types of resources that accounts for the variety of asymmetric power relations (enabling or constraining) that characterize all human social institutions.

- **Social organization:** The connectivity that characterizes all societal systems is the product of a diverse array of social, political, economic and ideological linkages. These comprise networks of interactions that act to generate various types of order and organization. In the most generic sense, networks arise as a solution to coping with complex societal problems. Social networks are usefully conceptual-ized as distributed systems; that is, a *heterarchy* comprising clusters of relatively decentralized social groups, rather than a single all-inclusive hierarchy. Control in such systems is not so much absent but is fluid, circular, and essentially discontinuous. What is most significant, is that within such a heterarchy, comprising a diverse array of semi-autonomous nodes – for example: local, regional and national administrative bodies – a novel structure can emerge spontaneously from the increasing and decreasing rates of connectivity across the system enacted by political decision-making processes.

The difficulties in conceptualizing such 4-dimensional dynamics are clear and can only imperfectly be captured by a 2-dimensional figure. Perhaps the best way to grasp the co-evolutionary framework is to conceive of it as a topological 'rubber sheet' model with a variety of possible stretching and folding capabilities as it is 'pushed' and 'pulled' in a number of directions over time. This sequence of asymmetric topologies best defines the self-organizing features of evolutionary development.

The real advantage of a co-evolutionary approach is that it challenges our conventional scientific methodologies, forcing us to think in terms of 'wholes' instead of 'parts'. However logical this may seem, its implementation is not easily achieved for it requires us to jettison reductionist models upon which scientific enquiry has been based for the past 200 years. Co-evolution is attractive precisely because it presents us with a model of reciprocal human–environment dynamics which is intuitively satisfying and, moreover, suggests new pathways along which we can confront complexity. On the other hand, from a practical perspective, any approach that cuts across disciplinary boundaries carries with it a particular set of difficulties (and even mistrust) that comes with any attempt to restructure conventional scientific discourse.

Such an epistemological shift has the added advantage that it encourages a pluralistic approach to knowledge acquisition and hence actively reconfigures the territory of decision-making. Practically, this involves a move from a search for deterministic causal linkages between risk and planning strategies to an arena of negotiated solutions, for a *dialogic* methodology (cf. McGlade 1995). This proposal is consistent with Norgaard's (1994, p. 102) call for 'conceptual pluralism' and the promotion of a more democratic situation – one based on increasing decentralization and local community participation.

In what follows, we shall attempt to operationalize the co-evolutionary framework by applying its principles to an empirical example – the mining industry in South Yorkshire and more specifically, the region's coalfield communities.

SOUTH YORKSHIRE MINING COMMUNITIES:
A CASE STUDY

The insights and appraisals we present were constructed following a series of qualitative interviews conducted between the months of July and November 2002. A total of 41 men who worked in the mining industry for varying periods of time were interviewed, according to a semi-structured interview format designed to cover the many assumptions that persist concerning the closure of the mines across South Yorkshire and the subsequent effects upon local mining communities. Coupled with a review of the literature surrounding mining and the development of coalfield communities, the results of the interviews form the main subject base from which the findings, understanding and subsequent inferences regarding the nature of resilience and the ever-changing co-evolutionary process within these traditional social networks are made.

As well as providing a useful taxonomy for conceptualizing different patterns of change-related behaviour displayed by industrial systems, the distinction between engineering and ecological resilience is also significant in applying the concept to the case of former South Yorkshire mining communities, which, given their historical, geographical, economic and cultural independence can be viewed as both highly specialized and identifiable social systems. Keeping in mind the non-neutrality of human systems (the role of agency), it is argued that these regionally-specific human systems can be characterized by, and modelled as a rigid, hierarchical and stable form of *engineering* resilience, similar to that which has been observed in the local industrial dynamic with which the workers were strongly synonymous. Despite the widespread disappearance of the industrial networks upon which communities were formed, the social structure and cultural processes remain largely unchanged and a sub-optimal, though belligerently stable organization persists. This idea is captured by Warwick and Littlejohn (1992, p. 7):

> Our approach will parallel that of recent sociological work which has stressed, despite predictions of their demise under the impact of social change, the continuity of traditional social networks – based on kinship, friendship and neighbourliness in household and community settings. Repeatedly our data point to the significance of such networks as bases of continuity and as resources to be drawn upon in a period of change. (p. xii)

This resource similar to social capital, has been termed 'local cultural capital' by the authors, in acknowledgement of its importance to these post-industrial localities in supporting the longevity of local values, identity, structure and ideology. Somewhat paradoxically, while from a historical perspective these ideas were crucial to the integrity and survival of such isolated systems, the strength of these structures was ultimately responsible for the prevailing inertia and reluctance to consign old knowledge in favour of the new ideas introduced by the changing environment. Without criticism of its purpose, this influence and the social networks in which it resides, should be understood as a significant driving force behind insufficient resilience, and consequently non-adaptation in the region's coalfield areas. Indeed, very little evidence of an adaptive and more fluid form of resilience can be cited following research into these systems given, amongst other indications, persistently high levels of unemployment coupled with chronically low levels of new knowledge and retraining acquisition.

Further evidence of this conscious reluctance to accommodate and adapt to changes in the system's environment and thus to thwart the natural course of evolution can be outlined systematically through an application of the proposed co-evolutionary framework. Each of the model's domains are discussed in turn with reference to the case study, while keeping in mind the interconnectedness (through self-organized dynamics) and feedback effects which continually shape the essence of each process and the degree of influence on the overall nature of change experienced by the system. The way in which these processes interact and affect both the structure of the system and its evolutionary trajectory is then outlined more explicitly with reference to Figure 6.3.

Social Organization

The process of social organization must be understood in relation to the reciprocal influence of many processes, though we shall argue that the most significant of these is that of *values*, viewed here as a common solidarity between workers and a bond that stems to form a social capital, common culture, shared risks, kinship and camaraderie. Little evidence exists for the claim that despite a more or less unified local understanding or schema, an even distribution of capital (economic or social) has ever really existed. In fact a clear hierarchy was observed in mining communities across the country: 'The whole ethos of mining communities was a respect for social order, even a respect for those in the local social hierarchy' (Turner 2000).

The question of power is addressed in relation to agency and resources, though more in reference to organizational influence. The social organization of coalfield communities was historically determined by mine owners who both built and rented out dwellings to their workforce, even employing 'Knocker Uppers' to govern the time at which each miner would rise for work. From such early productivity-driven bases of social connectivity and interaction, followed political and ideological commonalities. It was from these networks that we see the emergence of incipient union organizations representing a new form of agency with control over authoritative resources as previously described although as with the industry for which its members worked, a clear hierarchy was to develop.

Monoculture

Mines were created where accessible seams of coal had been located. Shafts were sunk, workers recruited, and a village to house these miners built. New communities were created that had but a single reason for existence. Despite an uneven distribution of capital, there was a pattern of monoculture in all the lives of those connected to mining.

> There is nowhere else like the coalfields. Their long history as the engine of the nation's industrialization meant that they developed a cohesion, a reliance on a single industry and an independent existence with few parallels. This was their greatest strength when the mines were producing and now it is their greatest weakness. (DETR 1999, p. 1)

This situation was confounded once the pits were brought into public ownership under the auspices of the NCB in 1947. The local ethos and way of life became unified at a national level. Now all those living in mining villages owed their livelihood to the one employer, the 'Board'. One body, the Union, represented their interests. Miners communicated only with other miners or those connected with mining and lived in distinct communities where it was automatic to reinforce the self-esteem of the community; an esteem fuelled by social capital, the nature of their work and the skills needed, as well as the comparatively high levels of remuneration. This outlook inhibited resilience and the ability for social structures to accommodate change, and the end, when it came, was therefore all the more shattering. It was not just jobs that went, but a way of life for an entire community.

> People did have a regular source of a reasonable income. There were structures in place which bolstered that stability: family and friendship ties; the union; the fact that you could nearly always get a job, if you wanted one. When the coal industry was closed down, that stability was destroyed. Once redundancy monies were spent, incomes dried up. Mining villages were not the kind of places to attract inward investment and, at least in West and South Yorkshire, not places where there had been a high emphasis on education. (Turner 2000, p. 1)

With the destruction, not only of jobs, but more importantly the destruction of their communities, miners were being asked – and were expected –

to embrace a whole ethos that was diametrically opposed to that which had served them well for generations:

> But it was an unquantifiable spirit that held these places together. A spirit which had developed over generations, based on collectivism, kinship, advancement by co-operation rather than individuality. The social institutions that characterized the places were all symbolic of that: the Co-op; the miners' welfare; the club trip; the union. The spirit that those trying to foster an 'enterprise culture', where the engine was individual effort and the motivation was individual gain, [was] never quite understood. (Turner 2000, p. 4)

Values

Values are held to be of critical importance in understanding the very fabric of social identity, group appraisals and consequent behaviour. In fact, in discussing this integral concept, a knowledge of this identity common to the subject group is necessary, in that it is seen to underpin both the creation and development of a community's value set, with direct consequences for social organization. A reciprocal influence develops between these two processes later in the system's evolution; a connection which constrained resilience and remains as a barrier to adaptation (Figure 6.3).

> Your life was a particular way because you were a miner, or because you were married to a miner. It influenced every thing you did. You were in a trade union because you were a miner; you drank in particular places because you were a miner, you married particular people because you were a miner. (Turner 2000, p. 65)

The strength of values and identities meant that historically such networks were not subjected to change, thereby resisting social or economic diversity. The ex-miners interviewed in our research displayed a very strong family tradition of employment in the mining industry with 40 (97.6 per cent) reporting an average of three generations of their family having worked in mining. The closure of the mines meant not only a loss of jobs but also a loss of identity and a loss of structure and meaning to their lives. In general, in a society where identity is largely defined by what we do, the unemployed are defined by what they are not – or at least, not any more (Kelvin and Jarrett 1985, p. 45). Moreover, take away the prospect of re-employment in the field that the person has been operating in and this sense of identity is further eroded. To put it more colloquially, 'they just don't know who they are anymore' (Marsden 1982, p. 155).

> They [the Government & Coal Board] never thought what it would be like for someone who had worked in a totally different environment for 25 years and that they [miners] would be like a fish out of water. [JT: Case 41]

In the case of the mining communities, this process does not happen in isolation but as a part of the wider disintegration of the community. The single structures (Coal Board, NUM) that provided a framework for individual and community identity and values have gone, though these concepts and beliefs remain. Faced with this, it is not surprising that the 'fortress mentality' (Rees and Thomas 1991) should become a more likely behavioural mode than one of risk-taking entrepreneurship, or one of embracing new (and strange) challenges in new work environments in new locations.

It becomes clear that the physical conditions in which miners worked are of great relevance in understanding both the creation and resilience of certain sets of values.

> The danger . . . was all part and parcel of the job, and we accepted the danger and in some ways it made you special. Nobody can be a proper miner unless they're born into the community. It's something in the blood. [SB: Case 4]

> When you first start you need to soon get a really close group of friends. It's the camaraderie and the thing that you're all in it together; it's like the wartime spirit, like the armed forces. [NM: Case 5]

In addition to this the necessity of a mutual dependency and behavioural predictability in order to minimize risk of injury, has meant that any notion of enterprise or 'maverick' behaviour was intensely discouraged and has led to an under-developed sense of individual enterprise. The nature of mining work and the pressures experienced in such an environment led to what has been described in the interviews as an overwhelming sense of 'camaraderie'. Others spoke of the intense bond extending to communities, though with hindsight they sensed it was not an outlook suited to change. The sense of solidarity vital in pit work has made it more difficult for miners to adjust to post-pit employment opportunities.

> As they were close knit, they were united, and all the very positive things, that close knitness and unitedness has ended up pulling them down. I think they'd be better ripping out communities completely, rather than letting them fester and die. Split 'em up. If you've got close knit, but it's all destructive at moment, or seems to be. . . . [MG: Case 25]

The consequences for those who were perceived to have contravened this collectivist obligation to social cohesion were dire and social exclusion inevitably followed. For those men who were unwilling, even unable to continue with strike action, no degree of compassion was shown:

> We all stuck together, all looked out for each other, except when strike come, after strike, that did split a lot of people and communities. If you went back to

work, you had to move house, else your windows would be through every night. [PD: Case 18]

The development of both implicit social support networks as well as a very explicitly recognized union upholding the common value set, is perhaps an unsurprising event in the system's evolution when we take into consideration the historic struggle for power over resources and the huge number of workers who felt disadvantaged. As with any process however, its state is not continual nor can simple linear causalities be observed. This has important consequences for regeneration initiatives which do not acknowledge the significance of a community's values in responding to alternative employment. Many of the belief systems and social codes of conduct akin to the miners' former sense of proud identity remain, despite the industry's collapse and the social discipline exerted by the union no longer being present.

Knowledge

Highly specialized knowledge of the industry and extraction process is developed over a great number of years. Such skills are not by and large transferable to any other industry or line of work.

> I think that there are a lot of miners who will never have a chance because they can't retrain to do anything else, you put a shovel in their hands, they were bloody good, but they can't be bricklayers, they can't be plasterers, they can't do jobs that require fine skills. The people who are capable of being retrained have started into an industry, ten or fifteen years behind the people who are already in that industry. [NM: Case 5]

> Skills what you did down pit wouldn't be any good anywhere else . . . apart from digging holes in road or something like laying cables where you're doing manual work. Did a lot of manual work down pit. I don't know what kind of training. [Pause]. Mining's unique isn't it? [AG: Case 9]

The problem is confounded by the fact that large numbers of ex-miners who have failed to secure alternative work commonly fail to express a desire to acquire new knowledge. In the course of our interviews, a reluctance to retrain was reported, many interviewees seeming resigned to unemployment:

> When it's a 6 month course, you're not going to learn a great deal. I mean, you can't go on a course and then 6 months later, say, 'I'm a plumber, I'm an electrician', it just don't work out does it? [RD: Case 19]

When asked how helpful the various agencies involved in retraining have proven to be, the most common response (n=16, 39 per cent) was that they had no contact. Of those who did report some experience of such agencies, the majority described them as being unhelpful. Similarly the number of subjects reporting that they had received no retraining (from agencies or elsewhere) since leaving the mining industry is higher than those who reported experience of retraining (n=23, 56.1 per cent).

It should be made clear that the observed reluctance to retrain is by no means due to a lack of ability on the part of former miners. Moreover, it appears to be the unsuitable nature of the retraining that was offered, rather than the principle of retraining which may be held more accountable for low levels of uptake.

> Yes, they need better direction in what would be the best job for them. Miners were consistently underestimated, I was underestimated, and I therefore under-estimated myself. There was a lot of clever lads down the pit, a lot cleverer than me, and I see these lads now and I don't feel that society has harnessed their ability, they've got to be encouraged to go for it. [SB: Case 4]

Consideration however, must be given to the lack of emphasis on education prevalent in a great number of mining communities. Academic attainment had never been a high priority for those whose working destiny was the coalface. Low levels of education were indeed observed in the subject group with 24 (58.5 per cent) of those interviewed reporting that they had no educational qualifications. The NCB introduced exemplary apprenticeship schemes that were generally regarded as providing a bench-mark level for other heavy industry sectors to emulate. These schemes commonly included subject areas, basic literacy and numeracy for example, that lay more in the province of schools rather than that of employers. In a sense therefore, and no doubt introduced through necessity, the 'Board' rein-forced the idea prevalent in mining communities that school education was less important. School children from these communities would leave at the earliest opportunity. The boys especially would then go to the mine and learn a trade.

On an industrial level, a failure to monitor stocks of knowledge, other than those directly related to production and optimization, meant that change in any relation to its eventual true scale and nature, was largely unpredicted and entirely unprepared for.

Agency

The role of agency is clear when considering former mining communities given the strong boundaries kept in place by staunch loyalty to the union and solidarity between miners. The most notable groups included the NUM, regional mine management bodies (National Coal Board, NCB)

and government. Following nationalization of the industry, the government and the appointed NCB are considered to be almost synonymous,
just as the NUM is with the huge majority of miners. These two regularly
opposing agents are by far the most significant to our case. In focusing on
the most wide-reaching and purposive human intervention, Thatcher's
government proved to be the most significant agency in bringing about the
industry's rapid decline. Conversely, in looking further at the application
of 'means' to achieve 'outcomes', the 1984 national miners' strike called by
the NUM is noted as an enormous undertaking given its breadth, commitment and duration.

> There can be little doubt that coal mining and coal miners played a central role in
> helping to shape the economic, social and political landscape of Britain in the
> industrial age. This was still the case just 25 years ago, when the miners' strike
> and the three-day week demonstrated not only the industrial power that they
> held, but the pivotal contribution that the coal industry made to the national
> economy and to prosperity in general. (Gore *et al.* 2000, p. 18)

The following section on resources gives some notion of the power the
NUM were able to exercise over miners, coalfield communities and the
NCB alike. 'The union was part of the social structure. It was part of your
life, day-in, day-out.' (Turner 2000, p. 141).

When analysing the process of agency in relation to our case study, it
becomes clear that the union exerted considerable power over the structure
and boundaries of social networks. The strength the union held was
regarded by some to have been detrimental to individuals and to have kept
many from being offered work. Post-strike however, the might of the union
fell, in line with huge numbers of its members being made redundant. The
contraction of a formerly dominant power reflecting their common interest
has proven very difficult to accept and of those left in the industry, union
membership is no longer assumed.

> We've got about two hundred men on site, nearly half of them are in the Union.
> The others are either keeping their head down because they're frightened of site,
> or because they think that the Union is ineffective, partly because we haven't got
> recognition, but we haven't recognition because them daft buggers won't join
> the Union. There's a big difference, the power that we had before is gone. [DD:
> Case 2]

Resources

Since the very beginning of the industry an inadequate relationship
has existed between allocative and authoritative resources. Upon the discovery of a great abundance of coal seams within the region it was the

landowners who were to capitalize on this allocative natural resource very early on in the industry's development, with (in the absence of workers' unions, safety or employment legislation) seemingly endless amounts of money to be made. Mines were then bought and the resources to extract the coal more efficiently developed by the new mine owners/companies and much later the coal board and government, post-nationalization in 1947. As acknowledged, control over authoritative resources, that is social inter-actions and to a large degree, behaviour, has been largely exercised by the NUM since its beginnings (as the Miners' Federation of Great Britain, MFGB) in the late 19th century. By 1908 the membership of the MFGB was over 600 000, giving the MFGB tremendous strength as the organiza-tion represented over a quarter of all trade unionists in Britain. The MFGB became the National Union of Mineworkers (NUM) on 1 January 1945, retaining a membership of 533 000.

The relationship between the coal and the communities coincides strongly with the processes involved in agency, most notably the distinction between power 'over' and power 'to'. Further to this, an important consid-eration has to be the politics and ideologies of the agents involved. An almost inevitable breakdown in relations came about when the right-wing government, preoccupied with 'market forces' came up against the will of a left-wing union stubbornly resistant to change. The union's power 'over' the social networks, interaction and behaviour of miners and their commun-ities became obsolete when the power 'to' deindustrialize was exercised.

UNDERSTANDING INDUSTRIAL AND SOCIETAL TRANSFORMATION: AN APPLICATION OF THE MODEL

Having outlined the nature of each of the co-evolutionary processes detailed within the framework in relation to our case study, the specific transformations each locus of processes undergoes needs to be made more explicit. In applying the framework to the socio-economic system of the South Yorkshire coalfield, we provide a real world example of how histor-ical events interact in unplanned and unpredictable ways leading to irre-versible historical outcomes.

Figure 6.3 highlights the way in which self-organizing processes act to generate the system's evolutionary character. Four periods in time have been selected to show how the sequence of asymmetric topologies can be used to demonstrate self-organization. In attempting to model the non-linear relationships, the size and tone of each process is representative of its influence in shaping the evolution of the mining and community systems

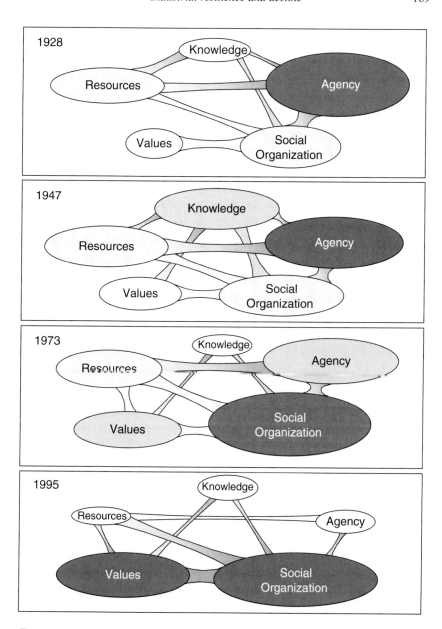

Figure 6.3   Historical patterns of mutual interaction

as a whole. The stretched links symbolize the strength of connection and the different sizes represent the specific nature and pattern of influence. As previously stated, the connectivities involved are periodically weak and strong as expansion and contraction is continually occurring.

1920 marked the decade which saw the height of employment in the UK coal industry with 1.25 million miners working in many hundreds of privately owned enterprises across the country (Church and Outram 1998). Conscious human intervention in this period is seen to be the main catalyst to the development of both industrial and social systems, as agency and resources (primarily allocative) determine both the organization of coalfield communities (built around seams with the sole purpose of aiding in the extraction process by maintaining an on-site workforce) and knowledge acquisition, as mine owners were able to fully dictate the conditions of employment. A sense of values and common identity is growing in strength yet remains in development at this time, as many of the workers employed by the mines were drawn from different parts of Britain (Taylor 2001). The main governing union of the time, the MFGB, though large in terms of membership, was yet to become a significant force of agency. The developing social organization and the nature of work did, however, mean that knowledge was shared and some level of mechanization followed from technological development implemented. This evolving social organization initiated by powerful agents would continue to influence the growth of a value set, culture and social identity that persist today.

At the time of nationalization in 1947, 147 NCB collieries were in full production in the county, less than half of the 450 which had existed at the turn of the 20th century (Taylor 2001). The impetus to nationalize in the Labour Party's first term of post-war government came from a desire to achieve economies of large scale production. Huge investments were made in implementing technologies to increase the efficiency of the industrial process. Nationalization however, did not appear to significantly reduce the high number of local strikes which would continue for another two decades, and labour relations remained strained. Value processes developed strongly over this period and a collectivist identity emerged. This began to have an enormous effect on the social and economic evolution of the system as a whole, as strong unions and political and ideological organizations grew in line with common aspiration. Values and identity influenced resources as the NUM exercised authoritative control over aspects of social organization and behaviour, in turn becoming significant to the diversity of processes involved in agency as a new power 'over' the workforce is formed.

As the NUM was able to exert greater influence on social networks (from which it grew), their power spread to govern social conduct and influenced identity throughout the region's pit villages. Resources as a process not only included this authoritative power 'over' the workforce, but in exercising this, the union was able to demonstrate an allocative power 'to' control the most significant means of production in what remained a labour intensive industry. This strength was to be demonstrated by mass strike action and the eventual defeat of the 1973 Heath Conservative Government. Now coal became a political issue. The source of power for the nation became seen as a struggle for power *over* the nation.

It was Margaret Thatcher in her second government (1983–1987) who felt confident enough to take on the perceived might of the NUM. Just as Heath had been fatally weakened in his struggle against the miners by international events outside his control (the arbitrary raising of oil prices by the OPEC cartel), so Thatcher's strategy was helped by external events in the emergence of alternative power sources, primarily the increasing flows from the North Sea oil and gas fields, and the sourcing of cheaper coal supplies from Eastern Europe. The near terminal contraction of the industry came with a series of pit closures in the 1980s and early 1990s. The scale of this decline may be judged by the fact that in 1981 there were 211 operational collieries in Britain; this has shrunk to 14 (Figure 6.4) and several of these are currently under threat. Over the same period, the number employed in the industry fell from 279 000 to fewer than 7000 (Gore *et al.* 2000, p. 18) (Figure 6.5).

Given the dramatic reduction in the number of collieries remaining in operation in the region coupled with dwindling union membership, previously strong processes of agency and resources exhibit a greatly reduced significance by 1995. Values and social organization became the most dominant processes behind the system's structure and evolutionary character, coupled with a common reluctance to consign old knowledge in favour of new learning. As previously outlined, this inability to incorporate change and perturbation inhibits system resilience and adaptive propensity, a situation which remains today in many of the more isolated coalfields. History, it seems, had become an inhibitor to change. Their culture, evolved over more than a century, meant that even when it became clear that alternative fuel sources, smoke free zones, financial restraints, production costs, market forces and inflation would all contribute to an eventual progressive decline (this had been happening since the turn of the century even throughout nationalization), miners still neglected to seek new skills, retrain or contemplate changes in employment, location or lifestyle.

In applying our co-evolutionary model we are able to visualize complex nonlinear interaction as opposed to the tendency to look for simple cause and effect in analysing collapse. Further, the true significance of historical events and transformations to the continuing evolution of the system is

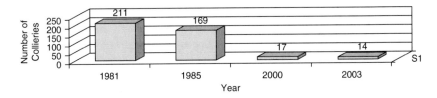

Source: Gore *et al*. 2000

Figure 6.4   Number of collieries in Britain

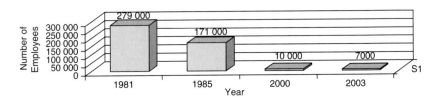

Source: Gore *et al*. 2000

Figure 6.5   Employment figures for the British coal industry

more fully understood. There is a pressing need to develop such models in advocating a more holistic approach.

CONCLUSION: RESILIENCE, COMPLEXITY AND ADAPTIVE MANAGEMENT

What the foregoing discussion demonstrates is that the degree of system collapse and the inability to effect sustainable strategies for transformation, effectively condemned the South Yorkshire coalfield to a type of slow death. Local communities were caught in an ever downward spiral, as they appeared powerless to cope with the changing circumstances brought by alternative sources of energy and the threats posed by an increasingly competitive global marketplace. This failure to absorb change as we have seen was essentially a failure of system resilience; that is, the degree to which system structure is capable of self-repair and internal self-organization of its constituent parts. Crucially, we can see that the mining industry in this region lacked sufficient institutional flexibility to anticipate and combat changes wrought by a rapidly shifting political and economic landscape. In many ways the South Yorkshire coalfield was a prisoner of its own history – a history of success that had locked it on to a rigid set of knowledge structures and values. In fact, the tight grip exerted by social and cultural traditions that had formerly provided the core values of community spirit and collective solidarity was to become an obstacle and ultimately a source of inaction. Thus, during the long slow decline from the 1970s to the 1990s, it was this inertia inherent in the system and its attempts to deny the reality of changing economic and social conditions that worked against the establishment of new ideas and/or learning opportunities.

But perhaps the worst failure was the system's inability to manage change, to anticipate likely futures (however unpalatable), that was to signal the death knell of the industry. It is this ability to manage under conditions of uncertainty and to create flexible planning strategies – those designed to withstand the impact of unintended consequences – that is the hallmark of system resilience. The demise of the South Yorkshire coalfield provides us with a spectacular example of the consequences of the loss of system resilience coupled with a linear and blinkered view of the future. From a management point of view it is above all a failure to understand that the mining industry, as with any socio-economic system, must out of necessity be viewed as a complex nonlinear system, one that is characteristically far from equilibrium and hence prone to the irruption of unanticipated, emergent outcomes. The message of complexity theory is that under such circumstances the ability to make future predictions is severely compromised. By contrast, the prevailing wisdom in the mining industry seemed to be based on a 'knowable' future – one in which there would always be a market for coal, and consequently there would always be a need for a coal industry.

What we have stressed is that while industrial decline is an exceedingly complex problem with multiple causes, it is clear that from a management perspective there has been a failure to acknowledge the importance of long-term strategic thinking. Planning has been characteristically short-termist, and decisions have frequently been retroactive; that is, they have been concerned with 'sticking plaster' or coping solutions, rather than the implementation of long-term adaptive management strategies. By contrast, what we have attempted to argue here is that successful adaptive management requires a more holistic reading of socio-economic systems and this can best be found in the adoption of a co-evolutionary perspective, one that recognizes the centrality of institutional flexibility and change. Herein lies the basis of system resilience and long-term survival.

By way of conclusion, this chapter has provided a real-world example of growth and decline dynamics emphasizing the importance of co-evolutionary approaches over conventional scientific methodologies and particularly the importance of a holistic approach to unravel the complex evolutionary behaviour of socio-economic systems. Significantly, our research has identified certain value-laden facets of society so deeply entrenched as to be apparently immovable. What this suggests is that in all probability it will take generations before fundamental changes begin to emerge. Findings suggest that if we are unable to influence processes involved at the level of a community's value system, then we may be powerless to effect real system change, and hence our ability to effect the knowledge-flows which generate resilience will be severely compromised. Societal systems that fail to incorporate change as an intrinsic aspect of system growth and to incorporate this within management policy are in real danger of collapse. Moreover, our study has provided a prime example of the way that historical path-dependent processes can act as a barrier to the acceptance of change; that is, the historically situated attitudes and identities within the industry created a type of 'lock-in' preventing the assimilation of novel ideas and practices. The inward-looking, inertial processes that accompany such a philosophy can only lead to atrophy and the type of economic marginalization experienced by the British coal industry as it struggled to retain its relevance in the face of a rapidly changing economic landscape. Finally, what our discussion underlines above all, is the crucial need for a long-term perspective as the basis for understanding any evolutionary dynamic and with it an acknowledgement of the central role played by history in creating the enabling and constraining conditions within which socio-economic systems co-evolve.

NOTE

1.   This is consistent with Alain Touraine's (1977) argument when he states that understanding human societies from an evolutionary perspective is not just about production per se, but more importantly, the process of self-production.

REFERENCES

Allen, Timothy F.H. and Thomas B. Starr (1982), *Hierarchy: Perspectives for Ecological Complexity*, Chicago: University of Chicago Press.
Arthur, W. Brian (1989), 'Competing technologies, increasing returns and lock-in by historical events', *Economic Journal*, **99**, 116–31.
Berkes, Fikret and Carl Folke (1998), *Linking Ecological and Social Systems*, Cambridge: Cambridge University Press.
Church, Roy A. and Quentin Outram (1998), *Strikes and Solidarity: Coalfield Conflict in Britain, 1889–1966*, Cambridge: Cambridge University Press.
Critcher, Chas, Klaus Schubert and David Waddington (eds) (1995), *Regeneration of the Coalfield Areas: Anglo-German Perspectives*, London: Pinter.

De Angelis, Donald L., Wilfred M. Post and Curtis C. Travis (1980), *Positive Feedback in Natural Systems*, New York: Springer-Verlag.

DETR (1999), *Making the Difference: A New Start for England's Coalfield Communities*, London: DETR Publications.

Dublin, Henry T., Alan R.E. Sinclair and Jacqueline M. McGlade (1990), 'Elephants and fire as causes of multiple stable states in the Serengeti-Mara woodlands', *Journal of Animal Ecology*, **59**, 1147–64.

Faucheux, Sylvie, Martin O'Connor and Jan van der Straaten (eds) (1998), *Sustainable Development: Concepts, Rationalities and Strategies*, Dordrecht: Kluwer.

Giddens, Anthony (1979), *Central Problems in Social Theory*, London: Macmillan.

Giddens, Anthony (1984), *The Constitution of Society*, Cambridge: Polity Press.

Gore, Tony, Gordon Dabinett and Jonathan Breeze (2000), *Improving Lottery Funding Access and Delivery in the British Coalfield: Coalfields and Lottery Study Phase II. An Independent Report to the Department for Culture, Media and Sport and Lottery Funding Bodies*, London: Department for Culture, Media and Sport.

Gunderson, Lance H., Crawford S. Holling and Stephen S. Light (eds) (1995), *Barriers and Bridges to the Renewal of Ecosystems and Institutions*, New York: Columbia University Press.

Günther, Folke and Carl Folke (1993), 'Characteristics of nested living systems', *Journal of Biological Systems*, **1**, 257–74.

Holling, C.S. (1973), 'Resilience and stability in ecological systems', *Annual Review of Ecology and Systematics*, **4**, 2–23.

Holling, Crawford S. (1986), 'The resilience of ecosystems: local surprise and global change', in William C. Clark and Robert E. Munn (eds), *Sustainable Development of the Biosphere*, Cambridge: Cambridge University Press, pp. 292–317.

Holling, Crawford S., Dixon D. Jones and William C. Clark (1977), 'Ecological policy design: a case study of forest and pest management', in Geoffrey A. Norton and Crawford S. Holling (eds), *Proceedings of a Conference on Pest Management, October 1976*, pp. 13–90.

Kelvin, Peter and Joanna E. Jarrett (1985), *Unemployment: Its social psychological effects*, Cambridge: Cambridge University Press.

Marsden, Dennis (1982), *Workless: An Exploration of the Social Contract Between Society and the Worker*, London: Croom Helm.

McGlade, J. (1995), 'Archaeology and the ecodynamics of human-modified landscapes', *Antiquity*, **69**, 113–32.

McGlade, James (1999a), 'Archaeology and the evolution of cultural landscapes: towards an interdisciplinary research agenda', in Robert Layton and Peter J. Ucko (eds), *Anthropological and Archaeological Approaches to Landscape*, London: Routledge.

McGlade, James (1999b), 'The times of history: archaeology, narrative and nonlinear causality', in Tim Murray (ed.), *Time and Archaeology*, London: Routledge, pp. 139–63.

McGlade, James (2002), *Landscape Sensitivity, Resilience and Sustainable Management: A Coevolutionary Approach*, AQUADAPT discussion document, Montpellier, 24–26 October.

Norgaard, Richard B. (1984), 'Coevolutionary development potential', *Land Economics*, **60**, 160–73.

Norgaard, Richard B. (1994), *Development Betrayed: The End of Progress and A Coevolutionary Revisioning of the Future*, London: Routledge.

O'Neill, Robert V., Donald L. De Angelis, Jack B. Waide and Timothy F.H. Allen (1986), *A Hierarchical Concept of Ecosystem*, Princeton, NJ: Princeton University Press.

Peterson, Gary (2000), 'Political ecology and ecological resilience: an integration of human and ecological dynamics', *Ecological Economics*, **35**, 323–36.

Pimm, Stuart L. (1984), *The Balance of Nature*, Chicago, IL: University of Chicago Press.

Rees, Gareth and M. Thomas (1991), 'From coalminers to entrepreneurs? A case study in re-industrialisation', in Malcolm Cross and Geoff Payne (eds), *Work and the Enterprise Culture*, London: Falmer.

Schubert, Klaus and M. Bräutigam (1995), 'Coal policy in Germany', in Chas Critcher, Klaus Schubert and David Waddington (eds), *Regeneration of the Coalfield Areas: Anglo-German Perspectives*, London: Pinter.

Sinclair, A.R.E., P.D. Olsen and T.D. Redhead (1990), 'Can predators regulate small mammal populations? Evidence from house mouse outbreaks in Australia', *Oikos*, **59**, 382–92.

Tainter, Joseph A. (1988), *The Collapse of Complex Societies*, Cambridge: Cambridge University Press.

Taylor, Warwick (2001), *South Yorkshire Pits*, Barnsley: Wharncliffe Books.

Tilman, D. and J.A. Downing (1994), 'Biodiversity and stability in grasslands', *Nature*, **367**, 363–5.

Touraine, Alain (1977), 'Science, intellectuals and politics', *Scientific-Technological Revolution: Social Aspects. 8th World Congress of Sociology*, London: Sage.

Turner, Royce (2000), *Coal Was Our Life: An Essay on Life in a Yorkshire Former Pit Town*, Sheffield: Sheffield Hallam University Press.

van der Leeuw, Sander E. and James McGlade (eds) (1997), *Time, Process and Structured Transformation in Archaeology*, London: Routledge.

Walker, Brian H., Donald Ludwig, Crawford S. Holling and Richard M. Peterman (1981), 'Stability of semi-arid grazing systems', *Journal of Ecology*, **69**, 473–98.

Walters, Carl J. (1986), *Adaptive Management of Renewable Resources*, New York: Macmillan.

Warwick, Dennis and Gary Littlejohn (1992), *Coal, Capital and Culture: A Sociological Analysis of Mining Communities in West Yorkshire*, London: Routledge.

7. Diversity and uniformity in the evolution of early information and communication technologies

Elizabeth Garnsey, Paul Heffernan and Simon Ford

INTRODUCTION

The creation of novel forms and the effects of their subsequent selection or elimination is a central theme in complexity studies. Complex processes are at work whenever their outcomes impact on further activity in iterations that generate recurrent feedback processes. 'Evolutionary processes' are not simply a biological metaphor applied outside the natural world; they refer to a distinctive mode of transformation in arenas that include the evolution of languages, the development of scientific knowledge and the advance of technologies. There are common processes at work involving the generation of variety, the operation of selection forces and the propagation of selected variants, though these are manifest in distinctive ways in different arenas. Natural variety is generated through random genetic mutation and combination, blind to selection forces. But in the economy, intelligent agents can anticipate the rewards and sanctions exerted by selection forces and so experience incentives to respond to them.[1] Consumer demand, the allocation of investment, and competition have operated as selection forces shaping the advance of information technologies in recent years.

The questions addressed here concern diversity creation and standardization in information and communication technologies. The virtues of diversity are extolled in evolutionary economics and complexity studies for their capacity to generate new solutions and a richer economic habitat, but in many ways our world is becoming increasingly homogenized. What are the constraints on diversity? A co-evolutionary perspective throws light on the limitations of diversity in an arena that has wrought transformations by generating new forms of diversity. In Darwinian theory, sources of variation are independent of the selection that occurs through the elimination of non-adaptive variants. But in the evolution of technologies there are close linkages between the selection and generation of variants and their propagation. While in natural systems the generation of variety is random and blind, in social systems learning takes place and variety creation is guided by desired outcomes in the light of what has been learned about selection processes. We will see that uncertainty as to outcomes encourages a variety of responses, but also promotes forms of standardization. We conclude that some uncertainty reduction through policy and institutions may be needed to provide the incentives for the renewal of diversity.

It is increasingly recognized that co-evolution operates as a meta-evolutionary process in which the interaction of participants contributes to the collective creation of a habitat that shapes their prospects (Goodwin 1994). Co-evolution is the collective outcome of responses (whether or not intentional) and feedback effects that accommodate other participants in the system. Selected forms of mutual accommodation or symbiosis can occur without intentionality when blind accommodating responses are rewarded by survival, as where fitness rewarded by natural selection depends on capacity to fit into a co-evolving ecosystem.

The linkages between evolutionary mechanisms in the emergence of new technologies are here explored through examples in semiconductors, personal computers and electronic messaging. In these sectors, new ventures have been the agents of variety creation, as they were in the introduction of the telephone, the electric light, radio broadcasting, photocopying and bio-synthesized medical entities (Nairn 2002; McKelvey 1996). An evolutionary perspective throws light on why under-resourced newcomers are able to generate innovations overlooked by established players. We pursue three further questions about evolutionary mechanisms in connection with ICT innovations.

1. What were the origins of the knowledge exploited by entrepreneurial ventures to produce innovations?
2. What were the mechanisms connecting *variety generation* and *selection processes* in the evolution of these technologies?
3. What were the mechanisms connecting *selection processes* and the *propagation* of these technologies?

Answers to these questions shed light on unexplored connections between variety generation and variety reduction – diversity and uniformity – as manifested in technological innovations.

A complexity approach is used here to explore how small beginnings led to world-changing developments. The outcomes of evolutionary feedback processes cannot be forecast in any detail in natural or social systems subject to interactive feedback effects. But a complexity perspective can identify common dynamic processes that are not evident from the historical record alone, nor from cross-sectional analysis.

INDUSTRIES AND INNOVATIONS

Co-evolution occurs within an environment made up of producers and users. The conventional definition of industries is in terms of competing producers of classes of products (Barney 1997). When the focus is the characteristic structure of an industry, the unaddressed issues are how industries emerge and are transformed over time. It has been proposed that a new industry consists of competing producer webs or networks: 'a broad group of firms struggling to shape or influence the perceived value, nature, and technique for carrying out a particular activity' (Munir and Phillips 2002, p. 294). According to this perspective, it is not until an emerging technology matures that industries take on their characteristic structure after an early period of producer network activity. But from a complexity perspective, network activity is not confined to producers but extends to user or consumer groups and related organizations including professional organizations and standards bodies. These networks make up ecosystems of related production and consumption (Moore 1996). Production webs are not a transitional feature of emerging industries but persist and change over time as participants interact in an evolving business ecosystem.

In the next section we review the early emergence of the information technology and communications sector. We attempt to trace feedback connections between variety generation, selection and propagation. We go on to examine the swarming of innovations that occurred as the density of complementary technologies increased, and view the boom and slump as a further manifestation of complexity.

Semiconductors: the Integrated Circuit and Central Processing Unit

It was in the R&D laboratory of a successful early entrant to the electricity industry, Bell Laboratories, that the transistor was created in 1947. Constructed from semiconductor materials such as germanium and silicon, the transistor allowed the magnification of electronic impulses. It required less current, generated less heat, and was over fifty times smaller than the vacuum tubes earlier used for this purpose (Wolfe 1983). With US government grants that continued into the Cold War, Bell Labs was funded in some respects like a public sector research institute. Within about five years, transistors were reliable enough for commercial use. They were exploited not by established companies, but by a maverick employee of Bell Labs,

William Shockley, one of the co-inventors of the transistor. Returning to his home town Palo Alto, he set up Shockley Semiconductors in 1955 to pursue opportunities opened up by the transistor.

This was the origin of a swarm of entrepreneurial endeavours that created the semiconductor sector in Silicon Valley, largely through multi-generational spin-outs. Shockley fell out with his employees, who left and started up their own firms. The first spin-out was Fairchild Semiconductors, originally a joint venture, and the first company to work exclusively in silicon. It was by combining a number of transistors, diodes, resistors and capacitors onto a single piece of silicon that Robert Noyce invented the integrated circuit at Fairchild Semiconductors in 1959. Ten years later, Noyce had spun out his own company, Intel, with Gordon Moore. Within two years, Noyce and Moore had developed the 1103 memory chip, the size of two letters in a line of type, each chip containing 4000 transistors.

> At the end of Intel's first year in business, which had been devoted almost exclusively to research, sales totalled less than three thousand dollars and the work force numbered forty-two. In 1972, thanks largely to the 1103 chip, sales were $23.4 million and the work force numbered 1,002. In the next year sales almost tripled, to $66 million, and the work force increased two and a half times, to 2,528. (Wolfe 1983)

Other semiconductor ventures were drawn by these high returns, the numbers fuelled by large numbers of engineers produced by universities in the US and by employee departures to found new start-ups. By 1972 there were 330 semiconductor manufacturing firms in the United States (Freeman 1995, p. 234).

At Intel, Noyce aimed to hire the best people. One of these was Ted Hoff, who had spent over ten years in research at Stanford University when he was invited to join Intel. He designed a microprocessor[2] at Intel in response to a request from a Japanese manufacturer for specially designed chips to be used in their desktop calculators.[3] He packed all the central processing unit (CPU) functions of a minicomputer onto a single chip. At first the Intel marketing team were not convinced of the prospects for the microprocessor because the processing power was viewed as insufficient. But the improved Intel 8080 that came out in 1973 was twenty times faster than the first 4004 chip. Intel's core business was in computer memory, a sector which it dominated despite the numerous firms entering the sector (Grove 1996). It did not at first recognize the importance of the microprocessor, but the miniature size and increasing power of Intel's new products provided the core technology for the microcomputer industry.

The Microcomputer

Digital computers were developed in the 1940s, heavily funded by defence spending at IBM and elsewhere. During the 1960s and 1970s computing facilities became progressively more accessible with the introduction of timeshare systems and minicomputers. However, computers remained complex and expensive until the mid-1970s when the invention of the microprocessor made possible the development of the microcomputer.

The early days of the microcomputer provided new scope for entrepreneurs. The first ideas came largely from amateurs keen to gain access to digital computing. Entrepreneurial ventures experimented to create a variety of kits for these hobbyists, connecting up electronic components to the increasingly powerful chips available from young semiconductor companies. The first commercial microcomputer, the Altair, launched by a small business, MITS, in Albuquerque in 1975 had as its core Intel's 8-bit 8080 microprocessor. Hobbyist user groups supplied ideas for applications, such as games, music, databases and personal accounting. Small third party suppliers sprung up to provide software and add-ons. A compiler for the BASIC computer language was provided by young drop-outs from Harvard, Bill Gates and Paul Allen. Demand for the Altair outstripped supply and imitations were soon available based on the S-100 bus architecture and CP/M operating system of the Altair. New ventures, drawn to the emerging market, were experimenting with alternative designs and by 1977 a number of improved products were available, including the Commodore PET, Tandy TRS-80 and Apple II, each using their own operating systems and a variety of chips (for example Motorola 6800; Zilog Z80). The Apple II, conceived as a consumer product by the young Steve Jobs, attracted customers well beyond the hobbyist market, and sales increased from $750k in 1977, to $983m in 1983. At this early stage, the design of microcomputers included most of the now familiar elements: a microprocessor unit, a keyboard, a storage device and a monitor.

Users fuelled demand for microcomputers. In established computer companies, engineers were ordering their own microcomputers to bypass interaction with the mainframe computers which then dominated the business market. As the 'toy computers' improved their performance, they made inroads into the markets of both mainframe computers and the more recent generation of minicomputers, produced by companies like Digital Equipment Corporation and Wang.[4]

The emerging market also attracted the attention of what was then the world's largest computer manufacturer, IBM. The first IBM Personal Computer (PC), launched in 1981, was innovative in introducing the first 16-bit microprocessor used in a microcomputer, the Intel 8088 chip. IBM's entry into the microcomputer market attracted buyers in the business sector, faithful to its brand. IBM calculated that an open standard would encourage the production of software and IBM-compatible complementary products, enhancing their product. Users and suppliers were ready for a new standard that would allow for variation around a common format. The advent of the IBM PC contributed to the early industry shakeout and closure of many firms with 8-bit products. Apple co-founder Steve Wozniak explained the need for markets to set standards in terms reminiscent of complexity ideas: 'You've got to let end users develop their own standards . . . when a new market evolves like PCs did, there's a period of time when you've got to let the world go in random directions and eventually it will subside because it wants standardization' (Langlois 1992, p. 45).

Apple did not make its proprietary technology available as an open standard.[5] This prevented the pioneer from gaining licensing revenues and creating an alliance of companies using its operating system. In the UK, another pioneer, Acorn Computers, also followed a proprietary strategy, not anticipating that in an industry reliant on complementary products, customers would soon shun a minority system incompatible with the industry standard. After the emergence of a dominant design in the form of the IBM PC, the numbers of exits from the industry exceeded the number of entries, resulting in a fall in producer numbers reminiscent of other complex assembled product industries examined by Utterback (1994).

IBM had not themselves anticipated the widespread imitation of their PC, which they viewed as a provisional product for a small market. The company secured very limited intellectual property for their system. By outsourcing the PC's operating system from Microsoft without requiring an exclusive licence beyond the first 12 months, IBM encouraged other producers to provide peripheral complementary products that enhanced the value of the PC. But they also made it easy for competitors to produce rival products, PC clones, which also worked on Microsoft's operating system using components readily available on the market. The most successful of the companies to introduce PC-compatible models, Compaq (founded in 1982) was soon in direct competition with IBM and achieved revenues of over $1000m by 1987.

In 1987, in an attempt to regain control of the standard, IBM introduced its PS/2 Personal System product range with proprietary logic chips and interface standards. IBM ceased production of its previous PC models, but this only encouraged sales of PC clone makers; Compaq's profits tripled in three months in 1987 as exits from the industry rose. But ultimately, it was not the hardware producers that came to dominate the PC industry;

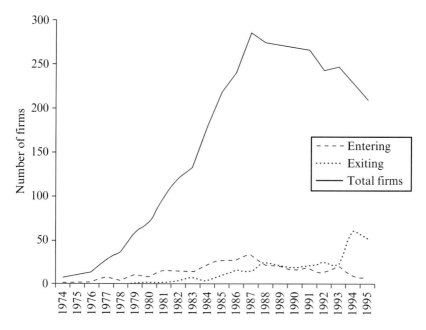

Source: International Data Corporation PC database

Figure 7.1   Entry, exit and total number of firms, PC sector 1974–1995

hardware and software are interconnected and the user experience is more closely associated with software. By 1987, Microsoft's operating system, MS-DOS, was in use in hundreds of cloned products and had become the basis for a multitude of other software applications. Other companies with operating systems technically superior to MS-DOS found to their cost that the market was locked into MS-DOS. European producers of PCs were soon eliminated in the international market as Figure 7.2 shows for leading UK producers.

Microsoft and Intel emerged from the industry shakedown as the dominant players in the industry. Microsoft had begun as a small supplier, but gained crucial leverage through its partnership with IBM when it was able to license the DOS operating system to PC clone producers. Microsoft's revenues grew with the rapid expansion of the PC market, taking off around 1987, the year when the dominance of the PC was established.

As microcomputers reached a wider range of users, ease of use and accessibility became important factors. The Graphical User Interface (GUI), first demonstrated by Xerox in the mid-1970s, was seen as a way of

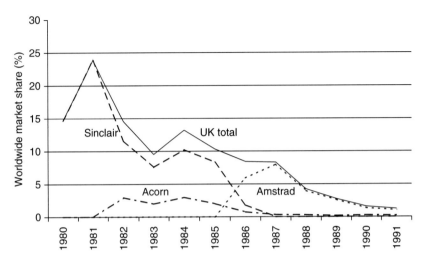

Source: Langlois 1992, pp. 34–35

*Figure 7.2   Worldwide market share of leading UK producers of
microcomputers*

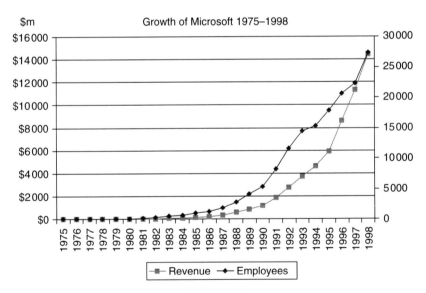

Source: Calculated from Cusumano and Selby 1996

*Figure 7.3   Microsoft's growth took off with the market expansion
of the PC*

facilitating human–computer interaction, and received clear customer endorsement when successfully implemented by Apple. In response to this perceived threat, Microsoft introduced its Windows product in 1985, a graphical front-end to DOS. Maintaining DOS beneath Windows ensured backward compatibility and avoided alienating the established customer base. Though it would be a further five years before Windows could be regarded as a fully functioning GUI, Windows software became a feature of the dominant PC design.

The personal computer industry provided a market for a wide range of components and complementary products. The PC provides an example of diversity reduction (convergence onto a basic product design) giving rise to extensive variety generation around the new standard. More firms entered the industry because they were confident of a market for products compatible with the standard. Thus, even as diversity diminished in the architecture of the PC and its office software, new generations of improvement were made in components and peripherals. For example, DRAM (dynamic random access memory) increased in speed by a factor of 500 between 1975 and 2003, while prices have reduced by a factor of 190 000. Hard disk drives also increased in both speed and capacity while reducing in price, from 5MB and US$2000 in 1980, to 120GB at US$125 in 2003. Meanwhile printers advanced from monochrome dot-matrix models to low cost colour inkjet and laser printers with similar reductions in cost. The rate of change was enshrined in what has come to be known as 'Moore's Law', which has been used since the late 1980s to refer to exponential increases in computing performance.[6] The factors supporting this empirical generalization were complex. Market forces were operative, but US government funding of information technologies and South East Asian government support for their emerging semiconductor industries were enabling factors making possible the massive improvement in the performance and yield of computer chips and increasing miniaturization.

A Critical Transition to Connectivity: Electronic Messaging

By the early 1990s, the computing power of the desktop PC had reached a level achieved by minicomputers and workstations only a decade earlier. Largely as a result of the advances in IT supported by these developments, a critical shift took place in the key attribute of PCs. Improvements in memory and processing speed had become required rather than winning attributes for sales, since competing PC makers used the same semiconductor chip suppliers. It was the connectivity of PCs that provided opportunities for meeting user needs in a new way, leading to the emergence of a new communications sector, electronic messaging.

The standardization of communication protocols was first required for PCs to become the vehicle for a new form of electronic communication. TCP/IP protocols had been developed as part of the US Military's ARPANET, the origin of the Internet.[7] These had become the standard for connecting PCs to local computing system servers and servers to each other. The development of the World Wide Web facilitated Internet usage as it provided a common set of protocols for access and storage of information through the Internet. The Web was made possible by small amounts of European public sector funding at CERN and discretionary time being accorded to one employee, Tim Berners-Lee (Berners-Lee and Fischetti 2000). He saw that uniformity of standards was needed to support new forms of diversity. His entrepreneurial efforts were directed towards social rather than commercial returns. The Web illustrates the unintended impact of public sector funding in enabling work that was required to achieve standards but would not offer a commercial payback.

Once again the role of new entrants in taking up opportunities for this form of variety generation is demonstrated. Lack of insight among newly established players can be observed in the failure of Microsoft and IBM to anticipate the importance of the Internet. As in the case of the microprocessor and the microcomputer, new ventures were the first to seize the new opportunities opened up by the ease of communication between users' microcomputers. Netscape and Cisco Systems were set up by entrepreneurs who transferred technologies that had been developed in universities. Founded in 1994, Netscape's predecessor Mosaic was a spin-out from the government-supported computer science department at Michigan University and pioneered a graphical web browser. Cisco was a spin-out from Stanford based on federally funded LAN research. It provided the servers and routers necessary for large scale PC network infrastructure. Netscape was one of the first companies to base its success on freeware. Nurtured in the 'gift culture' of the government-funded IT community, Netscape's entrepreneurs were among the first to see that propagation might require giving its product away initially and earning returns on enhancements or future related products.

The technology and standards underpinning the Internet and the World Wide Web (WWW) serve as enablers for a wide range of applications, from e-commerce to online gaming. Connectivity extended the use of the PC beyond word and data processing to the provision of a data and communications portal. In the office, more people were using a computer for Internet-based tasks (including e-mail) than for word processing or desktop publishing, and user-to-user contact through electronic messaging proved to be the most common use of the Internet (BLS 2001).

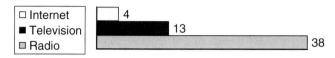

Source: Meeker 1996

Figure 7.4 Time taken to reach 50 million users

After nearly twenty years in which electronic mail had been used by professionals to communicate with each other, PCs in wide use had the computer power, and the Internet infrastructure was in place to make it possible to link users to each other on a massive scale. Pioneering firms experimented with business models aimed at providing this new form of communication from 1993. Influenced by Netscape, Hotmail's entrepreneurs conceived the idea of providing free e-mail accounts on the Internet, thus leaving users to set up their own account with Internet Service Providers and reducing Hotmail's costs to the point where, with revenue from advertisers, they could provide a free service. By 1997, 400 further new entrants swarmed into the sector as participants in the Internet boom of the late 1990s (Hugo and Garnsey 2002).

Established companies did not initially detect that the Internet had commercial potential as significant, if not more so, as hardware and applications for isolated PCs.[8] But the expansion of e-mail communication was unprecedented. Between 1993 and 1997 use expanded to reach a reputed 50 million. Hotmail alone acquired 7 million users between 1996 and 1997.

As soon as the success of the Internet pioneers came into view, Microsoft was quick to engage in Schumpeterian imitation, pursuing its policy of acquiring new entrants with promising technologies. The best known was Hotmail, acquired for $400m in 1997. Adapting the concept of providing free software in order to attract customers, Microsoft soon bundled its web browser with Windows software. Since Microsoft software was standard with PC purchases, Microsoft's browser, Internet Explorer, effectively put Netscape out of business.

DISCUSSION: UNIQUE DEVELOPMENTS AND COMMON PROCESSES

We return to the questions raised in the introduction concerning linkages between variety creation, selection and propagation processes and ask them of the ICT sector. A complexity approach reveals a persistent dynamic operating between the diversity of user needs – met by multiple technical solutions – and the uniformities that make interchange possible. This dynamic interplay between variety and uniformity has provided the impetus for complementary and compatible innovations. As complementary technologies matured, increasing returns promoted an economic boom, but as asynchronies built up they precipitated the ensuing slump, a recurrent feature of rapid technological advance.

The Agents of Variety Generation and the Origins of their Knowledge

Co-evolution did not occur immediately. Unrelated experiments took place around an enabling technology before producers came up with products at a price and with specifications attractive to consumers. Entrepreneurial firms hit upon innovative solutions as they sought to exploit business opportunities in the face of stringent resource constraints. Early periods of ferment of this kind have been identified in many other industries (Utterback 1994; Nairn 2002). Variety generation was in each of these examples made possible by new knowledge developed with the support of public funding and made available in the public domain. Entrepreneurs with relevant experience and expertise were able to perceive and pursue the opportunities offered by knowledge newly entering the public domain.

A pool of knowledge representing an investment of time and effort takes form outside the market arena for two main reasons. Firstly, scientific knowledge undergoes its own evolutionary processes and advances create an independent problem-solving potential that may have unexpected market applications. Secondly, the payback anticipated from funding the commercialization of research seldom attracts market investors, who look for earlier and more certain returns on capital.[9] In the case of transistors, microcomputers and electronic messaging, established companies had access to scientific and technological knowledge, and in some cases involvement in their development, with support from public funds. But unlike incumbents, entrepreneurial ventures had no vested interests in prior technologies and ways of organizing business. They had no existing customers to alienate or reputation to sully by offering a product based on immature technology.

In semiconductors, technological performance depended on a pool of resources provided by the public sector, no less than on market forces. Although the transistor, integrated circuit and microprocessor were invented in private companies, Bell Labs, Fairchild and Intel, there were years of technical expertise funded by government behind their inventions. Major federal contracts supported development work and the Small Business Innovation Research programme (SBIR) made it possible for new entrepreneurial firms to access this funding (Wessner 2003). Shockley,

Fairchild and others employed large numbers of PhD graduates trained in universities supported by government funding. At Intel, the creator of the microprocessor, Ted Hoff, came straight from research at Stanford. The US defense department supported scientific and technical education in universities on an unprecedented scale (Lowen 1997).

The microcomputer is often cited as an industry that was the product of pure enterprise without government subsidy (Fong 2001). But here too the costs of developing the technologies that went into such features as the graphical user interface (GUI), the mouse and the local area network (LAN), were not borne wholly by the market. The Defense Advanced Research Projects Agency (DARPA) was heavily involved. DARPA provided extensive support for selected computer science departments throughout the US, including UC Berkeley and Stanford. DARPA funds made possible the accelerated development of graphics through the sponsorship of the CAD industry and through support for the computer scientists who developed GUI advances and LANs (Hafner and Lyon 1996). DARPA employed and supported the knowledge generation of many of those who were later active in Xerox PARC in Palo Alto, the home of developments that inspired Apple's Macintosh computer and ultimately Microsoft Windows (Fong 2001). Much DARPA related business was carried out at Xerox PARC itself (Hafner and Lyon 1996, p. 238). Without Cold War defence funding, the microcomputer industry could not have grown so quickly. A pool of knowledge funded outside the market and accessible to new ventures compensated for the short-term focus of capital markets. The success of these sectors made possible the expansion of commercial venture capital.

Both the Internet and the World Wide Web, which were necessary underpinnings for online electronic messaging, emerged from government-funded activities, the former from the US ARPANET, and the latter from the work of Tim Berners-Lee at CERN. Again, it was entrepreneurs who identified and acted to exploit the opportunities in a variety of ways apparently not foreseen by the original developers and funders. In these sectors, variety generation was facilitated by historically and culturally specific conditions. The San Francisco Bay area provided a creative and unconventional culture that encouraged innovation. The 'gift culture' in IT, which stimulated technology diffusion, was made possible because US defence expenditure provided munificent resources for IT development during the Cold War. The anti-trust tendencies of the judiciary led large companies to make available innovative technologies, including RISC and UNIX, for licensing on favourable terms (Mowery and Rosenberg 1998). Scientific knowledge created with government support was not sufficient to create an IT economy. This is illustrated by the contrast with the Soviet

Union, where the absence of incentives and market mechanisms for trans-forming scientific advances into industrial innovation prevented the command economy's transition to the information age (Mowery 1996). However, market mechanisms represented 'only one level and mode of selection' (Metcalfe 1994, p. 29). Cultural factors, government policy and institutions that included the universities and standards-setting bodies were part of the co-evolutionary process from which complementary innov-ations emerged in the US. In Japan, South Korea and Taiwan, public support for industrial research and production made possible the increases in corporate production capacity and skills that raised yields and sustained rates of improved performance of semiconductors alongside massive reduction of costs (Kim 1997). Asian public expenditure helped sustain Moore's Law.

Complex Dynamic Processes

Reflections

Having offered the reader a historical account of developments, we turn now to examine this period of intensive innovation from a complexity perspective. We start by looking at the way variety generation, selection and propagation were coupled by feedback processes. We consider the implica-tions of the stock market crash of the Millennium and the unintended impact of US policy during the Cold War in accelerating the pace of devel-opment in ICTs. In view of the difficulties of predicting co-evolutionary developments we go on to examine factors conducive to further rapid ICT innovation and counteracting developments that may be obstructive. We conclude by asking what kind of policy measures and conditions might support the sustained generation of diversity; a complexity perspective leads us to distinguish this from technological innovation as usually conceived.

Feedback mechanisms connecting variety generation, selection and propagation: user–producer interaction and learning

Technologies are not produced and selected in the marketplace on the basis of price and attribute considerations, as economists focusing on the price incentives for innovation assume. Products and services that could not be anticipated prior to technical advance have utility that cannot be accurately assessed ahead of time. Innovations are constructed and refined through a collaborative learning process (Bijker *et al.* 1987). Early input–output com-puting kits like the Altair became the personal computer through user involvement. Learning on the part of providers and users continues to shape developments as markets mature. Early customers for a new product, looking for a new solution, are prepared to accept relatively unreliable products with complex interfaces, and to pay a premium for the ability to do something new (Rogers 1983). As a wider range of users is reached, usability and reliability become key requirements. In the PC sector early adopters used the machines to write their own programs but by the early 1980s pre-packaged applications took over in consumer markets.

The emergence of technical standards and competition for dominance
In networked industries, users benefit as the number of users of an innovation increases.[10] Katz and Shapiro identified three sources of consumption externalities from which users benefit in networked industries. (1) The direct physical effect of the number of purchasers, as might be found with a telephone system where utility increases with the number of connections; (2) Indirect effects such as the availability of associated products, as might be seen with software for a particular type of computer hardware, or pre-recorded tapes for videocassette recorders; (3) Support effects, whereby the quality and availability of post-purchase service depends upon the experience and size of the service network (Katz and Shapiro 1985). If these benefits are to be experienced, products must be compatible with each other, calling for agreed, imposed or de facto technical standards.

There are advantages for producers in common focus on a given set of production problems. Pressures to standardize the wide range of new variants launched by the early experimental phase of a newly commercialized technology result in the emergence of a dominant design of an assembled product, as in the 'keyboard, monitor, processor' features of the PC. This is pivotal for the formation of an industry in the conventional sense of a set of producers producing competing products (Utterback 1994; Munir and Phillips 2002). A related development is a set of technical standards that promote interoperability. These include protocols for connectivity in telecommunications and the media or common interface modes in hardware and software.[11] In the three sectors examined, the selection of newly generated variants was coupled to the adoption of technical standards. Once a specific technical standard is selected, switching costs are created for consumers who have invested funds and knowledge in that standard. A path dependent lock-in of this kind helps to explain why the market does not always select the best performing technology (Arthur 1990; Rohlfs 2001, p. 43).

Network externalities reinforce selection
In the network products we have reviewed, the need for products to be compatible or support interoperability was a critical factor in determining the survival of firms offering early experimental designs. The emergence of

a preferred solution changes the competitive environment to provide an advantage to those firms that adopt the standard as compared with those that have non-standard products (Tegarden *et al.* 1999). For products in these markets, selection and propagation are not empirically separable. The rapid propagation of winning products results in the selection of these products by new adopters, with increasing sales tipping the likelihood of further sales in the winners' direction.

The combination of selection and propagation acts as a self-reinforcing process so that the market power of dominant players is increased. When network effects operate at the limit, strong attraction is exerted by the emerging standard. This occurs as new users head for what becomes the market's preferred technology and some existing users are also attracted to this emerging dominant standard (see Figure 7.5).

A rapid shift of this kind occurred in the emerging PC industry. An incremental increase in sales of IBM PC software produced a cascade effect, leading to the selection of the IBM PC at the expense of Apple products. In 1982, software for Apple had made up about 85 per cent of the microcomputer software market but it fell to 35 per cent within a year with the rapid expansion of software applications for the IBM PC. Apple's market share halved between 1981 and 1984 and continued to fall, while IBM's expanded to 33 per cent of the global market by 1984 (Gabel 1991, p. 24). As early as 1987, over 80 per cent of the market was compatible with the IBM PC (Grindley 1995, p. 140). Buyers' preference was the overt mechanism of selection in the PC sector which led to the near elimination of non-compatible systems such as Apple's.

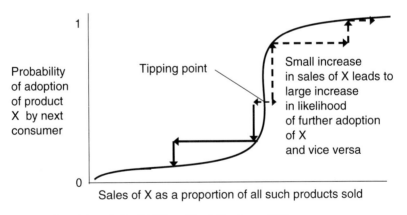

Source: Adapted from Agliardi 1998, p. 62 and Henderson 2003

Figure 7.5   Network effects illustrated by probability of adoption curve

Path Dependence and the Acceleration of Innovation

Innovation in the ICT sector took the form of specialist niche activity, as found in Peter Allen's models of complex dynamic processes associated with innovation (Chapter 2, this volume). Specialist niches provided a favourable environment for new entrant growth. As technologies matured, certain niches expanded to become mainstream markets attracting complementary activity. Those producers of bandwagon products who attracted a critical mass of users enjoyed competitive advantage. But some smaller niches where the needs of particular markets were met offered a habitat for specialist companies, which were well placed if their niches grew into mainstream markets.

The increasing diffusion and interoperability of PCs resulting from earlier advances drove the emergence of further generations of diversity. The distinction between innovations within semiconductors, PCs and electronic messaging illustrates the contrast between *variety* that occurs within a given structural form and *diversity* of form that changes the structural order. Electronic messaging ushered in a new order of mass communication, enabled by the Internet and World Wide Web. Further progress in PC processing and memory enabled advances in other hardware and software sectors, including sound and image processing for consumer entertainment and telecommunications. A new fusion of computer and communications technologies was to be seen in mobile devices and handheld computers. In each of these cases, technological advances built on what had gone before, in the path dependent mode created by cumulative feedback processes.

The pace of change was accelerated by interactivities, increasing the difficulty of predicting and synchronizing innovative products, services and modes of provision. Schumpeter argued that the swarming of innovations was responsible not only for 'leaps and bounds of progress' but also for setbacks 'carrying in their wake not only the primary disturbance, inherent in the process, but a whole string of secondary ones and the possibilities . . . of crises' (Schumpeter 1928, p. 384). He recognized that difficulties in assimilating bursts of disruptive innovation can set off periodic disturbances in the economy.

As complex dynamic systems, industries are prone to surge effects in the intensity of innovative activity. Such surges provide impetus to technological progress, but they create asynchronies and disturbances with unpredictable outcomes. There are historically specific factors at work. In the late 1990s, when stock market speculation led to the boom and bust of Internet ventures, incentives exerted by increasing use of share options for managers and the rapid dismantling of regulatory controls were among the precipitating factors (Stiglitz 2003). Speculative bubbles have in the past

Source: Yahoo Finance http://finance.yahoo.com

Figure 7.6   NASDAQ exchange monthly closing values 1984–2002

arisen as returns from new forms of investment rose well above the other sources of return on capital (Nairn 2002). Even once it was clear that share values of technology ventures were out of line with possibilities for real returns, investors feared losses from pulling out too soon (Cassidy 2001). Events then precipitated a sudden shift in investor sentiment through tipping effects, as demonstrated by the NASDAQ Index before and after the Millennium (see Figure 7.6).

When a speculative bubble bursts it is more difficult for new projects to obtain funding, so bringing about a lull in variety creation. The disturbances predicted by Schumpeter spread throughout the telecommunications industry and indirectly affected funding for biotechnology ventures after the year 2000.

DIVERSITY, UNIFORMITY AND INNOVATION

Despite contrary historical evidence, we tend to assume that the future will be like the past. A complexity approach leads us to expect that continuity will be challenged by reactions to current conditions and consequent feedback effects. In this final section we explore some of the difficulties of predicting co-evolutionary developments when complex dynamic processes are at work.

The Darwinian evolution of life forms takes place unimaginably slowly, the evolutionary mechanisms of variety generation, selection and propagation occurring independently of each other. The random emergence of new variants and the elimination of those that are less adaptive takes place over 'deep time'. Survival rewards for mutual accommodation have been found to underlie co-evolution (Goodwin 1994). In the natural world, collaboration is not pursued because its benefits are envisaged, but through blind responses that sustain mutual advantages.

In contrast with the Darwinian process, advances in IC technologies have been occurring ever faster as evolutionary mechanisms in ICT have become more closely coupled. While there are reasons to expect the acceleration of innovation to continue, other considerations remind us that the continuity of earlier patterns is far from inevitable and that innovation does not equate to diversity generation. Successful innovations are the product of competition, which is essentially a variety-reducing force. The further generation of new forms is needed if diversity, along with future innovation, is to be sustained.

Factors favourable to the sustained pace of innovation relate above all to the level of technological knowledge that has been reached and to inherent features of ICT. There have been cumulative processes advancing the depth and range of knowledge about electricity from the 18th century, with advances building on prior knowledge as science and practice broke through earlier barriers. From the beginning of the 20th century, when Hertz's discoveries fed Marconi's efforts at broadcasting radio waves, through to mid-century advances in solid state physics, knowledge accumulated so that by the end of the century it had reached a critical mass that made possible an effervescence of technological advance. Complementary innovations were forthcoming in anticipation of the positive selection exerted by demand. Although some co-evolving developments were unintended (for example text messaging along with mobile telephony), overt collaboration has been common. We have seen that early selection of a variant by the market fostered its propagation as network effects took hold. Amplifying forces created dominant standards which provided the basis for further variety through complementary innovations.[12] These coupled evolutionary mechanisms were self-reinforcing.

Unique features of information and communication technologies contributed to the rapid rate of innovation: their generic nature, scalability and modularity. ICTs have uses across multiple industries and sectors. Increasing returns in software production make software innovations highly scalable. The modularity of ICT innovations is conducive to further innovation because it allows diverse products and infrastructures to be interoperable through the use of interfaces that promote connectivity. There remain myriad markets that have yet to be penetrated by ICT, especially in developing countries, which offer prospects for new applications if technological capabilities and market needs can be coupled. Cost reductions in mobile telephony represent a striking illustration of this possibility.

Moreover it does not require radical advances in knowledge to give rise to radical innovations. Incremental innovations that are brought together from different domains may result in new species of technology. Different streams of technology, each developing gradually, can give rise to major advances. For example, gradual advances in magnetic data storage and in optical signalling were combined in established companies to provide the basis for video recording. Applications of newly combined technologies to entirely new domains of use can sustain innovation.

Uncertainties affect the Pace of Innovation

Forces favourable to continuing rapid innovation are not the only trends in evidence. There are counter forces at work that make outcomes unpredictable. 'The difference between systems that are predictable and systems that are not predictable lies in the numbers of degrees of freedom they possess' (Bass 1999, p. 236). Degrees of freedom are all the greater when industries have no enduring structure or boundary, contrary to assumptions in industrial economics (Munir and Philips 2002). In ICT industries in particular, the boundaries of industries were reconfigured as new products and sectors were spawned, through developments that encompassed workstations, handheld devices, Internet-based services and multiple applications in telecommunications.

Among forces that could counter rapid innovation are the intractable requirements of synchrony as industries mature and interconnect. On the supply side, the synchronization required for the co-evolution of technologies is continually challenged by delays between design and market readiness, and lags between investment and returns from sales. Market signals are celebrated for spontaneous coordination of supply and demand (Chapter 5, this volume). They are less effective at re-synchronizing temporal de-couplings. The stock market crash of the Millennium points to asynchronies that are not corrected by stabilizing market mechanisms but are instead exacerbated by their positive feedback effects. In financial markets herd behaviour prevails and the real economy pays for re-coordination through crisis and slump. The price may rise with the proliferation of derivatives which have increased the liquidity that facilitates exchange at the cost of potentially greater dislocating effects.

The enabling conditions of the late 20th century had a largely unanticipated impact on innovation. Federal investment in science was expected to foster innovation in large companies through a linear process in which scientific research eventuated in commercial and social returns (Bush 1960). Instead, the most important innovations of the information revolution were made by resource-constrained new entrants. This unintended outcome of policy was the result of contingent conditions that are not self-perpetuating.

Selection processes are increasingly supporting big laboratories and established paradigms rather than small innovative teams and new ideas. The bureaucratization of science and intellectual property arrangements that benefit established players could endanger sources of variety and the selection of new variants. In the US, the post-World War II judiciary applied an anti-trust regime that made it possible for new entrants to challenge established players (Mowery and Rosenberg 1998). More recently, established players who could defend their patents have been favoured by intellectual property arrangements and rulings. Pressures on companies to focus on short-term share price gains have also increased (Stiglitz 2003). The slump following the 'correction' to share prices in 2000 greatly reduced the availability of venture capital for experimental new entrants. Such risk-averse investment conditions make it difficult for new entrants to play the role of agent of change.

In Europe, the standardization of selection conditions has been a goal of policy. These are less favourable to the rise of new species of activity than diverse economic habitats providing a variety of different selection conditions. Market selection may not provide independent mechanisms for variety generation when expected returns from a known set of selection forces determine the variants launched on the market. The prospect of low returns have limited the extent of innovation in drugs for common diseases and ICT suited to conditions in low income economies.[13] Rather than becoming more equal, the distribution of income within and between countries has become less equitable, limiting the purchasing power of potential consumers of ICT innovations and creating the 'digital divide', a societal segregation between those with access to ICTs and those without. A key influence on diversity will be new selection conditions in emergent economies and the response of innovators there to information technologies.

Physical limits to improvements in technical performance have brought waves of innovation to an end in the past (Freeman 1983). But before such limits are reached, there are other factors at work that can alter the pace of innovation as technologies and industries mature, notably the lock-in of consumers to dominant technologies and asymmetries of market power. Established firms can use returns from past successes to innovate. Both Microsoft and Intel, alert to potential competition, have attempted regular product updates and innovations. But incumbent firms have only rarely shown the capability and incentive to introduce radical innovations (Utterback 1994; Nairn 2002). It was not until pioneering new entrants had demonstrated the returns to be obtained from microcomputing and the Internet that incumbents imitated their initiatives.[14] As the Xerox PARC case illustrates, even established companies promoting advanced R&D faced inertia that prevented assimilation of the knowledge they generated in their own labs (Rumelt 1995).

Along with the acquisition of more innovative entrants, the most likely source of major innovations from incumbent companies is the application of a known technology to a new domain, often through new combinations (Levinthal 1998).[15] But there are factors relating to technical standards and strategic realities that affect the propensity for breakthrough innovation in established corporations. Owners of proprietary standards tend to inhibit innovations that could threaten their position. Modularity of design allows diversity of provision to coincide with standard interfaces, thereby opening up new domains of application, as in retail payment systems. But as Penrose pointed out, there are strategic limits to the new directions in which established companies can move (Penrose 1959). Companies with reputations at risk from uncertain new products prefer to manage risk by using tried and tested solutions, or incremental variations thereon. Groundbreaking innovations are by their nature risky and are adopted only in exceptional conditions by corporate decision makers (Christensen 1997). Managers under pressure to demonstrate short-term share price gains are unlikely to embrace uncertain new technology paradigms.

In sum, the evidence we have examined reveals the extent to which market exchange stimulates both the multiple variants of goods and services that meet diverse needs and the uniformities that make exchange possible. Amplifying processes reinforce emerging concentration and asymmetries of market power. Kauffman has shown that as networks mature and become interlocking, there is a reduction in the diversity of outcomes (Kauffman 1996). Whether or not this will apply to ICT technologies depends on the interaction of countervailing forces. The close coupling of variety generation, selection and propagation has accelerated innovation in ICT over the period examined, but this dynamic has depended on a contingent set of favourable conditions, including long-term investment in science and technology and incentives for technical entrepreneurs. Policy can be directed towards fostering favourable conditions but these are much more specific and difficult to provide than an ill-defined 'climate of enterprise'.

In the 20th century, government policies in the home of free markets helped to shape the very conditions of supply and demand that gave rise to innovations. Advances in science, the output of skilled technologists and an intellectual property regime favourable to innovation, were among the conditions of supply formed by US policy. Demand was influenced by public procurement, regulation and fiscal incentives, among other factors (Stiglitz 2003). It was an unintended consequence of Cold War defence policies that they created munificent conditions not only for science but for technology-based enterprise in the USA.[16] Radical innovation in the private sector resulted from the application of new knowledge made available in the public domain by massive public funding on IT research in US companies and universities (Mowery and Rosenberg 1998). In particular, government funding supported the advance of IT from invention to market-ready applications, bridging the gap between R&D and market, paving the way for profitable venture capital and public listings.

Policies that promoted ICT reveal that supply and demand do not operate as market forces independently of government measures and institutions. Supply and demand are the outcome of all the complex dynamic forces of selection and variety generation. These include the institution-based and publicly funded transactions that allocate resources, alongside the choices of private consumers and producers. There is no such entity as the market. Market signals are the emergent properties of complex processes of exchange.

While the US Cold War policies inadvertently enabled micro-diversity in ICT, this diversity can be deliberately fostered in other spheres. For example, current market conditions do not provide the capital required for the long term development and commercialization of innovative clean technologies. But the experience of ICT indicates that if environmental degradation is to be counteracted and the necessary conditions created for rapid innovation in clean technologies, public campaigns in support of the natural environment need to be funded as an all-out war. The record shows that overcoming incumbent and consumer inertia can only be achieved when selection conditions counteract asymmetries of power and wealth, allowing scope for initiatives at the micro-level enabled by public funding.

Ferment in the realm of knowledge is a critical feature of radical innovation. The progress of ICTs across generations of innovation shows that investment in knowledge yields returns more extensive than the capture of gains by originators. Entrepreneurial innovators are stimulated by new ideas and often act on them prior to shifts in supply or effective demand. Path-breaking entrants anticipate and respond to selection forces in a different manner from incumbents. It is because they have much less to lose that entrepreneurial ventures pursue opportunities overlooked by better resourced players. Although the rate of failure of new entrants is wasteful, this failure constitutes the overhead required to generate diversity (as discussed earlier in this volume in Chapter 2). Experimental entrants give rise to distributed forms of innovation, the costs of which are mitigated by serendipity and the triumph of the unexpected.

NOTES

1. 'while no treatment of innovation can ignore a stochastic element, it is also true that innovation represents guided and intentional variation purposely undertaken in the pursuit of competitive advantage. Economic agents learn from experience and anticipate future states of the selective environment in a way quite unknown in biological or eco-logical selection' (Metcalfe 1998).
2. A microprocessor is an integrated circuit designed to carry out most of the processing and control functions of a computer.
3. Texas Instruments, where the integrated circuit had been independently invented, become Intel's first competitor in the microprocessor market, coming out with their own chip to meet the specifications of one of Intel's customers.
4. Minicomputers were more accessible than mainframes but still costly and beyond the reach of ordinary consumers and small businesses.
5. Apple's new CEO John Sculley had previously guarded the Pepsi recipe, though he continued a policy that had been established by Apple's founders.
6. In 1965, Gordon Moore, then a Director of Fairchild Semiconductor, observed that the number of components on a cost-effective silicon wafer had doubled each year since 1959. He predicted that this rate of increase would continue for a further 10 years. In 1975, Moore extended his prediction, but this time referred to the maximum complexity over 2-year periods. The period of the effect is frequently quoted as 18 months (EC 2000; Cringely 1996).
7. TCP/IP stands for Transfer Control Protocol/Internet Protocol, two sets of rules that allow computers and networks to communicate effectively. The ARPANET originally used NCP, for communication, but the TCP was devised to enable ARPANET to communicate with other networks, that is the early Internet. It was adopted by the US DoD in 1980 and was introduced to the ARPANET in 1983 (Zakon 2003).
8. Until 1995, Internet use was limited to non-commercial applications, though some commercial activities had begun in the early 1990s.
9. This argument is by no means universally accepted. For instance, Kealey (1996) argues that government funding displaces commercial funding in a ratio of greater than 1:1. He suggests that the majority of government funding of science is only necessary because it is now the accepted norm. The evidence of the three cases presented here indicates that government funding played an important part in the generation of variety.
10. Bob Metcalfe hypothesized that the utility of a network was proportional to the square of the number of users (Rohlfs 2001). Rohlfs points out that this 'law' assumes that the value that users derive from a networked product or service is the same for all users, but in reality some users will derive more value than others and links with different users have differential value. While the insight is valid, this statement of it is incorrect and likely to overstate the value of large networks.

11. Connectivity protocols include TCP/IP for local area networks and IEEE 802.11 for wireless ('wi-fi') networks. Physical connections such as PCI, SCSI and USB provide hardware interfaces; device drivers and programming languages provide the interface between software and hardware.
12. An example of cross-fertilization is provided by storage devices developed for photographic images which turn out to have applications for other types of data files.
13. Geographic diffusion and diversity of selection regime have taken on new impetus with the growth of the Indian and Chinese economies.
14. Although IBM established the standard for the PC, it did not enter the market until the basic technology and architecture had been tested by more entrepreneurial ventures. This is consistent with the type of risk-reducing strategy that might be expected from a large incumbent firm.
15. As Darwin emphasized, many branches of the tree of life were eliminated by selection forces, but immense variety was possible among the remaining branches.
16. The US military provided an intermediary IT customer/funder in cases where market assimilation would have been too slow to provide incentives to invent and develop an innovation.

REFERENCES

Agliardi, Elettra (1998), *Positive Feedback Economics*, Basingstoke: Macmillan.
Arthur, W.B. (1990), 'Positive feedbacks in the economy', *Scientific American*, **80**, 92–9.
Barney, Jay B. (1997), *Gaining and Sustaining Competitive Advantage*, Harlow: Addison-Wesley.
Bass, T. (1999), *The Predictors: How a Band of Maverick Physicists set out to beat Wall Street*, Penguin edition 2001, New York and London.
BBC (2000) 'Text messaging grows up', http://news.bbc.co.uk/1/hi/uk/916337.stm.
Berners-Lee, Tim and Mark Fischetti (2000), *Weaving the Web: the Past, Present and Future of the World Wide Web by its Inventor*, London: Texere.
Bijker, Wiebe E., Thomas P. Hughes and Trevor J. Pinch (1987), *The Social Construction of Technological Systems: new Directions in the Sociology and History of Technology*, London: MIT Press.
BLS (2001), 'Computer and Internet use at work in 2001', www.bls.gov/news. release/ciuaw.nr 0.htm.
Both, David P. (2002), 'A short history of OS/2', http://www.databook.bz.
Bush, V. (1960), *Science: The Endless Frontier*, Washington: National Science Foundation.
Cassidy, John (2002), *Dot Con*, London: Allen Lane.
Cavalli-Sforza, Luigi L. (2001), *Genes, Peoples and Languages*, London: Penguin.
Chandler, Alfred D. (2001) *Inventing the Electronic Century: the Epic Story of the Consumer Electronics and Computing Industries*, New York: Free Press.
Christensen, Clayton M. (1997), *The Innovator's Dilemma: When New Technologies Cause Great Firms to Fail*, Boston: Harvard Business School Press.
Cringely, Robert X. (1996), *Accidental Empires*, London: Penguin.
Cusumano, Michael A. and Richard W. Selby (1996), *Microsoft Secrets*, London: HarperCollins.
Darwin, Charles (1985), *The Origin of Species*, London: Penguin.
Downes, Larry and Chunka Mui (1998), *Unleashing the Killer App*, Boston: Harvard Business School Press.

EC (2000), *European Competitiveness Report 2000*, Commission Staff Working Paper, SEC (2000) 1823.

Fong, G.R. (2001), 'ARPA does Windows: the defense underpinning of the PC revolution', *Business and Politics*, **3** (3), 213–37.

Freeman, Christopher (1983), *Long Waves in the World Economy*, London: Butterworth.

Freeman, C. (1995), 'The National System of Innovation: historical perspective', *Cambridge Journal of Economics Special Issue on Technology and Innovation*, **19** (1), 5–24.

Gabel, H. Landis (1991), *Competitive Strategy for Product Standards*, London: McGraw-Hill.

Goodwin, Brian (1994), *How the Leopard Changed its Spots*, London: Orian.

Gould, S.J. (1980), 'Is a new and general theory of evolution emerging?', *Paleobiology*, **6** (1), 119–30.

Grindley, Peter (1995), *Standards Strategy and Policy*, Oxford: Oxford University Press.

Grove, Andrew (1996), *Only the Paranoid Survive: How to Exploit the Crisis Points that Challenge Every Business and Career*, London: HarperCollins.

Hafner, Katie and Matthew Lyon (1996), *Where Wizards Stay Up Late: the Origins of the Internet*, New York: Simon and Schuster.

Henderson, R. (2003), *Developing and Managing a Successful Technology and Product Strategy*, CD 1, Cambridge, MA: MIT/CMI Compact Disc.

Hugo, Oliver and Elizabeth W. Garnsey (2002), 'Hotmail & Co.: the emergence of electronic messaging and the growth of four entrepreneurial entrants', in Wim E. During, Raymond P. Oakey and Saleema Kauser (eds), *New Technology-Based Firms in the New Millennium*, Amsterdam: Pergamon.

Katz, M. and C. Shapiro (1985), 'Network externalities, competition and compatibility', *American Economic Review*, **75**, 424–40.

Kauffman, Stuart A. (1996), *At Home in the Universe: The Search for Laws of Self-Organization and Complexity*, London: Penguin.

Kealey, Terence (1996), *The Economic Laws of Scientific Research*, Basingstoke: MacMillan.

Kim, L. (1997), 'The dynamics of Samsung's technological learning in semiconductors', *California Management Review*, **39** (3), 86–100.

Langlois, R.N. (1992), 'External economies and economic growth: the case of the microcomputer industry', *Business History Review*, **66**, 1–50.

Levinthal, D.A. (1998), 'The slow pace of rapid technological change: gradualism and punctuation in technological change', *Industrial and Corporate Change*, **7** (2), 217–47.

Lowen, Rebecca S. (1997), *Creating the Cold War University: The Transformation of Stanford*, Berkeley: University of California Press.

McKelvey, Maureen D. (1996), *Evolutionary Innovations: the Business of Biotechnology*, Oxford: Oxford University Press.

Meeker, Mary (1996), *The Internet Advertising Report*, Morgan Stanley US Investment Research.

Metcalfe, J.S. (1994), 'Technology systems and technology policy in an evolutionary framework', *Cambridge Journal of Economics*, **19**, 25–46.

Metcalfe, J. Stanley (1998), *Evolutionary Economics and Creative Destruction: The Graz Schumpeter Lectures*, London: Routledge.

Moore, G.E. (1965), 'Cramming more components onto integrated circuits', *Electronics*, **38** (8), 114–17.

Moore, G.E. (1975), 'Progress in digital integrated electronics', *IEEE International Electron Devices Meeting, IEDM Technical Digest*, **21**, 11–13.

Moore, James F. (1996), *The Death of Competition: Leadership and Strategy in the Age of Business Ecosystems*, Chichester: Wiley.

Mowery, David C. (1996), *The International Computer Software Industry: A Comparative Study of Industry Evolution and Structure*, New York: Oxford University Press.

Mowery, David C. and Nathan Rosenberg (1998), *Paths of Innovation: Technological Change in 20th Century America*, New York: Cambridge University Press.

Munir, K. and N. Phillips (2002), 'The concept of industry and the case of radical technological change', *Journal of High Technology Management Research*, **13**, 279–97.

Nairn, Alasdair G.M. (2002), *Engines that Move Market: Technology Investing from Railroads to the Internet and Beyond*, New York: John Wiley and Sons Inc.

Penrose, Edith T. (1959), *The Theory of the Growth of the Firm*, Oxford: Blackwell.

Rogers, Everett M. (1983), *Diffusion of Innovations*, New York: Free Press.

Rohlfs, Jeffrey H. (2001), *Bandwagon Effects in High-Technology Industries*, Cambridge, MA: MIT Press.

Rosenberg, Nathan (1994), *Exploring the Black Box, Technology, Economics, and History*, Cambridge: Cambridge University Press.

Rumelt, Richard P. (1995), 'Transformation and inertia', in Cynthia A. Montgomery (ed.), *Resource-Based and Evolutionary Theories of the Firm: Towards a Synthesis*, London: Kluwer.

Schumpeter, J.A. (1928), 'The instability of capitalism', *Economic Journal*, **38**, 361–86.

Smith, Douglas K. and Robert C. Alexander (1988), *Fumbling the Future: How Xerox Invented, Then Ignored, The First Personal Computer*, New York: William Morrow.

Stiglitz, Joseph (2003), *The Roaring Nineties*, New York: W.W. Norton.

Tegarden, L.F., D.E. Hatfield and A.E. Echols (1999), 'Doomed from the start: what is the value of selecting a future dominant design', *Strategic Management Journal*, **20** (6), 495–518.

Utterback, James M. (1994), *Mastering the Dynamics of Innovation*, Boston: Harvard Business School Press.

Wessner, C. (2003), 'Sustaining Moore's Law and the US economy', *Computing in Science and Engineering*, **5** (1), 30–38.

Wolfe, T. (1983), 'The tinkerings of Robert Noyce, how the sun rose on the Silicon Valley', *Esquire Magazine*, December, pp. 346–74.

Zakon, R. (2003), Hobbes' Internet Timeline, http://www.zakon.org/robert/internet/timeline/.

Afterword

Simon Ford, Elizabeth Garnsey and Michael Lyons

The chapters of this book are all concerned with impetus and response, action and reaction, feedback and cumulative consequences – the workings of complex dynamic processes in socio-economic settings. These are explored with reference to the spatial configuration of cities and landscapes, with the workings of markets, production systems and evolving technologies, on the basis of evidence that ranges from the historical *époque* to recent technological history. The chapters reveal ways in which complexity at the micro-level is manifest through collective behaviour on the larger scale, demonstrating the phenomena of emergence, feedback, self-organization and their role in co-evolution.

In the complexity models explored by Allen and others in Chapter 2, and applied to markets and other interactive systems, it is shown that diverse activities and strategies are necessary to achieve outcomes in which all participants benefit rather than one or two protagonists dominating at the expense of others. Chapter 3 by Batty and others present an approach to the emergence and evolution of cities, modelling the interactions between elements of a system that bring about self-organization and co-evolution. In Chapter 4 McGlade continues the theme of human settlement, tracing the way in which interactions between agents, resources and their physical environment operate through co-evolutionary processes that transform whole landscapes over long historical periods. Another set of integrating themes is taken up in Chapter 5 by Metcalfe and Ramlogan, who demonstrate how knowledge-based market economies are continually co-evolving and why they cannot operate in equilibrium. The conceptual approach presented in Chapter 4 is revisited in Chapter 6, where the South Yorkshire mining community case study applies it in a contemporary context, revealing a co-evolving system failing to adapt to its environment, with path-dependent lock-in creating inertia and inhibiting local resilience. In Chapter 7, Garnsey and others take up the theme of co-evolution in relation to the emergence of the technologies of the information revolution. In tracing the development of technologies and business ecosystems, the authors also show that diversity is a source of renewal, as seen in Chapter 2, but that, nevertheless, certain uniformities are required to enable exchange to take place. Common standards enable the creation of further variety but also create conditions for lock-in to a given structure. These exemplars highlight the distinction between varieties within given structural form and diversity of form that changes the structural order. Transformation of this kind is effected by emergence, feedback and self-organization as complex dynamic processes operate in diverse settings.

The chapters in the volume demonstrate that models are an invaluable tool in understanding complexity; Chapters 2 and 3 present formal simulations while the remaining chapters use models as organizing schemas for making sense of scattered evidence by tracing the complex interrelations between apparently unrelated phenomena. Simplification is a necessary feature of modelling; the aim is usually to gain a better understanding of the whole by concentrating on a few key aspects of the system. But this raises the corresponding issue of interpretation. Ormerod notes that 'macro-economic models are unable to produce forecasts on their own. The proprietors of the models interfere with their output before it is allowed to see the light of day. These "judgemental adjustments" can be, and often are, extensive' (Ormerod 1994, p. 103). We interpret the output of a model in the light of our understanding of factors we know or believe could influence the output but are not included in the model itself.

The process of modelling is one of focus, while interpretation of the model involves re-introducing aspects of reality lost during the modelling process. To produce a sufficiently accurate representation of reality, the modeller makes decisions as to which elements it is necessary to include. The modeller derives learning from the process of constructing models through which insight is gained into how the elements interact and mechanisms operate in real systems. It is therefore unsurprising that when different people and groups interpret the same issue they often develop radically different models, and that different conclusions can be drawn from the use of the same model. When simplifying assumptions about how the 'world works' are needed, models that explicitly set out these simplifications have the advantage of being open to criticism and modification. Quantitative models (computer-based simulations) have the additional advantage of enabling humans to overcome some of their cognitive limitations (Lyons 2004).

Decisions are made on the basis of the underlying assumptions of the implicit or explicit models we hold of the world. Complex systems thinking disturbs our reliance on specific models, recognizing that while a model is necessarily simpler than the subject matter under inquiry, a great deal depends on the considerations that led to the particular simplification being made. Allen (1997) identifies five simplifying assumptions made in conventional modelling:

1. Boundary assumption: a boundary of the system can be defined so that a distinction may be made between a 'system' and an 'environment'. Such an assumption arises on the basis that the interactions across a boundary are much weaker than those within it.
2. Classification assumption: classes of objects in the system can be identified. While it may be assumed that we know how to classify correctly, Allen warns that such decisions are often made intuitively.
3. Stereotypes assumption: individual entities are either identical or distributed normally around the average. Allen warns that this assumption eliminates micro-diversity, along with the evolutionary effects that can lead to change in individuals, functionalities and typologies over time. With this lost, the model becomes increasingly static.
4. Smooth processes assumption: this assumption concerns the averaging of processes in the system, whether they are behaviours, mechanisms or interactions. This effectively eliminates 'noise' or serendipity from the system. According to Allen, this diminishes the capacity of the system to self-organize its structure.
5. Equilibrium assumption: as we have seen, this assumption maintains that systems move towards a natural state of equilibrium and that such a state is desirable. When the system is in equilibrium, the different variables of the system are in fixed relationship to one another.

Each of these assumptions is made with the intent of decreasing the complexity of reality so as to make it more tractable and make generalization possible. Each assumption affects the ability of the modeller to represent aspects of the system being modelled. Allen identifies the models that result from the application of each successive assumption, and orders them according to their ability to represent reality. This enables the user to identify what assumptions underlie different types of model and to decide whether the models are too far removed from reality for their purposes. As Allen points out, the gradual elimination of evolutionary and adaptive effects is the consequence of applying successive simplifying assumptions. This places resultant limits on the ability of such models to address questions about change.

Even a simple step, such as assuming a boundary, has implications since change does not occur only inside or outside the boundary; endogenous and exogenous changes co-evolve. Feedback takes place across system boundaries as well as within them, and these lead to changes and adaptation. Modelling approaches such as system dynamics, though acknowledging the influence of feedbacks, limit them to within the system boundary and as a consequence limit the analysis of change to that taking place within the system. The relationships within the system are not capable of qualitatively changing themselves as the model is constructed, yet the real question is how reconfigurations occur in practice as the elements of a system impact on each other and the environment. This highlights the limitations of formal models as representations of reality; they are created in an effort to simplify the world enough to support decision-making, but there is a temptation to view the world as being as predictable and controllable as the illusion created by the model.

As long as this is recognized and avoided, models developed for academic purposes also have uses for policy and practice, as shown by Lyons (2004). Complex adaptive systems anticipate the future by means of various internal models that are simplified representations of the environment (Holland 1998). The distinction has been made between a tacit internal model that prescribes current action under an implicit prediction of future state, and an overt internal model that provides a basis for explicit (internal) exploration of alternatives (Holland 1998). This distinction provides a means of justifying the use of models of this kind in strategic decision-making. A successful modelling approach involves taking tacit internal models (held by individuals) and turning them into overt internal models which can be debated, criticized and simulated (Lyons *et al.* 2002).

Complexity models demonstrate how the potential for change is based on the ability of system elements to adapt to external change, and collectively to alter their environment. For a system to be adaptable it must have 'hidden diversity or mechanisms that can produce diversity as and when required . . . This means that some overhead of maintaining an underlying diversity or of a diversity creating mechanism must be carried' (Allen 2001). In practice, some of the costs of the high rate of failure associated with experimental new ventures commercializing new technologies could be taken to represent the 'overhead' carried by capitalism to accommodate the adaptability provided by entrepreneurial innovation (Chapter 7).

Among other common strands woven throughout this book, the central theme of co-evolution recurs across the chapters in relation to production systems, markets, communities and settlement. The tensions between stability and change and between uniformity and diversity are seen to be of particular significance in co-evolving systems. The distinction between variety and diversity distinguishes variants from radical difference, a matter of degree and category. 'Variety concerns a selection of possibilities that share a common attribute space, but diversity concerns a selection that spans different attribute spaces' (Allen 2001). For example, a classification distinction is possible between variety in bird types (web footed, wingless and so on) and diversity among creatures that fly (insects, bats, fish, birds). Similarly, there is variety among types of proprietary software (word processing software, spreadsheets and so on), with diversity provided by nonproprietary Open Source software.

Diversity of ideas, technologies and community organization is explored in the various chapters. As Ramlogan and Metcalfe explain in Chapter 5, in a knowledge-based economy it is the co-evolution of ideas that underpins economic change. But there is tension between the status quo of accepted ideas and paradigms and the conceptual changes necessary as new knowledge emerges. Neoclassical economics provides an example of intellectual lock-in; recognition from some of its practitioners of the extent to which prevailing models and assumptions oversimplify reality to the point of obscuring understanding has not overturned the paradigm. Financial institutions, multinational corporations and governments, along with places of learning, continue to rely on the simplifying discourse and equations of neoclassical thought. This paradigm legitimizes a particular type of selection environment in which variety in consumer goods and service provision is stimulated, but differentiation of variants in this sphere does not enrich diversity of a new order, as is needed for adaptation to changing conditions in the natural environment.

Garnsey *et al.* describe the tension between uniformity and diversity in the electronics industries in Chapter 7. They first set out recent developments in the history of information technology without commentary before highlighting the complex evolutionary processes inherent in these developments. For technologies subject to network effects, uniformity through standardization was required to facilitate interactions between users. User switching costs, the development of complementary technologies and production scale effects all contributed towards the emergence of a dominant design and standard protocols. The need for interoperability resulted in the consolidation around dominant microprocessors and operating systems alongside the market dominance of their providers.

While many variants of technological innovation have been supported by dominant standards, the stifling of diversity through various forms of lock-in remains a possibility. Conditions are needed that support the generation of variety around common platforms but also promote new combinations, so enabling technological speciation in new domains and offering the possibility of new forms of diversity. This is where scientific knowledge can be a source of diversity, evolving as it does through its own form of selection (the scientific method and peer review) based on a different logic from that inherent in commercial pressures.

Entrepreneurial activity is needed to move such knowledge into use against the forces of inertia in the economy.

Inertia brings a halt to the relentless change associated with contemporary innovation. Complexity thinking suggests that the reinforcing processes that propagate certain types of accumulation, seen as forms of co-evolution in which a limited range of retailing, banking and other economic organizations are hegemonic, will not endure indefinitely. Amplification effects of this kind ultimately give rise to reactive forces, whether endogenously or through global and local feedback processes.

The tendency for reinforcing processes to set in and for feedback to create counter-reaction confounds expectations and undermines prediction. While amplifying trends are under way, 'more of the same' is the general expectation, and yet reactions against current reinforcing trends are to be anticipated from complexity theory and from history alike. This is demonstrated by all the chapters on varying timescales, from those on human settlement through to the account of Internet boom and bust. Among the many challenges to predicting outcomes in complex dynamic systems, as discussed in the Introduction, is the inherently unpredictable timing of tipping points, or the transition from dominant trends to reactive developments. These issues have particular significance in the social sciences because of the strength of the view that only prediction can validate research efforts. But as Prigogine argued, understanding, that is, making sense of evidence and imbuing observation with meaning, is no less a goal of science than is prediction. Many types of system are inherently unpredictable. This tends to be attributed to the workings of chance, but what appears to be random may ensue from systemic causal sequences that can only be understood when feedback effects are traced through and different system boundaries are drawn. Doing so reveals causal interactions too complex to be amenable to the cross-sectional analysis dominant in the research literature. However, the forging of understanding in the social sciences is amenable to the logic of scientific inquiry in so far as expected findings and received interpretations are continually challenged by new ways of confronting evidence with new perspectives and fields of observation.

The concept of sustainability, whether connected to environmental or corporate concerns, is a major challenge to the received idea that we can rely on innovations to counteract over-dominant forms and solve current problems. What the chapters in this volume demonstrate is that it is the ability to generate diversity and to adapt that makes complex systems not only innovative but also sustainable. During the early periods of human settlement and emergence of cities described in Chapters 3 and 4, the pace of technological change was relatively modest; occasional advances were followed by decades in which inventions were adapted and adopted to meet human needs. But the rate of technological advance and accompanying economic change has been increasing exponentially. If businesses, cities and communities are to survive the pace of change, they must possess a high degree of ecological resilience and adaptability. In the South Yorkshire mining community case presented by McGlade *et al.* in Chapter 6, resistance to change was ultimately destructive. The path-dependent lock-in experienced by the community arose from the legacy of a rigid set of knowledge structures and values, leaving participants ill-equipped to adapt to a reduction in demand for the coal they produced. This case study raises important questions as to how such communities and their members can be assisted when such dramatic changes occur and how flexibility and adaptability can be built into such systems. These questions are relevant across the scale, from the education and training of individuals through to national production systems and industries. It is of particular concern in the developing world where a legacy of colonialism is specialization in the production of a restricted range of commodity goods. The examples in this book have implications for government policy and strategic decision-making as complex dynamics operate across multiple scales from the macro government scale to the micro-scale of personal interactions.

Policy makers and strategists seldom recognize the long term impact of their decisions. Complexity studies warn us against the assumption that the future will resemble the past, since even inertia will manifest itself in new ways in different contexts. Over time incremental change set off by individual actions may accumulate and give rise to exponential change. Amplifying forces, such as those that arise from positive feedback effects, can lead to cataclysmic changes in the operational environment.

The recognition of the way these forces operate in the economy can inform policy making. Whether at the level of the firm or government, interventions can help to create the conditions for diversity. For example, providing conditions for diversity in sources of investment (entrepreneurial reinvestment, corporate venturing, informed private and sustained public investment) is more likely to stimulate sustained expansion in new areas and renew industries than is reliance on any one major source of investment. Where technological standards can facilitate variation, policy makers can do much to support international bodies that promote effective standards, and can encourage diversity through procurement measures, rather than allowing standards to reflect market power that perpetuates inferior technologies. Most obviously, variety occurs through differentiation of output, but structural diversity may be generated by firms that act differently, for example by collaborating with their competitors in innovative networks.

Those policy makers alert to reinforcing processes anticipate and counteract congestion, resource shortages and the impact of external shocks

(Allen 1997). In the face of the runaway tendencies of self-reinforcing dynamic processes, policy can favour countervailing measures, such as those practised by the West German Central Bank in a way that made it easier to support the transformation of mining communities at a time when British monetary policy was exacerbating business cycles. Countervailing measures can be taken, for example to counter market asymmetries of power through anti-trust measures, while positive feedback effects can be harnessed, to promote spatial clusters of leading-edge activity. Local competition and collaboration effects, along with an increasing pool of complementary suppliers and specialist knowledge, can lead to firms in such clusters becoming competitive on an international scale, as demonstrated by the clustering of IT innovations in the US (Chapter 7). In view of the key role of individuals, the agents of micro-diversity, strategists and policy makers who want to initiate change could seek out local champions who have the capacity to set off chain reactions.

Individual actors and organizations have throughout history set off cascade effects that shaped the course of events, to an extent largely neglected in the social sciences with their emphasis on structures and tendencies. In mainstream social science, including economics, individuals are excluded from the analysis (Garnsey and Lawton Smith 1998). This is an important respect in which the complexity perspective provides a basis for overcoming the rift between historical and social scientific approaches. Allen points out that underlying our stylized representations of the world:

> is the richer, more difficult, microscopic reality of diversity and individual subjectivity, which in fact provides the basis for the adaptive responses of the system and its creativity . . . moments of instability and structural change in a system are precisely when the macroscopic average description breaks down . . . [Theory must encompass] the individuals and local events within the system who, cumulatively and at critical points are . . . the source of diversity and change. (Allen 1997, p. 2)

In complexity theory, the significance of specific individuals, so evident in historical analysis, does not have to be averaged out, but is integral to the analysis. Technology and business history reveal the key role played by specific individuals, whose actions bring into being, sustain and renew developments which might have been otherwise without their critical initiatives. The approach avoids reductionism by uncovering the way collective influences come into play at the different levels of system aggregation, showing how social structures are constituted by self-reproducing patterns of action.

Engagement with the complexity discourse calls for reconsideration of the nature of causality and the process of evolution. Variety may require uniformity as a platform for interaction and exchange. Causes become effects, effects causes, when feedback operates. This poses a number of fundamental questions for the representation and modelling of complex socio-economic systems. Modelling has to date had a relatively narrow focus, with approaches directed at the development of appropriate computational structures (for example in multi-agent, dynamical systems and computational analysis). Contributions to this book show that it is also necessary to examine qualitative relationships, including those articulating agency and structure, that are central to understanding the nature of complex societal systems.

The use of a spectrum of approaches across the chapters demonstrates that there is no need for recourse to a single epistemology or methodology in exploring complexity. From the modelling approach of the first chapter to the empirical analysis of the last one, context and purpose guide the way in which complexity ideas are applied. This conceptual pluralism is in contrast with scientific reductionism. Complexity is not viewed as a new 'master narrative' but one that can enlarge our understanding of social, economic and environmental action and interaction. Adopting such an approach helps unravel the dynamic mechanisms and processes affecting emerging phenomena in the social world, their ramifications for the natural world and vice versa. This understanding can be applied to new developments in order to provide greater scope for adaptiveness and sustainability.

REFERENCES

Allen, Peter M. (1997), *Cities and Regions as Self-Organizing Systems: Models of Complexity*, Reading: Gordon and Breach.

Allen, P.M. (2001), 'A complex systems approach to learning, adaptive networks', *International Journal of Innovation Management*, **5**(2), 149–80.

Garnsey E.W. and H. Lawton Smith (1998), 'Proximity and complexity in the emergence of high technology industry: the Oxbridge comparison', *Geoforum*, **29**(4), pp. 433–50.

Holland, John H. (1998), *Emergence: from Chaos to Order*, Oxford: Oxford University Press.

Lyons, Michael H. (2004), 'Insights from complexity: organisational change and systems modelling', in Michael Pidd (ed.), *Systems Modelling: Theory and Practice*, Chichester: John Wiley & Sons.

Lyons, M.H., M.I. Adjali, D. Collings and K. Jensen (2002), 'Complex systems models for strategic decision-making', in Gerry Frizelle and Huw Richards (eds), *Tackling Industrial Complexity: the Ideas that make a Difference, Proceedings of 2002 Conference of Manufacturing Complexity Network*, Cambridge: Institute for Manufacturing, pp. 1–25.

Ormerod, Paul (1994), *The Death of Economics*, London: Faber and Faber.

Index